THE LAWRENCE STONE LECTURES

SPONSORED BY
The Shelby Cullom Davis Center for Historical Studies
and Princeton University Press

*A list of titles in this series appears at the back of the book.*

# Living I Was Your Plague

## MARTIN LUTHER'S WORLD AND LEGACY

## Lyndal Roper

PRINCETON UNIVERSITY PRESS

PRINCETON AND OXFORD

PUBLISHED BY PRINCETON UNIVERSITY PRESS
41 William Street, Princeton, New Jersey 08540
6 Oxford Street, Woodstock, Oxfordshire OX20 1TR

press.princeton.edu

Library of Congress Cataloging-in-Publication Data

Names: Roper, Lyndal, author.
Title: Living I was your plague : Martin Luther's world and legacy / Lyndal Roper.
Description: Princeton : Princeton University Press, [2021] | Series: The Lawrence stone lectures | Includes bibliographical references and index.
Identifiers: LCCN 2020032384 (print) | LCCN 2020032385 (ebook) | ISBN 9780691205304 (acid-free paper) | ISBN 9780691205311 (ebook)
Subjects: LCSH: Luther, Martin, 1483–1546. Classification: LCC BR332.5 .R66 2021 (print) | LCC BR332.5 (ebook) | DDC 284.1092 [B]—dc23
LC record available at https://lccn.loc.gov/2020032384
LC ebook record available at https://lccn.loc.gov/2020032385

British Library Cataloging-in-Publication Data is available

Editorial: Priya Nelson and Thalia Leaf
Production Editorial: Sara Lerner
Text and Jacket Design: Chris Ferrante
Production: Danielle Amatucci
Publicity: Maria Whelan and Kathryn Stevens

JACKET ART (Top and bottom rows): Portrait of Martin Luther by Lucas Kranach the Younger, 1543 / Ian Dagnall / Alamy Stock Photo. (Second row): AF Archive / Alamy Stock Photo. (Third row): Panther Media GmbH / Alamy Stock Photo. (Fourth row): Plastic figure of Martin Luther © Ottmar Hörl, "Martin Luther", 2019. Photo: Ottmar Hörl Archive

An earlier version of the lectures that appear here in book form were given as the Wiles Lectures 2015

This book has been composed in Adobe Caslon and IM Fell English
The Fell Types are digitally reproduced by Igino Marini, www.iginomarini.com

Printed on acid-free paper. ∞
Printed and bound in Great Britain by Clays Ltd, Elcograf S.p.A.

1 3 5 7 9 10 8 6 4 2

FOR RUTH AND FOR MARTIN

# CONTENTS

# PREFACE

IN SPRING 2017 I was asked to speak from Luther's pulpit. I knew that this would be an emotional experience, because I had spent the last twelve years of my life writing a biography of the reformer. Few biographers get so close to where their protagonist lived and worked, and others who had spoken from the Wittenberg pulpit had told me of its effect on their lives. I knew too that the event would bring back strong memories of my father, who had died just ten months before, and who had been a minister of religion when I was growing up in Melbourne, Australia.[1]

But I wasn't expecting what happened. I was very aware of my dad, and of what being a minister had meant to him, and I understood the stress that preaching brought for him in a new way as I climbed the pulpit stairs. To my surprise I found myself unable to stop thinking about something else too, the sculpture on the outside of the church, the Judensau. This fourteenth-century sculpture faces what once must have been the Jewish quarter, and it was put in place high up on the church tower; by Luther's time the Jews had left Wittenberg and there is no evidence of a community after 1422.[2] It shows a giant sow from which Jews are suckling, while a rabbi looks into the backside of the pig. It is labelled in a fancy later Gothic script *Schem hamphoras*, which means the ineffable name of God, words which according to Jewish belief should not be written down. It is a foul insult to Jews (who do not eat pork) and it is blasphemous.

The service was bilingual in English and German and members of an African church were visiting. Dressed in his long black coat and his starched white collar and ruff, the German preacher seemed like a sixteenth-century revenant. At the end of the service, we walked

o.1. Judensau sculpture on Town Church, Wittenberg. Anonymous, 1300s. City Church of St Mary in Wittenberg, Germany. © Friedrich Stark / Alamy Stock Photo.

out into the sunlight, and he told me that we would now move to the church hall, 'where you will answer questions from the congregation for 45 minutes'. This had not been mentioned in the invitation; and sure enough, the first question was his: 'Why did you say that Luther was anti-Semitic? Surely he was anti-Judaic?'

I stumbled out a reply in my inadequate German, when another member of the congregation stood up: 'Of course he is anti-Semitic! We have looked at all the passages [and here he named the key ones], we have spent years analysing them and we just have to admit it and see what it means. This is part of the history of our church'. He gave a highly articulate, deeply knowledgeable speech that was fluent, bold and inspiring. Who was this man?

It was Friedrich Schorlemmer, a famous East German academic and pastor, an opponent of the East German regime, a civil rights and peace activist who was spied on by the Stasi and who has written many major books on Luther's theology. And soon I realized that the woman who had done the many readings in the church service seemed somehow familiar too. I had seen her face in the giant photograph in the Cranach studio museum from 1989, taken when a group of Wittenberg citizens smashed the lock on the door and finally went in to try to save the building, just two weeks before the East German regime collapsed. They are all standing in the ruins, wearing hard hats, and smiling. The artist Lucas Cranach was the court painter of Frederick the Wise, Luther's ruler, and he lived in Wittenberg and was a close friend of Luther's; the group in the photograph had been trying for years to get the crumbling building preserved. The woman I met in the church is now the Director of the Cranach-höfe, a fine, restored building, and still a citizens' initiative which invites people from all over the world with some or no artistic experience to come to stay and to spend time creating art in the studios. On the Wittenberg town square later that day, I ate eggs and fried potatoes with her and with the pastor, the comforting dish that always reminds me of the old East. The pastor told me about the weekly protests calling for the Judensau to be taken down, and spoke of his shame at preaching in a church which, as he said, insults another religion.

I couldn't get the pastor's question out of my head, which I now understood differently. I felt I had to think again about Luther's anti-Semitism, even though I had written about it before. Was it a religious as well as a racial hatred, and if so, how far did it contaminate Luther's theology and his concept of the church? The event reminded me why I was so gripped by Luther, and why I was fascinated by Germany—the imagination and creative idealism that it took to found the Cranach-höfe, the openness of German society to outsiders like me, the matter-of-fact way in which learned academic debate was just expected to be part of a congregational discussion after a service. No-one, not even a pastor in a white collar and ruff, is immune from having their sermon scrutinised and debated; and Lutheranism remains a profoundly non-hierarchical, non-structured denomination, just as its founder Luther had no formal position in the church and was only ever a professor of Holy Scripture. In the end, I too will have my views assessed, and I hope that my view of Luther's masculinity and his knotty character may open up the discussion further about how we commemorate great men without losing sight of their frailties and violence.

LIVING I WAS YOUR PLAGUE

# INTRODUCTION

THE ANNIVERSARY OF Luther in 2017 was not just an event
of local Wittenberg history or even primarily of the Lutheran church. Because Luther has so long been linked with
German-ness itself, the event was a secular commemoration as well, an
occasion to ask about what being German means today. Even though
the country was formally reunited in 1989, the difference between
the former East and the former West is still unmistakeable. The East
remains noticeably poorer, and thirty years on, its idealism is different
too, with an abiding commitment to equality and communitarian
values, and an ingrained suspicion of the power of the state. If the
anniversary were meant to do anything politically, it was intended
to bring East and West together. Yet those formed in the education
system of the East approached Luther very differently. They wanted
to know about the economic side of the indulgences trade, and the
wealth and status of those who supported him, topics which were
not really considered during the centenary celebrations. They asked
different questions too; scholars from the former East who worked in
monument conservation, for instance, undertook the archaeology on
Luther's house and transformed our view of the family's wealth. But
far from uniting East and West, it felt as though the questions and
outlook of the former East was often silenced during the anniversary
year in favour of a more anodyne commemoration of the reformer
as the translator of the Bible and inventor of the German language.

Celebrating Luther has often been politically fraught, and linked to
questions of German identity. The first centenary of the 95 Theses was
celebrated on the eve of the Thirty Years' War, the catastrophic conflict that unleashed a generation-long religious and political military

struggle and left much of Germany devastated. In 1917, the posting of the 95 Theses was commemorated in the midst of war and on the brink of revolution and defeat. Now, in a reunited Germany, with the commemoration happening on the territory that had once been that of the former East Germany, celebrating Luther was also an attempt to escape defining Germany's history solely in terms of Nazism and the holocaust—to find, that is, a 'usable past'.

How Luther was commemorated was therefore a question of national significance.[1] This difficult hero, with his stodgy determination, his love of beer and pork, his relentless hatreds, his penchant for misogynist quips, and his four-square masculinist stance, has always been a divisive figure. Embracing him would not be easy. It could only be done with self-mockery, and could succeed only if religious divisions proved to be distant enough for denominational identity to be surpassed by a more indulgent attitude towards the colourful characters of the sixteenth century. But the fact that the Göttingen professor of church history Thomas Kaufmann published a book on Luther's Jews that acknowledged Luther's anti-Semitism once and for all, and which did not excuse it as a product of his times, meant that this issue in particular became a subject of national debate, the first time it had been confronted head on since the Second World War.[2]

Luther, it seemed, always raises issues of cultural and national identity that reach far beyond his theological legacy. A colossus of the stature of Bismarck, every age seems to appropriate him as its own—erasing him as a historical figure. People either love him or hate him, and even today, he elicits strong emotional reactions. How this anniversary unfolded, and what rituals of remembrance took place, revealed a lot about German culture and politics: here, surely, cultural history had much to say. It could help us examine Luther's cussed character, his lumpy masculinity, the depth of his appeal, and it could explain the pervasive legacy he has left in German culture, musical, linguistic, material, and visual.

As the commemorative year wore on, I pondered how the biography I had written of Luther had itself become part of the memorial cult, and I often felt uncomfortable. Partly because of my own experience when I spoke from the pulpit in Luther's church, I realized that I had not done enough to interrogate Luther's anti-Semitism or to ask how far it extended into Lutheran theology. And I sensed that I needed to confront the less comfortable sides of his legacy. Most of all, I needed to look more critically at one of the aspects I loved most about Luther: his rambunctious masculine posturing. Here studies of masculinity didn't really seem to offer the tools I needed. Years before, I had felt impatient with historians who divided masculinity into 'good', responsible house-father masculinity and rough, disruptive male behaviour. Surely you could not have one without the other; the upstanding patriarchs of today were yesterday's tearaways. Indeed, because state power so evidently relied in the end upon force in the early-modern period, authorities needed their young men to have mastered the use of weapons (towns were defended by citizen militias); and while law-makers might inveigh against drinking to excess, male bonding rituals—then as now—usually involve collective consumption of alcohol.[3] I felt irritated with histories that adopted the authorities' moralising tones towards the young rowdies of the past, and impatient with those who claimed to be shocked by Luther's crudeness, or who air-brushed out his aggressive polemics against those he disagreed with. This, to me, was part of Luther's anarchic attractiveness, his refusal to be a plaster saint. And yet, the commemoration year led me to re-consider my tendency to integrate Luther's obstreperous qualities into a relatively positive assessment of his personality, and to draw out more the dangers of his habitual aggression.

Thinking about masculinity—one of the major growth areas of gender history over the last thirty years—can help us think differently about Luther. You could, for example, write a history of the Reformation through Luther's facial hair: the tonsured, shaven monk gave way to the shaggy, bearded, mustachioed Luther once he was in hiding in the Wartburg, disguised as a nobleman. The mature Luther adopted a clean-shaven look but the stubble on his jutting jaw is usually visible. The Cranach workshop was at pains to show Luther as a virile, potent man, a figure very different from a diffident monk. Indeed, it could be argued that the Reformation marked a genuine moment of transformation in the history of masculinity, as it rejected the ideal of celibacy, mocked the pope as effeminate, and abolished monks and priests as different models of manhood. Protestant pastors were meant to be patriarchs like the city fathers and stately bureaucrats

0.2. The Luther Shrine triptych. Veit Thiem, 1572. Collection of the St Peter und Paul (Herderkirche), Weimar. © Heritage Image Partnership Ltd / Alamy Stock Photo.

who employed them. Instead of a multiplicity of different kinds of masculinity, Lutherans valued only one.

Cultural history of this kind has its seductions, but our story must be more complex, because masculinity is never uniform and individuals craft their sexual identities, albeit in dialogue with social forms. After all, from early on, Luther was paired in portraits with the much less potent-looking Melanchthon. Unlike Luther, the younger man wore a wispy beard; and as Melanchthon never was a monk, he did not have to repudiate celibate masculinity; but both men knew Melanchthon was the better scholar. The reformer's masculine strutting was of a piece with his bullying antagonism to the Jews. In his final years he ordered German rulers, including his own elector, to take measures against the Jews and he castigated the Brandenburg electors for being too tolerant, using the same polemical, prophetic mode he had developed early on to enable him to speak the truth (as he saw it) to power.

Luther revelled in his masculinity and liked to see himself as the hero of the Reformation. It was part of the way he established his dominance over his younger followers. It had playful aspects—one of Luther's greatest gifts was his sense of humour—but it also had much less pleasant sides. So, in 1530, when Melanchthon had to conduct the negotiations over the recognition of the Confession of Augsburg, Luther twitted him for his lack of masculine bravery and for weeping too much, cutting remarks that seemed to reveal less about sixteenth century masculinity than they did about Luther's penchant for bullying.[4] Or when, as the *Table Talk* (the notes Luther's students took on his dinner conversations) reveals, Luther mocked his wife Katharina von Bora for her failure to understand what 'rhetoric' was or pronounced that cleverness was the garment that suited women least, Luther's jolliness was also a way of shutting women up.[5] Luther's masculinist polemical mode, in fact, may have been part of the way he cemented his own position and made it less possible for others to speak. It also contributed to making compromise—with the Catholics or with the Sacramentarians—impossible. In this sense, the history of masculinity has much to offer, because this kind of rough-hewn, bullying manhood may mesmerise even those it grinds down. Why were Luther's followers, including women, willing to fall into line, at least for much of the time? And what did Luther's manly displays enable him to do, crossing the lines of what was acceptable, getting away with rudeness, and directing aggression at his greatest enemy, the pope? Luther's masculinity, it seemed, had its noxious streak.

Luther thought in binaries, and repeatedly split people into friends and foes. His ability to turn the world into an epic moral struggle—to see the Devil at work everywhere, to simplify, and to give names to things—was one of his greatest strengths, but also the source of his greatest weaknesses. This pattern is evident in his theological works as well: his ability to put a 'name' on something was key to his devastating polemic, but it was also one of his greatest gifts as a theologian. Looking for repetitive behaviour across all areas of Luther's activity helps us to understand his theology differently: the Luther who devised brilliant nicknames for his friends, calling the Wittenberg pastor Johannes Bugenhagen 'Dr Pommer' (he came from Pomerania and so spoke Low German, and his sermons were too long) and his enemy Johannes Cochlaeus 'the snail' (he was always several steps behind Luther), also had the knack of summarising complex theology in a word.[6] Naming is after all about the relationship of language to reality, a fundamental issue for Luther philosophically as well as theologically. These essays are an attempt to do theological history in a different way. Instead of treating ideas as independent agents, with their own lineages, this book tries to understand them in relation to the person who produced them, and not to distinguish them from their unconscious and semi-conscious usages. It looks for patterns and habits of mind as much as for explicit statements.

Binaries structured much of Lutheran rhetoric and a good deal of the Reformation's propaganda too. Central to this was its apposition of the pope and Christ, and the movement developed an unrelenting anti-papalism in which Luther was the hero who revealed the Papacy for what it truly was: the Antichrist. Even as Luther died, he repeated the anti-papal prophecy which is also a curse: 'Living I was your plague, O Pope, dead I will be your death'. This bitter aphorism was surprisingly pervasive in Lutheran memorial culture from the sixteenth century on. Nowadays the offensive words have frequently been erased, but even when they are not, it can be easy to overlook their presence in some of the most familiar images of the Reformation. For example, Luther's binary thinking was mirrored in the image-making which the Cranach workshop invented for the new movement, with clear vertical divisions into good and evil and anti-papal caricatures which at times bordered on being images of hatred. The movement's obsession with the pope is revealed in the insults his opponents flung at him, both radicals and Catholics. Müntzer dubbed him the Wittenberg Pope, accusing him of 'play[ing] the hypocrite with the princes' and 'set[ting] himself up in place of the pope'.[7] He is 'Pope of the Elbe', complained another former supporter.[8]

And yet the Cranach workshop did far more than manufacture images of hate. It also created novel Reformation iconographies, in particular, Law and Gospel, which—though they use binary forms—do more than contrast opposites. Both Law and Gospel are needed, for the Christian needs the Law to recognize their sin. The image-form the workshop devised required the viewer to meditate on different sections of the image, to incorporate it into their own devotion, and to follow words and sign so as to 'get' the key theological ideas.

There was more, too, to Luther than just the bullying patriarch. Dreams are not normally part of the field of investigation for ecclesiastical historians. But one cannot fail to be haunted by reading Luther's account in a letter to his confessor, Staupitz, of a dream he had when he was feeling abandoned by him, in which he wrote that he felt like a child 'weaned from its mother'. Weaning is a foundational human physical experience, for the mother as for the child, and yet we rarely talk about it.[9] When a child is weaned, he or she gradually separates from the mother and the interdependence of their two digestive systems, which begins at conception, finally comes to an end. For mother and child alike, it means the loss of a deep source of physical connection and pleasure. Both have to find comfort without that oral link, and the child must learn to comfort himself or herself.

Yet while this is a universal human experience, what is revealing is how Luther chose to invoke it, and what this might tell us about a specific historical time. As Luther wrote in the letter, the words were taken from Psalm 131, a psalm which Luther later translated, using words that conveyed more of the child's experience of *being* weaned, and that left the agency of the child in the process unclear. And yet in translations by others, the child is content, having reached its own separation from its mother. Mistakes and imprecisions are usually revealing, often more so than we readily realize, as Freud pointed out long ago: Luther 'remembered' the psalm as conveying a feeling of abandonment and not the child's arrival at its own contentment. This profound ambiguity in how Luther recalled what was a very important biblical quotation for him helps us to understand the depth of his attachment to Staupitz. It also suggests that he was groping his way towards independence as he set off on his own theological path, revealing some of the pain and abandonment that parting from the Catholic church entailed.

A conventional psychoanalytic interpretation might attempt to divine Luther's relationship with his mother through this dream, but that might be a reductive path, narrowing a complex character to problems in weaning and development, about which we know nothing in Luther's case. So also, a psychoanalytic analysis which derived Luther's theology from his relationship with his parents would be unsatisfying—though his complicated relationship to his father, against whom he rebelled by becoming an Augustinian friar, gave him unusual insight into the paternal aspect of the Christian's relation to God, and how that can lead to struggle with God. Psychoanalytic ideas are not much use to historians if they lead them to pathologise an individual. They serve then merely to cheapen complex inner lives and they do not help us understand their thought over time, organically revealed in all their habits, patterns of mind, conscious and unconscious inclinations, and in their actual relationships with others. As we start to tease these out, we can see how dreams—which raise issues about the nature of divine inspiration and prophecy as opposed to the letter of scripture—were connected to central dilemmas of Luther's Reformation. By approaching questions at a tangent, by looking at issues that are on the periphery of our scholarly vision, new and unexpected connections often emerge. So, for example, one of the central theological divisions of the Reformation was linked to the status of dreams. The revolutionary firebrand Thomas Müntzer was scathing about Luther's support of the rich and powerful, and derived his own authority in part from dreams and visions. For his part, Luther was always sceptical about them, preferring to rely on scripture alone—but of course, scripture too features prophetic dreams and visions. Luther could never entirely disavow dreams, and his apparent scepticism masked a fascination with them.

Dreams communicated hopes and fears for people in Luther's circle, allowing them to talk indirectly about them by arguing over possible interpretations of their dreams. They wondered, for example, if the eagle, who became a cat in one of Melanchthon's dreams, stood for the emperor. He was the focus of much of their anxieties at this time as they waited to present their confession of faith to him at the Imperial Diet of 1530 at Augsburg, the document that founded their new church. They worried about this while being unable to talk to Luther, who could come no further than the castle of Coburg. Psychoanalytic ideas could therefore help illuminate not just the psychological dilemmas of individuals, but might disclose the richness of relationships between groups of people—and it was these collective dynamics which were crucial to the Reformation's implementation. They were not just harmonious relationships of co-operation, but often of rivalry for Luther's attention, and they could on occasion include attacks on each other's manhood, as in every movement with a charismatic leader. To look at these undersides of the nascent church is not, of course, to belittle what the Wittenbergers accomplished together; it reminds us how important that Wittenberg collective was to the movement's self-perception: one of the abiding iconographies of the Reformation, not just within Lutheranism, but copied even within iconophobic Calvinism, was that of the reformers sitting together around a table.

Images were central to Lutheranism and museum exhibitions featured prominently in the celebrations of 2017. Perhaps the most inspiring was 'Luther und die Avantgarde', held in the nineteenth-century former jail in Wittenberg, with each artist given a prison cell as a canvas on which to develop their ideas about Luther. Containing a ramshackle series of installations, videos, mixed media artworks, and sculptures, the crumbling building was as much a part of the show as the exhibits, for it juxtaposed the architectural legacies of state institutions with Western cutting-edge art (having been a prison in the Third Reich and in the DDR, the building had lately become a depot for storing official records). Not all of it worked. Some artists seemed to think that Luther was an iconoclast who wanted to destroy all religious images—he was no such thing—while others thought he stood for the freedom of the individual. But some of the displays conveyed aspects of Luther that scholarship had been unable to deal with. In particular I was struck by Erwin Wurm's orange fist that greeted the visitor on arrival at the exhibition, which conveyed that masculine aggression so much part of Luther's style (see figure 1.19).[10] Another was a dizzying prison of clear plastic tubes in a cage-like structure by the Chinese artist Song Dong, filled with sweets and placed on top of a mirror that filled the floor space—it somehow managed to recreate the self-referential quality of Luther's thought, conveying how such a liberating theology could yet turn inwards on itself, repeating its key concepts to infinity.[11] Above all, the sheer creativity and inventiveness of this exhibition showed that Lutheranism is far from being confined to museums, and can inspire extraordinary art.[12]

As it did from its inception. There is no other Protestant sect which could have hosted such an amazing number of exhibitions, because none fostered such a rich material and visual legacy. Most other protestant sects shared iconoclastic instincts, mistrusting sumptuous altarpieces that might seduce the senses, and favouring white-washed walls or simple words from scripture. Not so Luther: from the outset, he remained closer to the Catholicism he had left, and though Lutherans remodelled their churches to include didactic art, with paintings of

Christ blessing the children that underlined the importance of infant baptism, or of Law and Gospel, they decorated their places of worship with appealing and fashionable mannerist designs. They also furnished their churches with images of the reformer himself. The artist Lucas Cranach was one of Luther's oldest friends and earliest supporters, and as the *Lutherjahr* demonstrated, he did more than any other artist to shape the remarkable churches of Saxony and Thuringia, to make Luther's face well known, and to stamp the 'look' of early modern Lutheran print.[13] Lutheranism was as much a visual and material culture as it was a musical one. And if we think that we can 'know' Luther as an individual, that is largely because we are so familiar with the Luther the Cranach workshop made, the man with the deep-set, far-seeing eyes, the confident four-square stance, and the wayward curl, poking out irreverently from underneath the doctor's hat. If this book can occasionally seem critical of Luther, or point to less comfortable features of Lutheranism's legacy, I hope that this will be taken in the spirit of Lutheranism I so admire: its profound anti-authoritarianism, its political engagement, and its insistence on argument, discussion, and critical appraisal of its own history.

0.3. Portrait of Martin Luther. Cranach the Elder, 1528. Kunstsammlungen der Veste Coburg.

CHAPTER I

# The Luther Cranach Made

THE COLLABORATION BETWEEN Luther and the artist Lucas Cranach the Elder contributed perhaps more to the Reformation's success than anything apart from Luther's own writings. Cranach lived just around the corner from Luther and his workshop produced a series of likenesses of the reformer, as well as designing books, illustrating the German Bible, and creating the look of the new churches. Court painter to Luther's ruler Frederick the Wise, he produced dramatically original, striking works, like his luscious scenes of the Fountain of Youth, his Adam and Eves, or his seductive nudes. By comparison, the workshop's portraits of Luther are artistically poor, and yet they proved perhaps to be the most successful of all his image-making because they made Luther recognizable, an effect which endures up to our own time: it is Cranach's Luther that graces the cover of just about every biography of the reformer on sale today, and it is his Luther who stares out even from the icing on the marzipan souvenirs in Wittenberg. Luther's face, moreover, became famous at an important juncture in the history of portraiture, newly fashionable amongst the rich burgher classes of sixteenth-century German lands, as artists broadened out from religious iconographies and began to produce likenesses of individuals for a lay market. Luther was probably the first non-ruler whose face became so universally familiar.[1]

A decade older than Luther, Cranach became court painter to Frederick the Wise, Luther's ruler, in 1504 and settled in Wittenberg. This was seven years before Luther moved there permanently, and he left only after Luther's death, dying in Weimar in 1553, after which his son Lucas Cranach the Younger took over the workshop. Luther and the artist seem to have soon become fast friends; Luther liked to look in on the painter's warehouse in the centre of town to see what was new from the Leipzig fair, for Cranach was not only a painter but the richest man in Wittenberg, holding a monopoly on fine wines and pharmaceutical goods.[2] The ties between the older and the younger man were close: Cranach modelled family life for Luther when he was still an Augustinian, and the two men later acted as godparents to each other's children. When Luther was waylaid and taken to the Wartburg after the Diet of Worms to go into hiding, it was Cranach to whom he wrote explaining he was safe.[3] An outlaw and then endangered by his support for the authorities during the Peasants' War, Luther was frequently confined to Wittenberg by ill health, unable to travel far from Saxony, so Cranach was the only artist who had access to the man himself. As the pair aged, we glimpse their sociability through the *Table Talk*, the notes Luther's students took on the reformer's dinner conversations, published after his death: they tease Cranach's son at his wedding for being besotted with his wife, and share an apple in the summer garden, making coarse jokes about the destination of the apple pips they have swallowed.[4] When Cranach's gifted elder son, Hans, died in Italy, Luther tried to prevent a grief-stricken Cranach and his wife from falling into melancholy, the distemper from which Luther suffered himself.[5]

Cranach occupies an ambivalent position in the pantheon of German artists. Overshadowed by his brilliant contemporary Albrecht Dürer, his adolescent s-bend nudes go in and out of fashion today. Periodic attempts are made to rediscover him as a bold and daring artist, an easier task with his early, arresting representations of St Catherine's martyrdom or his striking Holy Kindred incorporating Frederick the Wise and his brother Duke John amongst the Holy Family.[6] But it is harder to see much artistic merit in the identikit portraits of Luther that his workshop churned out, and which were so reverently brought out of storage in galleries all over the world in 2017.

Seeing Cranach—the man dubbed the 'fast painter' by his contemporaries—as an Artist in the great tradition of Western European art, is fundamentally misconceived.[7] He was above all an image-maker, a man who witnessed the explosion of the new medium of print, who himself owned a printing press for a time, and who was fascinated by these new possibilities of multiplying images.[8] Dürer lived in bustling Nuremberg, crowded with artists and workshops and home to a thriving lay market of rich townsfolk; in tiny Wittenberg, a building site for much of his life, Cranach was the only major artist for miles around and had to import every panel and pigment.[9] His workshop was huge and its output vast; his pictures are patterned assemblages of distinct, repeatable elements that could be put together by a staff of hired assistants.[10] Order a Cranach, and you knew what you were getting. The Cranach 'look' became so recognizable with its signature winged serpent, that his second son Lucas Cranach the Younger barely altered the formula for another generation.[11]

Cranach's portraits of Luther are not artistically dazzling, but they have endured for several hundred years and done much to shape the style of Lutheran piety itself. Cranach aimed not at visual singularity but at instant legibility. The huge corpus of images of Luther the workshop produced fall fairly readily into six or seven categories, tracking his life course. There is Luther the monk, an image which had run its course by 1524; Luther in the Wartburg; Luther as a married man; the standard portrait; the full-body Luther; and dead Luther. Each of these was made famous by the Cranach workshop. Finally, there is a type I shall term 'Luther and Co.' which was produced only after Luther's death.

Just what the workshop achieved is evident if we look at the extraordinarily diverse early images of Luther, before Cranach became involved.[12] The very first, from 1519, was produced not in Wittenberg but in Leipzig by the workshop of Wolfgang Stöckel. It shows a young and rather insecure looking monk, dwarfed by a giant cowl, his face obscured by his massive doctor's hat. We know it is Luther because his name is clumsily written in the roundel, and because the Luther rose is shown, the humanistic symbol Luther had adopted as his logo.[13] This image appeared in the wake of the Leipzig debate of 1519, the event which made Luther famous in humanist circles, and it shows him with his hand raised, in the pose of a disputant. He has no books beside him, his name is written as Martinus 'Lvtter' (though it is spelt correctly in print above), and the text in clumsy mirror writing tags him as an Augustinian, from Wittenberg, and a doctor. At least one printing press made a better attempt at the design a few years

Qk. 198 .(18)

# Ein Sermon geprediget tzu Leipßgk uffm Schloß am tag Petri vñ pau-

li ym. xviiij. Jar / durch den wirdigen vater Doctorem
Martinú Luther augustiner zu Wittenburgk/mit
entschüldigung etzlicher artickel / ßo ym von
etzlichen seiner abgünstigen zugemessen
seyn/in der zeit der Disputacion zu
Leipßgk gehalten.

¶ Getruckt zu Leypßgk durch Wolffgang Stöckel im iar.15o9.

1.1. Woodcut of Martin Luther. *Ein Sermon geprediget tzu Leipßgk.* . . . Anonymous, 1519. Martin
Luther University Halle-Wittenberg.

later, with a version attributed to Erhard Schön almost solving the problem of how to place reversed letters in a roundel; the design now shows a more robust-looking and tonsured monk, his doctor title visible to the left of his head, and a dove suggesting he is inspired by the Holy Spirit.[14] Other images from this early period show a full-length figure dressed as a monk whose face is rather indistinct, whilst another, probably taken from an existing block, shows three Ref-

Martin Luther

1.2. Luther with the dove of the Holy Spirit. Erhard Schön, 1519–20. © Photo: akg-images.

ormation heroes, possibly Luther, Hutten, and von Sickingen, but it is anyone's guess which is Luther.[15]

Cranach's intervention in this profusion of likenesses was deci-sive. Around 1520 he produced two full-face etchings of Luther. The first version, which is best known today, seems to have been judged unsuitable at the time, for most of the surviving prints date from the second half of the sixteenth century, and show a doodle etched in the corner of the plate.[16] A revision of the etching, however, be-came hugely influential at the time—although it is barely used now and seems not to suit contemporary taste. Altered to show a far less threatening, peaceable Luther, it shows him standing in front of a niche holding a Bible.[17]

The difference between the two etchings is revealing. The first is psychologically gripping—this is the intense monk who could write such iconoclastic works as the *Appeal to the Christian Nobility*; the second is a milder, more saccharine saint. In the first we see only the young monk's head, and the artist focuses relentlessly on his phys-iognomy; in the other, we see his upper body and gesturing hands, along with a background niche. The change is a shift from inner to outer, from a man whose intense gaze unsettles, to a more distanced, broad-chested public figure, with less interiority. This was a decision Cranach made early on, and it would determine the nature of the

1.3. Martin Luther as an Augustinian Monk. Cranach the Elder, 1520. Metropolitan Museum of Art.

1.4. Portrait of Martin Luther. Cranach the Elder, 1520. British Museum.

portraits that followed, which became ever more clear, iconic, public, and, I would suggest, more psychologically shallow. They could be mass produced because they portrayed Luther in well-worn conventions, making him easy to grasp.

Just how effective Cranach's second, more bland image was can be seen in the range of pamphlets and presses which copied it for their title pages: there were versions from Strasbourg, Vienna, Basel, Augsburg, Erfurt, and Lübeck.[18] Within barely five years, an unknown monk in an academic backwater had become a face recognized across the Holy Roman Empire.[19] All images are based on the Cranach original, and were most often used on the cover of *On the Babylonian Captivity*, one of Luther's most daring assaults on the Church, although they continued to front later works as well.[20] This meant that the reader encountered Luther's text mediated by Cranach's version of his face. The monk holds a Bible and stands in front of a niche, but that is not why we know it is Luther. Unlike a saint such as St Catherine—immediately identifiable by the wheel she carries—it

1.5. Title page, *De captivitate Babylonica eccle-siae*. Martin Luther, 1520. Folger Shakespeare Library.

1.6. Portrait of Martin Luther, *Acta et res gestae D. Martini Lutheri*. Hans Baldung Grien, Martin Luther, 1521. Southern Methodist University—Perkins School of Theology.

is Luther's features, not his attributes, which make him recognizable: his deep-set eyes, strong jaw, dimpled chin, wide cheekbones, and thick neck. Hans Baldung Grien's own high-quality version, produced in 1521, removes the niche and adds a dove and halo to show him as a man with divine inspiration, and yet we know it is Luther *despite* these additional attributes because of his familiar face.[21]

At about this time, Cranach had bought a printing press which he ran together with his friend the goldsmith Döring, so he would have guessed how his image might be used and spread. The image was probably on sale as a single sheet at the Imperial Diet of 1521, where Luther defended his works in front of the emperor and all the assembled Imperial Estates, and it would have flown around the empire, copied in presses everywhere.[22] We know too that specially designed medals of the leading players at the Diet were also sold at Worms. Luther had become a recognizable individual.[23]

By contrast, the profile portrait Cranach produced around the same year was much less successful and did not take off so readily in cheap

1.7. Luther as an Augustinian friar, with cap.
Cranach the Elder, 1521.

print. Fitting perfectly into the medal design common for rulers and humanists, and modelled on classical coins, this Renaissance design shows Luther with his doctor's cap, underlining his scholarship more than his Augustinianism; and it gave rise to at least one medal. The effect of the profile is distancing; it invites neither intimacy nor identification. Luther looks away, his gaze cannot be penetrated, and his face is not haggard but fleshy, with the merest hint of a double chin. His ear suggests someone directly inspired by the Spirit, as does the soft halo brightening the face.[24] Only the vestige of a curl adds a touch of waywardness and personality. Daniel Hopfer copied it in 1523, adding more hair and increasing the saintly resonances of the image; Altdorfer produced another.[25] I know of only two further versions based on this profile: one, a profile portrait by Sebald Beham from 1520 or 1523 that shows Luther at a desk as if he were St Jerome; indeed, Beham has borrowed Baldung's dove as well as Cranach's halo.[26] The other dates from 1525 during the Peasants' War, when the Reformation was beginning to be riven with division, and it harks back to earlier images that were not influenced by Cranach's designs. It shows a standing Luther with bent knee, but the profile is puffy, the jowls weighty, no longer the passionate monk of yore.

It was with its three-quarter frontal portrait of Luther that the Cranach workshop created an iconography which spread across Germany and which helped turn Luther into the best-selling writer of his age. It was not yet universal; Cranach himself did not use this iconography in his own printing so far as I can see, and Wittenberg printings of the *Babylonian Captivity* never deployed it; nor did it truly break through into branding every item Luther wrote. Cranach lost

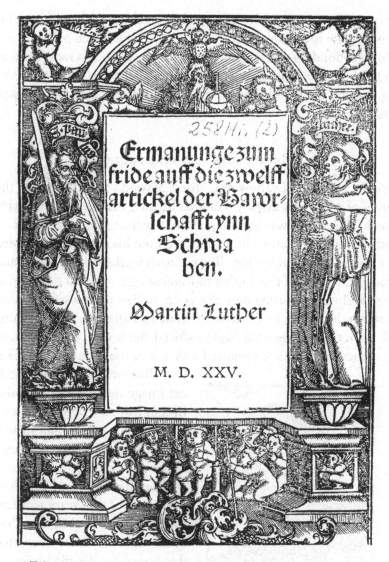

1.8. Title page, *Ermanunge zum fride auff die zwelff artickel der Bawrschafft*. Martin Luther, 1525. Herzog August Library, Wolfenbüttel Digital Library.

control of the image he had made, but his achievement was to create a physiognomy that other, cruder artists copied, and a face which the reader could recognize. Contemporaries remarked on Luther's remarkable, deep-set eyes: the papal nuncio Aleander thought them 'demonic'.[27] Readers of these pamphlets in Strasbourg or Lübeck who would never meet the reformer could nevertheless encounter his famous gaze for themselves, Luther looking out of the picture space while expounding scripture to them, his ear open to God's word as theirs should be. The inimitable face matched the style of the writing, because Luther's language was close to speech and, like his gaze, brilliantly direct.

## BACK FROM THE WARTBURG

Neither iconography, however, lasted beyond 1524. Indeed, by the spring of 1521 it was already outdated because the most recognizable man in the empire was in hiding in the Wartburg, disguising his face with a beard and moustache. Luther grew out his tonsure and dressed as a knight called Junker Jörg. The Cranach workshop responded and produced images of this Luther too, including a woodcut designed as a single sheet measuring over 21 × 34 cm in size and showing Luther in 1522 on his return to Wittenberg 'from his Pathmos', the Wartburg. We do not know when this was produced, but it was possibly around this time that Cranach produced a sketch of the reformer as Junker

Jörg. The verse below the woodcut image denounces perfidious Rome, Luther's persecutor, and other versions add small historical accounts of Luther's actions in the years 1521 and 1522.[28]

The Junker Jörg woodcut forms part of the creation of Luther as a historical figure. Cranach could not have circulated this image during the period of the reformer's stay in the Wartburg because his whereabouts and disguise were meant to be kept secret. After his return to Wittenberg, Luther donned his monastic garb once again, and it would take him some time to

1.9. Luther as 'Junker Jörg'. Cranach the Elder, 1522. Metropolitan Museum of Art.

decide he was no longer a monk. The image is not, therefore, showing him as he is in the present, but as he was at the moment of his return in the spring of 1522. It would not even have been wise to produce such an image soon after Luther's return because this was supposed to be taking place in opposition to the elector's will, though it was probably with electoral connivance.[29] Moreover, the mention of his 'Pathmos' would only have been familiar to those who had read the *Invocavit* sermons that Luther gave after his return to Wittenberg in 1522, or his letters circulating in manuscript in the 1530s and published in the late 1540s. These readers would have known that he liked to refer to the castle as his Patmos, an echo of John writing the Book of Revelation on his island.[30]

It seems therefore to be an image intended for pious Lutherans, who knew both Latin and their hero's life story. It reminded them of the drama that followed Worms, and pointed forward to their hero's return to Wittenberg, where he would deal with his erstwhile collaborator and now enemy Andreas Karlstadt.[31] While Luther had been absent, Karlstadt had spearheaded a Wittenberg Reformation in opposition to the elector's wishes; the reformer's return was therefore about the creation of Wittenberg orthodoxy. The Cranach woodcut was part of the heroic myth-making of Luther as the man who 'was first on the field of battle', as Luther put it himself in the *Invocavit* sermons of April 1522 in which he trounced Karlstadt.[32] It linked Luther's story to his loyalty to the Saxon house and to his undying opposition to a radical like Karlstadt.

A few painted versions of this Luther survive from the Cranach output, in Weimar, Leipzig, and Muskegon, Michigan, and they are not high quality. All have a green background, and the Michigan version is dated '1537'.[33] It seems possible, therefore, that this iconography was a later curio, catering to those with an interest in Luther's life story; the project at the German Historical Museum Nuremberg, which aims to date all the workshop's corpus, will likely settle the question.[34] With its striking corners and luxurious moustache, the beard is remarkably like that of Frederick the Wise, Luther's ruler, whose image the workshop was also propagating as part of a propaganda campaign by the later electors. One might almost speculate that Luther's extravagant facial hair in these images only makes sense in relation to the clean-shaved, balding Luther of the later portraits, as if to prove that he *could* have grown a beard had he chosen.[35] A later etching also trumpets Luther's manhood: this monumental Luther is so broad that he can barely get his legs together.[36]

## Double Portraits

In 1525, Luther married Katharina von Bora, a double outrage because it was the marriage of a monk and a nun who both broke their vows. From then on, painted double portraits of Luther and Katharina were produced by the Cranach workshop every year until about 1529, and they are mostly dated on the work itself.[37] At least twenty of them survive, and they are widely scattered, with versions in Milan, Stockholm, and in the Uffizi, Florence.

Luther's face in these portraits changes as he puts on weight and becomes more confident, until by 1528 we have a fully grown, masculine Luther. He is now a father with a household of his own. And yet the face is still recognizably that of the Cranach etchings of 1520 with the same visual features: the deep-set eyes with their penetrating gaze, the heavy jowls, bull neck, impressive stubble, and wayward hair. Only the ear is less evident now, hidden by a shock of curls.

These images are based on the double marriage portrait which was in vogue amongst the upper bourgeoisie, but they are subtly different. Unlike the commissioned portraits of patricians and rich burghers— such as the beautifully realized portraits of an unidentified couple from 1522 now in the National Gallery of Art, Washington, D.C.[38]— they are of poorer quality, copied many times and probably intended as diplomatic gifts. Their various formats reflect different functions: some are in circular frames that fit into each other so they can be kept in a plain round capsule; some have hinged rectangular frames which allow the pair to be shut and even closed with a hook, like a gaming board.[39] These portraits are evidently not intended for public display but for holding and contemplation. Others are, however, designed for conventional hanging on a wall—not to commemorate a private family history, but to proclaim a Lutheran, Saxon message. Cranach simplifies the faces, making the couple immediately recognizable and producing a double image which is more like a commentary on complementary sexual roles in marriage than a lifelike marriage portrait. As befits a noblewoman, Katharina wears a fashionable hairnet, not a wimple. Her waist is implausibly narrow, and her features vary more than Luther's do; indeed, she resembles Cranach's universal woman, with her catlike rounded face and slanting eyes, leaning slightly forward in the manner of all Cranach nudes, and collapsing her chest as if she can barely breathe.[40]

These portraits were unlikely to have been directed at a local market. Nor is it clear what influence Luther had over how he was depicted. We know that the Cranach workshop possessed cartoons of both von Bora and Luther that would have enabled them to standardise the image,[41] and yet they never produced woodcut versions of the paintings. Instead, Hans Brosamer, perhaps a former member of the Cranach workshop, provided a cheaper single-sheet woodcut for those whose purses could not run to the painted originals. His double portraits even have woodcut frames, so they could be pasted straight onto a wall without further ado.[42]

The Cranach workshop soon stopped producing such images and we know of very few after 1530; so far as I know, Brosamer did not produce a new design of the couple after 1530 either. The 'Luther marriage portrait' lasted little more than five years and seems to have functioned rather like the sixty or more portraits of the Saxon electors,

1.10a. Portrait of Martin Luther. Cranach the Elder, 1525. © Kunstmuseum, Basel, Switzerland / HIP / Art Resource, NY.

1.10b. Portrait of Katharina von Bora. Cranach the Elder, 1525. © Kunstmuseum, Basel, Switzerland / HIP / Art Resource, NY.

1.10c. Diptych with the portraits of Luther and his wife. Cranach the Elder, 1529. Hessisches Landesmuseum, Darmstadt.

1.10d. Portrait of Katharina von Bora. Hans Brosamer, 1530. Gotha, Duke's Museum (Landesmuseum).

1.10e. Portrait of Martin Luther. Hans Brosamer, 1530. Gotha, Duke's Museum (Landesmuseum).

painted by the workshop in the 1530s in identical formats and sent out as propaganda across the empire.[43] These too drastically simplified facial features and flattened the visual field, whilst a third of their pictorial space was taken up with rhymes recounting the electors' lives and works, painted so as to resemble typeface.

The broad diffusion of the Luther marriage portrait across Europe, including in lands which were not Protestant, may seem surprising. In one tantalising case we know a little of their history. The versions in the Uffizi derive from the Medici collection and have been there since at least 1561—and probably since soon after they were painted. We know that Cosimo de' Medici hung the portrait in his private chamber, not in the public rooms, and that the collection also boasted one of the standard-issue portraits of the Saxon ruling house produced in the 1530s. It is remarkable to think that a Catholic duke should have kept a portrait of the infamous reformer, and even more extraordinary that it depicted the marriage that was such an affront to the Cath-olic Church. The curators at the Uffizi suggest its presence could be explained by Cosimo's increasing hostility towards the Papacy—but this would not account for its appearance in the collection in the first place. It seems more likely that, along with the portrait of the elector, it was part of the electoral Saxons' visual propaganda campaign, an extraordinary and innovative use of what we might term 'semi-print'. Like posters, these images publicised Saxon characters, making them famous. It is a final historical irony that they now count as works of art and have even enjoyed their own commemorative show—at the Uffizi no less.[44]

The Reformation itself, however, never seems to have been fully comfortable with the Luther marriage portrait. It only returned in the late sixteenth and seventeenth centuries, as people became in-terested in their own movement's past. By the eighteenth century there were etching copies of the paintings, though these sometimes omitted Katharina altogether, as in the case of a reversed copy of the painting found in the library of Gottorff.[45] The etching improves on the original by adding the ring which Luther used to seal his letters, an anachronism, since he was given this by the elector only in 1530; he also holds his doctoral hat in his hand, something a Cranach Luther never does.

1.11. Martin Luther after Lucas Cranach the Elder, 1525. © National Portrait Gallery, London.

Already by 1530, the iconography had moved decisively away from Katharina. For years afterward Lutherans had trouble dealing with their hero's marriage. She had always introduced something disruptive into the ideal of the scholarly professor, and the marriage had become a target of Catholic ridicule too. Most sixteenth-century biographies avoid mentioning it, and the wedding is omitted from the sixteenth- and seventeenth-century picture versions of the reformer's life I have seen. The exception is an eighteenth-century Catholic satire, where Luther is shown first leading the nuns astray, and then marrying Katharina; he gets his final comeuppance as his coffin is ejected from the Wittenberg monastery and flies straight into the flames of Hell.[46]

In the place of Katharina, it was Philip Melanchthon who took the distaff position.[47] The unlikely pairing of the two Reformation talents was meant to represent unity in theology and leadership—though Luther as the larger is clearly the senior figure.[48] Like Cranach, Brosamer

1.12. Catholic satire on Luther's life, 1730. © Luther Memorial Foundation in Saxony-Anhalt.

1.13a. Philip Melanchthon. Heinrich Aldegrever, 1540. Metropolitan Museum of Art.

1.13b. Martin Luther. Heinrich Aldegrever, 1540. Art Institute Chicago, Clarence Buckingham Collection.

1.13c. Portraits of Martin Luther and Philip Melanchthon. Cranach the Elder, 1543. Galleria degli Uffizi, Florence.

also now replaced Katharina with Melanchthon in his new woodcut portrait; and the artist Heinrich Aldegrever turned his hand to an etching of the two men, reversing their positions. It was this, and not the marriage portrait, that became the variant that would last long into the seventeenth century. But the unity it depicted was spurious and the movement split bitterly after Luther's death between Lutheran loyalists and compromising Philippists.

The celebration of the double marriage portraits in leading art galleries around the world thus distorts our perception of how the Reformation liked to see itself. It was certainly not the most reproduced twin portrait of the reformer; that honour passed to the paired images of Luther and Melanchthon, of which there were many, many more.

### Full-Face Luther: The Standard Portrait

By 1530, the once gaunt, habit-wearing reformer was filling out and even putting on weight. This was the version of Luther that became standard and lasted for centuries in prints and etchings as well as on a welter of material objects, such as book covers, drinking vessels, tiles, and medals.[49]

This instantly recognizable design proved to be the workshop's lasting achievement. No other reformer spawned a similar visual culture: few images of Calvin survive, only a handful of Zwingli, and there are none of Karlstadt or Müntzer.[50] With far greater success than even that of the 1520 etching of the young Luther, Cranach's workshop created an icon for the movement itself. Luther's clothes would soon become stylised, with the red undershirt, collar, and black ribbon of the clerical uniform he invented, a variant of academic dress. Sometimes he wears the doctor's cap, sometimes not; his wayward hair perhaps hints at a rule breaker. The physiognomy builds on the earlier images and highlights the same facial features: the dark deep-set eyes on which contemporaries remarked, strong jaw, heavy jowls, dimpled chin, and broad cheekbones. No longer a monk, Luther has grown out his tonsure. Although he has returned to a clean-shaven look, we know that he *can* grow a beard, and the stubble does not let us forget his virility, even in black and white. A beautifully finished Cranach portrait on the inside of a presentation Bible—of much higher quality than most versions of the design—shows the five o'clock shadow in all its glory; and it gives Luther's hand as well, his signature dedication on the facing page transforming this printed book into a unique and precious gift.[51]

So influential was the classic Cranach pattern that it soon determined how Luther was represented everywhere. When Katharina commissioned the Katharinenportal for Luther's fifty-seventh birthday in 1540, she definitively turned Luther's former monastery where they lived into 'their' household. Rather than commemorating both herself and her husband with coats of arms, or with a double portrait, she had the Luther rose placed on one underside and a stone portrait of Luther indebted to the Cranach likeness on the other.[52]

The genius of this simple design of Luther's face is its boldness and clarity. It pretends to realism, yet the face is flattened and the monochrome background helps its lumpy features stick in the viewer's mind. It could translate easily into woodcuts, large and small, as these pamphlet covers show. But the legibility comes at the cost of interiority. The intensity of the gaze of the agonized monk of Cranach's first design has given way to a milder, diffuse benevolence. This is the face of a leader, distant and assured.

When Luther died in 1546 there was an outpouring of memorial images of the reformer, in pamphlet illustrations or on standalone single sheets, and the style became yet more ossified. Indelibly linked with the workshop, the Cranach winged serpent is an integral part of the design, proclaiming its authenticity. This Luther was copied by other painters, who now produced the images the new Church needed to hang in its churches or illustrate its books with. It could be translated onto pottery, or turned into green ceramic tiles.[53] Even satirists paid Cranach a backhanded compliment: their hostile images of the reformer follow his motifs to the letter, copying niche, collar, doctor's cap, and curls, because they and their audience knew the originals so well.[54] Luther's face, like Cranach's winged serpent, had become a brand.[55]

The rise of this iconography coincided with the development of Lutheranism as a separate Church. The first Saxon visitation was held in 1527, and in partnership with state officials, all the parishes of the territory were inspected. By 1530 the Lutherans presented their confession of faith to the emperor at the Diet of Augsburg. A move-

1.14. Portrait of Martin Luther. Cranach the Younger, 1570–1580. © Art Resource, NY.

ment which was a Church, but which did not have an ecclesiastical structure, found its expression in the face of its founder. His only props are his doctor's cap, proof of his learning, and his Bible, just as the only post Luther ever held was his professorship of Holy Scripture in Wittenberg.

## *Full-Body Luther*

The workshop soon produced a variant of the mature Luther that showed his entire body. Solid, four-square, and grounded, his face sits atop the plinth of his massive cassock, his massive boots poking out incongruously below. He is certainly not a saint. Gone was any hint of a halo, and the images could certainly not be used as devotional objects—Luther's face is simply too realistic to be worshipped. Instead, the workshop found a way to represent Luther's authority without relying on the trappings of his office as images of popes or bishops did. They showed the fleshy Luther, the anti-monastic reformer, who loved to eat and drink; and they conveyed his authority in his body by aligning his ample figure with the equally ample 'look' of the Saxon ruling house.[56] Such portraits resembled the full-body portraits of secular rulers in this period, and Luther's bulk conveyed his power in a similar fashion.

1.15. Portrait of Martin Luther, 11 parts. Cranach the Younger, 1560. © Luther Memorial Foundation in Saxony-Anhalt.

By the second half of the sixteenth century, big images of this kind were increasingly favoured.[57] Cranach the Younger produced one that could be assembled from eleven separate sheets and pasted up to make a life-size Luther. You could also swap his head for that of another reformer.[58] Matching life-size paintings of local reformers made to look like the hero himself soon proliferated. They have a sculptural feel, and they replaced the statues of saints that once adorned churches. Orthodoxy began to be represented by visual alignment with Luther, and instead of a church space that housed a variety of female and male saints, Lutheran church walls were lined with men in formless black semi-academic attire, sometimes in serried ranks of identical-size paintings that showed the succession through the years of similar-looking men—who might be related because parsons' sons so often followed in their fathers' footsteps or married parsons' daughters.[59] Full-body Luthers lasted into the eighteenth century and beyond, forming the centrepiece of one-page versions of the reformer's life.

## Dead Luther

The depictions of Luther reached their apotheosis when the painter Lukas Furtenagel was sent to Eisleben to paint the reformer on his deathbed. Those who were with Luther provided a complete account of his death, detailing his movements in his final days, and their description was published at Wittenberg, along with the funeral sermons and speeches. Lutherans had abolished the sacrament of extreme unction, so Luther had to die according to the new faith. The stakes were high

because a bad or disfiguring death, such as a stroke, would have suggested that Luther's doctrine was false. It was important therefore to proclaim that he had passed away peacefully, and the death-bed pictures provided public evidence. They too were soon copied, in woodcuts as well as paintings.[60]

There was no time to dispatch Cranach to Eisleben to paint his dead friend, but this image type owed a great deal to the physiognomy the workshop had already made famous, the dimple-cleft chin, unruly hair, and heavy jowls. Before long the workshop added it to its stock of designs, and at least six versions of Luther on his deathbed survive from the Cranach workshop.[61]

1.16. Portrait of Martin Luther on his deathbed. Cranach the Younger, 1546. Niedersächsisches Landesmuseum, Hannover.

33

The Saxon court painter Veit Thiem's Weimar triptych of 1572 provides the ultimate commentary and final chapter on the Cranach workshop's success at creating Luther's image (see figure 0.2).[62] On the left, it shows Luther the monk, now a deliberately archaic image; on the right, Luther the hirsute Junker Jörg; and in the centre in larger size, Luther, the icon he had become. Like the images of the Saxon electors, this work mixes print and image, and the words of the Bible in the image are a visual echo of the story of Luther's life below. Though the format plays with the form of the altarpiece, Luther is not a saint; there are no bones below and nothing to pray to. Instead there is just a person, a man whose face the workshop has made famous, and whose fame has made Cranach famous too. Luther is now so easy to spot that we instantly recognize him when he replaces St Jerome in Wolfgang Stübner's pastiche of Dürer's famous image.[63] We know Luther when we see him preaching from the predella of the Wittenberg altar, or when we see him in relief on the side of a beer mug today.

*Luther & Co.*

Finally, the image of Luther and the other reformers at table was not produced by the Cranach workshop and yet it owes a great deal to its designs. It sprang from the *Table Talk*, Luther's dinner-time remarks first published in 1566, a generation after Luther's death. The image first appeared on a pirated version of the text from Frankfurt in 1567, and it shows Luther and the other Wittenbergers sitting at a table, with four children in order of height facing them. We recognize Cranach's Luther, with his bulk, his untamed hair, wide forehead, and heavy jowls.[64] Each of the Wittenbergers is named in the roundel, and the Reformation is presented as team work: the image has shifted away from Luther the heroic individual to Luther as part of a community. The awkward reference in the image to the Last Supper must have disconcerted contemporaries, for it was soon rotated and given a Mannerist twist. The *Table Talk* was an instant classic, giving the reader an insight into Luther's home life and character. A generation after his death, they introduced Luther the man to a public that could not meet him, whilst also organizing his theology into bite-sized, easily digestible chunks.

1.17. "Colloqvia Oder Tischreden Doctor Martini Lutheri." Frankfurt, Peter Schmid, 1568.

Luther's children are on show in the image, but Katharina is missing. She may be hiding in the furthest right-hand edge of the roundel, though that would leave Luther a child short: the couple had six, four of whom survived. Crossing the boundary between household and scholarly group, public and private, this image type cannot quite combine the two successfully, and Katharina is muzzled, just as she largely is in the *Table Talk* itself, where she acts as a foil for Luther's jokes. Soon she would drop out of the image altogether, taking the children with her. Later versions of the image—and they continued to be used well into the eighteenth century—show only the reformers. The all-male version was easy to extend to images of the Reformation in general, to include Calvin, Zwingli, and the English reformers.[65] Unsurprisingly, this iconography offered an irresistible target to Catholic satirists. One grisly image by the Catholic propagandist Johannes Nas satirizes the divisions after Luther's death by showing the reformers sitting around a table, anatomizing and consuming not a pleasant supper but Luther's corpse.[66]

Though not by Cranach's workshop, the composition of the *Table Talk* woodcut owed something to the swift painter nonetheless, because it echoes Cranach's Dessau Last Supper altarpiece of 1565, which shows the reformers in the guise of the apostles, sitting around the table at the Last Supper.[67] Indeed, the 'Luther' of the *Table Talk* is the one Cranach had made familiar. In many of its editions, the volume of the *Table Talk* contained a second woodcut showing Luther's shoulders and face that conformed to Cranach's famous design, with his clerical uniform and jowls.

Cranach and his workshop created the face of the Lutheran movement. The process began in 1520 with three very different versions of the Luther portrait, and it was the milder monk, gesturing with his Bible, who won out. Copied by print workshops all over the empire, used on medals and sold as etchings, Luther the monk was famous. When Luther took a wife, the workshop changed tack and produced a series of portraits of the reformer and Katharina von Bora, presenting the shocking couple in the conventions of upper-middle-class portraiture. This double portrait design is perhaps today the best known of all the versions of his image, perhaps because Katharina's female presence intrigues modern audiences, and yet it was actually short-lived, soon replaced by double portraits of Luther and his less visually appealing co-worker Melanchthon.

Solo Luther meanwhile took final form as the Cranach workshop designed an iconic visage. The workshop made Luther's face, instantly recognizable, part of the message, whilst the Cranach workshop's winged serpent became intrinsic to the portrait too. The man Luther guaranteed the movement's message; the workshop logo guaranteed the image. Luther became a monument, and the workshop produced images of Luther's whole body, including Luther on his deathbed. Cranach's Luther must be numbered amongst the workshop's most influential and longest-lasting creations, perfectly adapted to the new medium of print, and ideally suited to a movement which relied so heavily on the personal charisma of its leader—never more so than when that leader was dead.

Cranach was so successful that his instantly recognisable Luther lives on even today in modern portraits of Luther, each of which is indebted to Cranach in different ways. For example, the East German artist Uwe Pfeifer's *Tischgespräch mit Luther* was completed in 1984, a year after the 500th anniversary of Luther's birth, which was celebrated in a series of events in East Germany.[68] The GDR had at first denigrated Luther, honouring Thomas Müntzer instead as the authentic revolutionary, but by 1983 it recuperated Luther into its pantheon of heroes. Pfeifer's work translated the *Table Talk* into what was then the most modern medium, television. Luther is a chat show guest and his interlocutors include a liberation fighter and a stolid media star, while Adam and Eve flank the triptych, Eve smoking, and Adam wearing headphones. The piece is three-dimensional, with a chair that invites the viewer to join the show.[69]

The work was intended for the University of Halle-Wittenberg, but it was apparently felt to be offensive. For a while it was displayed on the rear wall of an auditorium in Halle, but it is now kept in a conference room of the Leucorea in Wittenberg, where I stumbled upon it in 2017. The room is so small that the chair is in the way, and the work itself

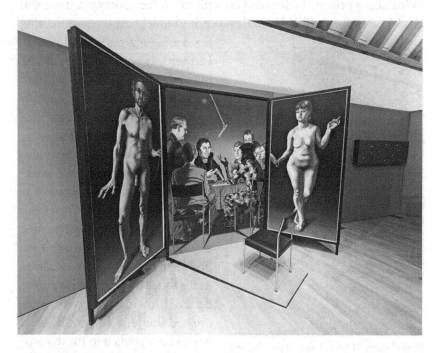

1.18. Table talk with Luther. Uwe Pfeifer, 1984. © dpa picture alliance / Alamy Stock Photo.

is hard to see. Pfeifer's piece is as much an engagement with Cranach as it is a meditation on Luther: the triptych shape itself is a reflection on the many Lutheran altarpieces, the Adam and Eve figures though based originally on Dürer's famous couple also echo Cranach's and fit perfectly with the wider culture of amateur nudist photography in the GDR.[70] Luther is immediately recognizable from Cranach's version and the central panel uses the conceit of the reformers at table which fronts the *Table Talk*. The picture could be read as an attempt to present Luther as a revolutionary who would have been a liberation theologian had he been alive in 1980s East Germany; or it might be viewed as an ironic updating of Cranach, the cultural heritage to which the East was then trying to lay claim. Pfeifer remains a significant artist whose reputation survived the fall of the Wall, and exhibitions of his work are held in Halle today, but this marvellous painting seems to have offended both East and West, falling into oblivion.

By contrast, the Viennese artist Erwin Wurm's lurid orange fist fronted the 2017 Luther und die Avantgarde show, held in the former Wittenberg prison.[71] Mounted on a plinth in the courtyard, it greeted all visitors. A powerful, dramatic piece, it uniquely captures something

few commentators have addressed: Luther's aggression. This is the man who boasted of having been 'first on the field of battle', Luther the pugilist who insulted the 'ass-fart pope', 'Pope Paula III'.

Wurm also pays unconscious homage to Cranach, whose workshop illustrated an edition of Fabian von Auerswald's *Ringerkunst* (*The Art of Wrestling*), first printed at Wittenberg by Luther's own printer in 1539.[72] There is something about the wily old instructor, deftly throwing his noble, well-dressed student antagonist, that would have spoken to the dynamics of Wittenberg at that time. By

1.19. Erwin Wurm's Boxing Glove Sculpture. Erwin Wurm. © 2020 Artists Rights Society (ARS), New York / Bildrecht, Vienna.

then the reformers were well into their fifties and Cranach himself over sixty. Formed in a very different world from their aristocratic students, Cranach's images of the old teacher still contriving to overwhelm his student must have struck a chord.

The final image of Luther is by a woman. Finished in 2017, 'Luther as an Anti-Semite' is by the Amsterdam artist Neel Korteweg, who was unable to find a Lutheran space to exhibit it. Her Luther is large and luxuriantly fleshy—soft, almost maternal, and slightly repellent. He has discarded his talar, formal clerical collar, and ribbon for a loose bathrobe that still displays the tailor's stitches, leaving him vulnerable and naked underneath, the man minus the uniform he invented. Instead of a Bible he holds a gold ring, the symbol Jews were forced to wear, and Korteweg intimates that this man with his dark piggy eyes is on the side of the propertied. This portrait is not sympathetic, and puts its finger on Luther's bullying masculinity, all talk behind its puffy frailty, that is such a feature of the Cranachs we have seen. This is Luther the anti-Semite, a riposte to Cranach's idealisation, on which it closely draws.

All three modern works engage in some way with Cranach's iconography, testifying to the influence of his creation. Cranach's workshop was an artisanal factory, breaking the artistic process into parts that could be reproduced by his assistants and assembled in new ways. He was fascinated by the multiplication of the image, whether through print, through paint as imitating type, or as the production of endlessly similar but slightly different images. He strove for a particular 'look', clear, instantly legible, and recognizable.

Luther too knew that he was recognizable by his style, and was proud of it. When he published an anonymous satire against Albrecht of Mainz, and was asked if he was the author, he replied that of course he was: 'I made it so that I would be recognized. And whoever reads it and has ever seen my thoughts or quill will have to say, "Das ist der Luther"!'[73] His written style was inimitable, and he would constantly address his 'dear reader', as if speaking directly to him or her. In the midst of theological polemics he would prove his point by referring to his own life, how he had stood up to the radicals or fought the papists. Reading Luther meant encountering a character and getting to know his life story; and so Cranach's Luther was the perfect foil for the reformer's rhetorical style.

1.20. Luther with the yellow ring. © Neel Korteweg. Amsterdam 2017, acrylic on linen 50/60 cm.

Cranach solved the fundamental problem of how to present Luther as a man and not a saint. Lutheranism famously rejected the cult of saints, and yet its founder constantly threatened to become another holy man. This was a tension some of the early images of Luther did not resolve, presenting their hero as divinely inspired or wreathed in a halo. But by finding a design which showed Luther as distinctive, manly, manageably plain, stout, and human, Cranach managed to square this circle. Luther became a character, not a saint. A new kind of man, he was not a celibate cleric, but a virile colossus whose power was reflected in his bulk and in his mighty stubble. Cranach achieved this at the cost of psychological complexity—the workshop portraits do not invite our curiosity, and betray little behind the flat, public mask. Luther had no formal position in his new Church, remaining 'only' a doctor of holy scripture. His authority depended on his masculine charisma, and so, in a sense, on the 'face' Cranach created.

Uniquely in Protestantism, Luther's image was *the* identifier of the new sect. It gave rise to a whole material culture of images of the reformer that outlasted Luther and the workshop. Indeed, Cranach's portrait proved so successful that it escaped the bounds of Lutheranism altogether and became a signifier not just for the Lutheran Church, but for German-ness itself. The costs of such a focus are high: they create a movement that is liable to split when its founder dies, making it hard to see the contribution of others, and they personalise ideas. Luther with the piggy eyes in the 2017 anniversary appears almost not at all, and Cranach's one-dimensional Luther still triumphs over a more complex understanding of Luther the man and his ambivalent legacies. But Cranach's remarkable image has survived for five hundred years, and its capacity to point beyond itself is why it still played such a central role in the celebrations of 2017.

## CHAPTER 2

# Luther and Dreams

ROM THE JESUIT Matteo Ricci's dream of God appearing to him as he returned to Nanchang to start converting China, to the remarkable prophetic dreams of Lucrecia de Leon about Philip II, dreams in the Reformation century offered a distinctive medium that was used to convey profound experiences. Dreams are experiences before they are texts, and they can encompass ambiguity, their meanings multiple and puzzling.[1] The Bible too is full of visions and dreams, from Joseph's dreams to the dream of Nebuchadnezzar. Divining the meaning of dreams has been an art stretching back to Antiquity, and dream books that matched each dream object with a particular significance were part of the cultural furniture with which everyone involved in the Reformation had grown up.[2]

With such a biblical precedent for the importance of dreams, quite apart from their cultural currency, it was no surprise that Luther's followers took them seriously. Melanchthon, Luther's co-worker, was the great dreamer of the Reformation; he could be relied upon to have dreams at the moments of greatest historical significance.[3] Rich panoramas, his dreams featured groups of angels, dragons, and asses on their hind legs pulling ropes, crowded with motifs that could have been taken straight from the artist Lucas Cranach's memorable Reformation tableaus. Melanchthon's dreams were so visually striking that Luther's table companions even attempted to sketch them.[4] Luther himself, whose dreams were less elaborate, was characteristically sceptical about the significance of dreams.[5] Theirs was the most important friendship of the Reformation, and part of its dynamic was that Melanchthon played the dreamer to Luther's sceptic. 'I prayed to God not to send me dreams',[6] Luther quipped, and he teased Melanchthon for being plagued by ills caused not by God or the Devil (as were Luther's many physical sufferings) but 'by the stars'.[7] Luther dismissed such things as 'lauter somnia', mere dreams, and he regularly labeled superstition, the views of his antagonists, Catholic dogma, and the beliefs of the Turks and the Jews as 'dreams'.[8]

But Luther also had potent dreams. As historians, we can recover what sixteenth-century people thought about dreams, their interpretations, meanings, and contemporary context. But dreams can also give us insight into the deepest emotional conflicts of our subjects, disclosing the patterns of their unconscious. Such an undertaking is of course fraught with difficulty because we cannot ask Luther to 'free associate' from the content of his dream—although we can use his later behavior as a test to see whether we have divined the emotional conflicts of his dreams correctly. We can contextualize the words and images of the dream in relation to his other writings and to what was happening to him.

The week his father died in 1530, Luther dreamt that a huge tooth fell out of his head, 'so huge that he could not stop wondering at it', a dream that encapsulates his complicated relationship with his father, against whom he had rebelled decades earlier by becoming a monk.[9] Luther's lost tooth was bone, part of himself, and losing teeth is also part of growing up. Luther freely admitted that he could be 'biting' in his polemic, so the dream with the lost tooth, and Luther's sense of losing his father, may also convey his identification with him. He was proud of his 'head', yet it also became a source of suffering, and at about this time he began to suffer from headaches so severe that he later kept a vein in his leg open so as to ease the pain.[10] The sources for this particular dream are problematic, as it comes from a later report of a letter of Luther's secretary to Katharina von Bora, and so an interpretation cannot be pushed too far. But it does suggest how interconnected dreams, Luther's body, and his emotional conflicts were in the way others saw him and in how he was remembered.

Luther, who spent most of his life in one tiny Saxon town, Wittenberg, is usually studied in grand isolation. He is the champion who brought about the Reformation on his own, fighting the Devil with ink. But because dreams so often focus on relationships, they can disclose just how much Luther depended on others, and how far his theology was shaped by his friendships and enmities—as well as suggest how his followers related to each other. Moreover, because they raised the issue of authority and the relationship to God, dreams went to the heart of the Reformation and illuminate the nature of Luther's own religiosity. Lastly, they shed light on how the Reformation dealt with shaping its own heritage. This chapter therefore draws some ideas from psychoanalysis, as well as conventional social and cultural history, to examine how contemporaries thought about dreams and used them to communicate what they could not otherwise express.

## DREAM I: STAUPITZ

One of the most extraordinary dreams Luther relates occurred in 1519, two years after the 95 Theses had been published and the Reformation had begun, but whilst Luther was still an Augustinian. He reported the dream in the course of an emotional letter addressed to his confessor, Johann von Staupitz. In the words of the psalm, he lamented that his confessor was 'deserting him too much', making him feel 'like a child weaned from its mother' (Ps 131).[11]

Why did Luther resort to such powerful language? Staupitz was Luther's great patron, who had persuaded him to undertake a doctorate; he had promoted Luther and a coterie of men about the same age, placing them in key posts in the Augustinian Order of which he was the Saxon provincial, and at the university in Wittenberg as he tried to reform the Augustinians. Of noble birth, Staupitz had grown up with Frederick the Wise, Luther's ruler. A shrewd negotiator and wheeler dealer, Staupitz was also the man who had helped Luther through his famous *Anfechtungen* or temptations, knowing just how to mix deflating humour and wise advice to guide his difficult confessional charge. Staupitz was the father Luther never had and the emotional bond between the two was deep. Long after his death, Luther acknowledged that 'I got everything from Staupitz'.[12]

Luther's letter was written on 3 October 1519, after the Leipzig debate in the summer which had made the issues of the Reformation a subject of discussion amongst all the intellectuals of the day. Luther had lost when it had become clear that the Reformation would divide the Church and Saxony, setting him on a path to martyrdom.

Luther was now insisting that Jan Hus—the Bohemian condemned as a heretic by the Council of Constance in 1415—had been right and that lay folk should indeed receive communion in both kinds, that is, they should have the wine and not just the bread. Up to this point Staupitz had supported his beloved Luther, but he would eventually part company, 'destitute of the other, oh sorrow, whose voice I never once hear nor whose face do I see', as he wrote mournfully to a friend a few years later.[13]

Luther's letter of October 1519 begins in chatty style with news; enclosed with it are two copies of Luther's recently published commentary on Paul's Letter to the Galatians.[14] Now a man of the world, Luther relays events from as far away as France, Bohemia, and the Netherlands as well as from within the Augustinian Order, and tells Staupitz about the progress of negotiations in his case with Rome. His own bishop has said, as he threw a log onto the fire, that he will not sleep soundly until Luther has been cast into the flames too—an anecdote reminding his confessor that he risks burning as a heretic.[15] After the extraordinary words about feeling like 'a child weaned from its mother', Luther continues: 'I am empty of faith, full of other gifts, Christ knows how little I desire these, if I cannot serve him'—an appeal to his confessor who, like no-one else, understands the 'Anfechtungen' which Luther would suffer from all his life and focused on his fear that he had no faith and love of God.[16] The tone shifts once again back to the conversational, but then comes a final paragraph in which Luther recounts the dream: 'This night I had a dream about you, as if you wanted to retreat from me, but I wept bitterly and suffered; but you waved to me with your hand and said "I should be calm, you would return to me', concluding 'this is surely true and happened this very day"'.[17]

This dream gives us a rare insight into the relationship between the two men, and what it cost Luther to set off on his path of opposition to the Roman Church. Luther had not heard from Staupitz for some time and was suffering from what he felt to be the older man's increasing coldness. Indeed, before long the rift between the two men would become irreparable; Staupitz refused to leave the Church or reject the pope, deserting Luther when he was excommunicated in 1521. In the dream, Luther's confessor leaves, just as he is deserting him in real life, but says he will return. The instruction his confessor gives him—'quiescerem', that 'I' should be calm—is exactly what was difficult for Luther to do. Indeed, Luther's previous letter to Staupitz back in February 1519 had opened dramatically with him saying he wanted to be 'still' (quietus) but was seized and driven by God, thrown into the noise.[18] The entire October letter is full of noise, news about disputations, envy, and argument. So what does the dream mean? Is Staupitz's moving hand—the only gesture Staupitz makes in the dream—reaching towards Luther or away? Is his return dependent upon Luther becoming 'calm', or indeed, on his keeping 'quiet', as the Latin 'quiescere' may also hint, that is, halting his struggle against the pope? Luther's assertion that 'this is surely true and happened this very day' adds five emphatics in one short phrase, as though the dream itself had brought Staupitz back.

The dream was psychologically prescient. Staupitz almost certainly sent back the copies of Luther's *Commentary on Galatians* enclosed with the letter, refusing his protege's gift: he could hardly have made it clearer that he would have no truck with the new theology.[19] Just a few years later, Staupitz left the Augustinian Order, which he tried to reform all his life, and, to Luther's utter disgust, became abbot at a rich Benedictine monastery.

The theology to which Staupitz dedicated his life grew out of the mystical tradition of Tauler and the *Theologia Deutsch*, combined with a radical Augustinianism.[20] It insisted on the sweetness of God's love, and stressed that human beings could not do anything to merit their salvation because all human action was mired in sin. Only by giving up the 'self' and all human ties could one allow God to enter, taking over one's will, a state that was termed *Gelassenheit*, a word which one might translate as 'relaxedness', or 'renunciation' in the sense of 'letting go'. Luther too admired the *Theologia Deutsch*—an anonymous German treatise written in the late fourteenth century which he published twice. He took different things from it, however, adopting the dour Augustinian assessment of human beings as utterly corrupt, their every action mired in sin, without sharing Staupitz's vision of a sweet, loving God, still less the ambition that you could ever make your will conform to Christ's. Luther never formally repudiated this strand of theology, but simply outgrew it. It is as if Luther's dream of Staupitz allows him to regain his confessor's comforting presence, only for him then to try to make the dream real by writing to him. He concludes his letter by bidding his friend farewell and asking him to pray for him, and yet Luther's wording of the dream as he tells it shows he grasped (at least unconsciously) just how serious the breach between the two truly was. It reveals Luther's awareness of his separate theological voice, and marks his independence as he weans himself from Staupitz.[21]

## Dream 2: Müntzer

Our next 'dream moment' comes from 1524. By this point Luther had defied the pope, the emperor, and all the Imperial Estates by insisting at the Diet of Worms in 1521 that the only authority he would accept was that of scripture—adding, as he may or may not have said, 'Here I stand. I cannot do otherwise'. This was the high-water mark of the Reformation. But already Luther's movement was splitting as one of his very first followers, Andreas Karlstadt, began to take a more radical line than Luther; and another, Thomas Müntzer, linked it to violent revolution. At stake, at least in part, was the status of dreams and visions. Luther himself insisted that he put no trust in dreams, asserting that the Word of God was enough for him; scripture was the only authority. But as some of his former followers saw it, scripture could be a 'dead' letter, and it could only be part of the living Word if the Christian were open to receiving God's Word now.

This was at the heart of Thomas Müntzer's attack on Luther in 1524, when he preached his powerful *Sermon before the Princes* to the Saxon Duke John and his son, taking as his text the Dream of Daniel.[22] Müntzer launched into an assault on Luther, calling him 'Brother Fatted Swine' (*Bruder Mastschwein*), a jibe that mocked Luther for his taste in pork and for his wealth and security. To become receptive to the Word of God, Müntzer insisted, 'God must free [a person] from his fleshly lusts', and if he wishes to know whether a dream is from God or the Devil, he must 'cut himself off from all distractions and develop an earnest concern for the truth', a classic statement of the theology of Gelassenheit which had once bound together Luther and Staupitz. The true spirit of the apostles, the patriarchs, and the prophets, Müntzer averred, is 'to expect visions and to receive them while in tribulation and suffering' and '[h]ence it is no wonder that Brother Fatted Pig and Brother Soft Life reject them'.[23] Luther's positive view of the flesh and of pleasure—oral and sexual—was linked, in Müntzer's eyes, with his rejection of dreams and visions; and this was why he was not willing to engage in revolution. Müntzer, in contrast, developed the mystical idea of Gelassenheit to the point that it enabled the revolutionary Christian to move into apocalyptic mode, giving up attachment to the honours and comforts of this life, willing even to undergo martyrdom in order to bring about Christ's second coming on earth. The true Christian has dreams of a new heaven and earth, a prophetic vision that enables him or her to imagine a new social order.[24] As preacher in Allstedt, Müntzer paid attention to his followers' dreams, and it was even said that his sermons were sparked by his daily interpretation of the dreams of an old local sage. During the anxious days when Müntzer was summoned to the castle to answer for his Sermon to the Princes and his radical theology, his followers dreamt of pears which became lumps of flesh and then became bread, of doors of blood, of mills and of floods—extraordinarily vivid and disturbing visions with resonances of the Eucharist. Back in 1522, Karlstadt, Luther's erstwhile follower, had boasted that 'I have said more about dreams and visions than any of the professors';[25] and for his part, Müntzer rejected religion that would revolve around the legalistic interpretations of the Bible by academics, who mistook the letter of scripture for the Spirit. 'Paul never once had a dream; they cite that as proof', he inveighed, well aware of the importance of Paul to Luther's bible-based spirituality. 'To the Devil with preachers like that', he continued, pointing out that Paul's apparent rejection of visions in Romans 4 actually rested on profound Scriptural acceptance of the active work of the Spirit through visions and dreams, and attacking the Lutherans as 'wild insolent disciples of Bacchus'.[26] Like Daniel with Nebuchadnezzar, Müntzer claimed the prophetic power to interpret the ruler's dream, articulating the word of God as it spoke through dreams and visions.

For Luther, all this was 'Schwärmerei' or enthusiasm, fanaticism, and he wanted nothing to do with it. He set it apart from rational interpretation of scripture, lumping together the revolutionary

Müntzer with the quietist Karlstadt. And he soon moved to linking their 'Schwärmerei' with what he held to be their key theological error: Müntzer and Karlstadt, both influenced by the idea of Gelassenheit, denied the Real Presence, that Christ was physically present in the elements of bread and wine at communion. Luther condemned their view and accused them of relying on dreams. In his 1524/25 treatise against those who denied the Real Presence, Luther rebuked their use of scripture as interpretation 'in whatever way their dream or fancy dictates', arguing that they 'understand nothing in the scriptures . . . and neither seek nor find anything therein but their own dreams'.[27] He alleged they were under the influence of the Devil: 'How else, without the influence of Satan, could such learned men possibly be so blind and pride themselves so haughtily on empty dreams, and advertise them in the world as the strongest of all grounds of faith?'. He lumped them together with those who 'think, when they dream something up, it is forthwith the Holy Spirit'.[28] It was a gift to Luther when the Swiss reformer Huldrych Zwingli claimed to have received his understanding of the key passage on the nature of Christ's presence in the Eucharist in a dream.[29]

Throughout this battle, Luther opposed 'dreams' and 'fancies' in favour of the clear word of scripture. Now the Reformation was splitting between Luther, who supported political authorities; Zwingli and the Sacramentarians, who denied the Real Presence in the Eucharist; and Müntzer, the religious revolutionary who had been forced to leave Zwickau and was expelled from Allstedt, and for whom dreams were the pathway to a God who revealed himself in visions. The believer, Müntzer proclaimed, must experience suffering and 'tribulation'. For his part, Luther was scathing about Karlstadt's divine inspiration: he has swallowed the Holy Spirit, 'feathers and all', he remarked.[30]

These battles between Müntzer, Karlstadt, and Luther were fought against the background of the impending Peasants' War. Up until 1524, the trusty peasant had been the evangelicals' hero and it had seemed as if there could be a unified movement of popular reform, led by peasants in alliance with miners and mercenaries. But in 1525 the peasants, inspired by ideas of evangelical freedom and led by preachers including Müntzer, rose up against serfdom in the greatest popular revolt in Western Europe before the French Revolution.

The Peasants' War was a great turning point of the Reformation. Luther emphatically sided with the lords and against the peasants. He even toured Mansfeld and the other mining regions in a fruitless attempt to prevent the miners downing tools, staying with the local count's leading official: he wrote a pamphlet against the Peasants' War from the comfort of the man's garden.[31] From then on, Luther, who liked to claim he was of peasant stock, feared for his life when travelling through rural regions. He knew he had forfeited forever peasant support. Müntzer made his last stand at Frankenhausen, telling his soldiers that no bullets would harm them; when the peasants lost, he fled, and was found with a bag of incriminating letters—the most infamous of which Luther then published.[32] Müntzer was executed on 27 May outside Mühlhausen, where he had been town preacher. With unfortunate timing, Luther's pamphlet 'Against the Robbing Murdering Hordes' had appeared just when the peasants had been defeated. Here, in an uncanny echo of Müntzer's own bloodthirsty language, Luther had advocated that all who could should 'stab, smite, slay' the peasants. 'If you die in doing it, good for you! A more blessed death can never be yours, for you die while obeying the divine word and commandment in Romans 13, and in loving service of your neighbour, whom you are rescuing from the bonds of Hell and of the devil'.[33] He seemed to be sanctifying the bloody slaughter of thousands of peasants which even many of his contemporaries felt had gone too far. For all that Luther would continue to speak his mind to secular princes, and for all his earlier insistence that some of the peasants' complaints were not unfair, there was no doubt where he stood. This was now emphatically a Reformation that was on the side of the authorities.

## DREAM 3: CAT IN A SACK

Luther's Reformation depended not just on him but on a network of close co-workers, a group riven by jealousies and bound together by long-standing friendship. These ties were a source of huge strength for the movement but they were also its Achilles' heel, because Luther's powerful personality was so divisive.

In 1530, the Diet of Augsburg was held in the presence of Emperor Charles V and it was intended to settle the issue of religion, so that war would be averted. Having been declared an outlaw, Luther could not attend the proceedings in Augsburg and so he spent the six months of the Diet's duration in the castle of Coburg, the fortress closest to Augsburg, still within the Saxon elector's territory, but where messengers could reach him quickly. Meanwhile, in Augsburg, Melanchthon had to organize the group of Wittenberg theologians and conduct the negotiations, although he could not make the final decisions on what concessions to make to the Catholics without first checking with the great reformer.

This situation set up keen tensions for the Wittenbergers. Arriving in the spring, they had to wait for the emperor, whose arrival kept being delayed. Augsburg, despite its strong evangelical movement, was anything but friendly since the rival Sacramentarians had won the day against the Lutherans. The Wittenbergers found themselves preaching to empty churches and had to watch while the local preachers attracted congregations of thousands. Emperor Charles V finally entered Augsburg in mid-June with a vast entourage of courtiers and armed men. Charles banned public Protestant preaching altogether: the only crumb of comfort for the Lutherans was that their competitors, the Sacramentarians, were banished from town. Eventually, Melanchthon presented the Confession of Faith that would become the founding document of Lutheranism. It encapsulates the key doctrines of the Lutheran Church, and indeed the Lutherans would later frequently be known as adherents of the 'Confessio Augustana'. But Melanchthon soon realized that he could only count on Saxony, Hesse, Brandenburg, Lüneburg, Anhalt, Nuremberg, and the small town of Reutlingen to support it.

In a hostile town full of bustle and pomp, the Wittenbergers somehow had to communicate with Luther and the rest of the inner circle back in Saxony. All letters were to be sent to Coburg, where Luther and his secretary, Veit Dietrich, would read them, and then on to Wittenberg. But there were few messengers, and they were monopolized by the important princes and dignitaries. Luther, meanwhile, lost in the vast castle and stuck with Veit Dietrich for company, periodically sulked. 'How are the gentlemen? Is there any news?' he pestered every messenger who came, furious with Melanchthon and the others for not letting him know what was going on. From his fortress in Coburg he penned his *Exhortation to All Clergy Assembled at Augsburg*. It was strong, knockabout stuff that mocked the pomp of the Diet, set out a strong Lutheran position, and sold like hot cakes. This was all very well for Luther, who could not see the sheer size of the opposition the Lutherans faced at Augsburg. Melanchthon, well aware that religious war loomed unless an agreement could be reached, had to conduct months of negotiations with the Catholics.

Facing all these challenges, how did the Wittenbergers communicate with each other? One important way was through dreams.[34] As Freud argued, dreams play jokes on us and are masters of the pun. The 'royal road to the unconscious', they trip us up, revealing things we thought were hidden, desires and fears we would rather not face. Dreams challenge any view of human action as determined by reason alone, and suggest we need to think about the irrational and emotional wellsprings of action. We might think that, in a post Freudian era, our understanding of the meanings of dreams is superior, because we know they reveal the inner self, and do not mistake them for prognostications about the future, as our ancestors did. In his *The Interpretation of Dreams* Freud criticised the old 'dream books', which equate particular dream objects with certain fixed meanings.[35] Sold in various editions, some sixteenth-century versions even had charts that allowed the dreamer to interpret their dream by looking up the object.

But these people paid enormous attention to dreams, with a subtlety and sophistication we should not underestimate. Indeed, one might perhaps argue that Freud's *Interpretation of Dreams* was the culmination of centuries of analysis of dreams. The very success of psychoanalysis may have helped put an end to the practice of telling each other's dreams, which had been so much a part of early-modern culture, because it made people abashed about what dreams revealed.[36] The dreams the Wittenbergers discussed during the Diet of Augsburg reveal how intently they examined their emotional significance, and how important it was who reported whose dreams to whom, and why. The Reformation was a collective event, but also one where Luther's various followers and friends jostled for position.

Early on in the Diet, Melanchthon had one of his famous dreams— and Luther's friend Agricola eagerly reported it. Melanchthon had dreamt that an eagle had appeared, but had been enchanted and transformed into a cat (since cats were associated with witchcraft, this was not good news for the eagle). Then the cat had been put into a sack, where it screamed. Luther then appeared and demanded that the cat be let out of the sack.[37]

The Wittenbergers keenly discussed rival interpretations of the dream, trying to work out what it meant. We might immediately think of the proverb 'to let the cat out of the bag', meaning to reveal a secret; but I can find no contemporary use of this proverb in German, where getting a cat in a sack is more likely to mean 'being cheated', that is, getting only a cat instead of good livestock in one's sack. At first, the Wittenbergers concluded that it might concern one of their number, Caspar, whose surname was Aquila, or 'eagle'; if so, it might betoken disaster to his house. Or it might be about the Saxon elector and the trouble he and the Gospel would get into unless Luther came to help. Or the eagle might represent the emperor, imprisoned by the nasty sophists and Catholics, who would become free only once he listened to Luther. The dream's ambiguity allowed them not only to choose different prophecies but to discuss these possibilities and so openly express the various anxieties they felt. That is, the discussion about the dream and its meaning is as important for revealing collective anxieties as it is for revealing an individual's inner feelings.[38]

The figure of the eagle is particularly interesting. Was it the emperor, the obvious meaning because of the imperial eagle? If so, the dream expressed the Wittenbergers' ambivalence, caught like Luther between intense loyalty to the emperor—determined always to believe the best about him and to condemn the pope as evil—and their knowledge that he was in fact a Catholic loyalist who had declared Luther an outlaw and would never relent. This loyalism would distort their politics, making it impossible for them at first to agree to take up arms against the emperor in defence of their faith. One interpretation of the dream allows them to see the emperor as weak, humiliated, and turned into a diabolic animal by the enchantments of the Catholic clergy, a ridiculous, howling cat—when he was in fact all powerful, the man who was going to accept or reject Melanchthon's Confession. The other interpretation, that it was the Saxon elector who was suffering at the hands of the monks, put considerable pressure on Luther to risk his life and attend the Diet. The different prognostications were different diagnoses of what was at stake politically, but also emotionally. In this way, prognostication can work as a proxy for the psychological meanings of dreams. Just as Freud pointed out how dream objects often hide their meaning through puns or significant words, so also the meaning of 'eagle' might be a word game or a symbolic association. If the dream were about the emperor, it enabled the Lutherans to vent the ambivalence about him that they could not otherwise express: would the emperor be let out of the bag? Was he enchanted by the evil papists? Even more importantly, the dream conveyed another anxiety: how would Melanchthon manage without Luther? Would they fail unless Luther himself came to the Diet to save them? This was surely why Agricola told Luther the dream.

Luther shrewdly spotted the emotional subtexts, and so he fired off a reply to Agricola. When he did not want to do something, he often ventriloquized his wife Katharina, his 'mistress' as he calls her, to explain, in this case why he could not come to Augsburg and sort matters out. He threatens that he has forwarded the letter to her, joking that he can prophesy what Katharina will say, what naughty boys they are, and how wrong they are to 'vex the good man' by putting pressure on him to attend the Diet. Treating the whole dream as a joke, he adds that he hopes Caspar Aquila has returned home and is no longer a cat. By taking the most mundane and unthreatening interpretative route, Luther seems to reject out of hand the idea that such a dream could be a prophecy.[39]

But Luther did not forget the dream. Three months later, when the Augsburg Confession of Faith had been presented to the emperor, Luther alluded to the dream again, this time in a letter to one of his close associates, the former secretary to Frederick the Wise and now churchman in Altenburg, Georg Spalatin. Luther was deeply irritated by the concessions Melanchthon and Spalatin seemed to be making to the Catholics: 'You see now that the enemies [the Catholics] are deceitful', he wrote. 'I don't need to write much', he went on curtly. 'If you concede something against the Gospel, I will come myself and free the eagle from the sack'.[40] Now the 'eagle', no longer disguised as a cat, stands for the gospel, and Luther is using the dream to threaten Spalatin, who would have understood exactly what he meant: if you continue compromising, I will come and take over from you.[41]

## Dream 4: The Devil's Dreams

Dreams were of three kinds, Luther once remarked. There were dreams that foretold the future: these were about governments and states; then there were dreams that sprang from physical imbalance; thirdly, there were dreams that came from the Devil. These last were the kind of dreams Luther increasingly experienced, especially from 1530 onwards as the divisions between him and the Sacramentarians became more bitter. For the last six months, he complained in 1532, he had dreamt of the Last Judgement.[42]

One of these dreams, which he discussed at table, conveys what he was experiencing. As ever, Luther told it with wry humour: 'My dream will come true. It seemed to me that I was dead, and I stood by the grave almost nude wearing nothing but mean rags'. Immediately he drew the theological lesson: 'Thus I who have long been damned yet live', that is, I who am a complete sinner am yet saved.[43] Part of the ongoing banter at table was about Melanchthon, whom Luther mocked for his faith in dreams: this was a dream that *would* come true because everyone will die. The dream has Luther seeing his own death and he is wrapped not in a winding sheet but in rags; that is, he is a total sinner. Yet this itself assures him that he 'lives'; that is, the 'I' standing beside the grave is not dead, and in real life, Luther lives on, to spite the Devil. In 1531 he wrote to his friend Jonas about a similar dream: normally he slept on his left side, but last night he was so tired he had slept on his right. The day before he had slept on into the day, 'carrying stones and wood in Hell', probably referring to the slavery of the Israelites in Egypt. Yet it wasn't the iron oven of Egypt from which God freed the Israelites, 'but such a one that you can't describe in words so that I seemed to me to be a corpse'. Again, Luther was quick to override the disturbing dream with a theological message: 'But I write all this so that you know that God does the opposite, Christ's weakness is strength, death, life'.[44] In each case, there was no comfort in the dream itself, but pure terror: the theological message of comfort came only as the waking Luther reflected afterwards.

For Luther, bad dreams were closely linked with the night and with the Devil. He quoted the old saying that 'Sleep is the brother of Death'.[45] On one occasion when he lay down to sleep in the afternoon

2.1. Allegorie auf Gesetz und Gnade. Lucas Cranach the Elder. National Gallery, Prague.

he dreamt that on the Feast of the Conversion of St Paul (25 January), the Last Day arrived and he had said, quoting Psalm 4, 'In pace in id ipsum requiescam seu dormiam!'[46] Bad dreams made him sweat.[47] These were the moments of despair that were connected to his Anfechtungen (temptations), integral to his religiosity and key to his relationship with his confessor, Staupitz, the man he had dreamt left him, holding out his hand and promising to return.[48] The Anfechtungen had driven the young monk to spiritual despair, and Staupitz, his beloved confessor, had helped him by pointing out that he was hating, not loving, God. The realization that God accepts us regardless of our sin helped relieve the Anfechtungen, and Luther seems to have thought he was free of them. But they returned with a vengeance. In 1527 he experienced a complete mental and physical collapse; from then on, Luther's illnesses dogged the Reformation. Time and again, meetings would have to be rescheduled or guests would have to come to Wittenberg, and Luther's acolytes would worry endlessly about the reformer's physical state.

What were these battles with the Devil? Luther said that his fiercest struggles happened at night, with Katharina by his side. 'Sad dreams come from the Devil', he said, for 'everything that served to death, fear, murder and lies is the Devil's handiwork. He has often driven me from prayer and poured in thoughts so that I had to flee'.[49] The bad dreams and temptations seem to have concerned salvation itself. They arose in relation to preaching, where Luther worried that 'you [Luther] alone started the whole thing; if it is wrong, you are guilty for so many souls, who go to Hell. In temptation I often went into Hell, until God called me back and confirmed to me, that which is the true Word of God and true doctrine'—an extraordinary description, which casts Luther in the role of Christ descending to Hell.[50]

For all that Luther insisted he had no need for dreams and scripture was enough for him, he worried about them, and drank before going to bed so as not to be plagued by them—his kind of 'fasting', he liked to joke.[51] He told the story of the nun who consulted her brother, a bishop, when she suffered bad dreams. The bishop gave her a good dinner and plenty to drink, and asked her in the morning whether she had experienced Anfechtungen and bad dreams. 'No', she replied, 'I slept very well and had no dreams at all'.[52] Luther loved to tell this tale because it proved that asceticism simply encouraged the Devil: melancholics should eat and drink. 'So keep your stomach and your head full, that helps even with dreams. For thus it is with me: when I wake up, the Devil comes and disputes with me, until I finally say, "Lick my arse!"'.[53] Luther presents a wonderful vision of the Devil engaging in disputation with him, the intellectual form of questioning point by point analysis that he used throughout his life to train students, test ideas, and to attack his enemies. In such instances, he short-circuited this kind of intellectual gymnastics—only excrement, the great leveler, can get rid of the Devil.

This was a bold way of turning the tables, because frequent encounters with the Devil opened one to the accusation of being inspired by the Devil. And that was precisely what Luther's Catholic antagonists alleged, claiming that his mother was a bath maid (a notoriously promiscuous profession) and his father a demon,[54] or that he had suffered from demonic fits. Many medieval saints had also experienced encounters with demons and these too had taken physical form, as demons threw them around the room and left them bruised. To an extent, therefore, Luther was using a mode of religious experience that was familiar. But whereas saints usually experienced visions of Christ to balance their diabolic warfare, Luther was not a visionary and he mistrusted dreams, as his dispute with Müntzer showed. For him, it was not beatific visions but the diabolic assaults themselves that proved he was on Christ's side—an inversion of the principle that every vision should be checked to see if it did not come from 'an angel of light', that is, the Devil. For Luther, it was the opposite: the Devil's presence was the touchstone of his spirituality. He and his followers showed remarkable courage in discussing his ongoing battles with the Devil, because these could so easily have been used as propaganda against him.

But what were the Anfechtungen, and what form did they take? Why did Luther increasingly associate them with the night, and with dreams?[55] Here we might think about Cranach's depictions of Melancholy, which in sixteenth-century thought was linked with creativity as well as with depression and the predominance of black bile. Cranach produced several representations of this theme, all of which are variants of one another. The figure of Melancholy is a woman and, as so often, there is an element of competition with Dürer, whose famous representations of Melancholy Cranach did not equal. Cranach adds, however, a view through a window onto a nighttime cavalcade of strange figures, including a goat, witch, and figures dressed nobly. This is not a witches' Sabbath, and Cranach avoided the kind of sexualized images of witches favored by Hans Baldung Grien and other artists: his rare depiction of witches in the woodcut—showing the executed corpses of four men and only one woman—displays no erotic interest in their bodies whatsoever. It seems more likely that the night cavalcade represents dreams that might be inspired by the Devil.[56]

If so, Cranach, Luther's long-standing friend, may have intuited the importance of Luther's Anfechtungen to his spirituality; certainly, the visual similarity of many of his images to Luther's mental world as revealed in language is striking. If Müntzer claimed authority through dreams and visions, Luther's nightmares may have arisen from the same spiritual place as his Anfechtungen, part of a distinctive theology in which doubt would always have its place.

2.2. Melancholy. Cranach the Elder, 1532. Musée d'Unterlinden, Colmar.

2.3. Melancholia. Cranach the Elder, 1528. National Gallery of Scotland, Edinburgh.

## Dream 5: Frederick the Wise

In 1617 a remarkable broadsheet appeared, entitled *The Dream of Frederick the Wise*. The broadsheet showed Luther wielding a giant quill pen, and below that was a full account of the dream, which Frederick supposedly experienced in Castle Schweinitz on the night before Luther posted his 95 Theses.[57] Here was a dream being used to commemorate the event's centenary in 1617.[58]

Three times Frederick falls asleep, and each time he dreams the same dream: that a monk with a giant quill (who is St Paul's natural son) asks permission to write on the door of the castle church. When he starts to write, the letters are so large that Frederick can read them from Schweinitz. The monk's quill grows so long that it stretches from Wittenberg to Rome, piercing the ears of the lion in Rome, and finally making the papal tiara itself wobble. Twice more the elector awakes, and the quill turns out to be a goose feather that is so hard it cannot

2.4. The Dream of Frederick the Wise, 1617. Wikimedia—ref. Museum Catharijneconvent.

be broken despite the elector's best efforts. The monk explains that it comes from a hundred-year-old Bohemian goose (code for the Bohemian heretic Jan Hus) and was given to him by a schoolteacher; its soul cannot be destroyed. Finally, lots of people in Wittenberg take feathers, which become strong like the monk's, and they all set to writing. Luther appears three times in the rather unwieldy woodcut: first and most obviously, nailing up the 95 Theses on the door of the castle church, then in the background preaching, and finally he is shown between Rome and Schweinitz, writing while God the Father and Christ look on from above, and a rather mangy dove—the Holy Spirit—inspires Luther's pen. In the foreground there is a goose, the emblem for Hus, whose feathers supply the quill, and a swan, the emblem for Luther, while Luther's followers take feathers from his quill.

Why should a dream have been chosen to represent the Reformation? At the most basic level, the dream plugged a gaping Reformation hole, for there was no contemporary or even sixteenth-century image of the famous posting of the 95 Theses, the event that the 1617 festival was designed to celebrate. Worse, as a Catholic postwar historian would later devastatingly point out, there is precious little in the way of source material to prove that Luther did indeed nail the 95 Theses to the door of the castle church.[59] Frederick's dream provided the next best thing, the closest we have to a visual representation of the event that sparked the Reformation.

The dream was highly successful, several versions circulating as huge single-leaf woodcuts that could be posted up like the original printed versions of the 95 Theses themselves. It found its way into numerous printed Bibles, often prefacing Romans, or as a frontispiece to the whole New Testament, and it lasted right into the eighteenth century. A roundel version condensed the complicated image into a simple design. Medals were produced with it and it became part of the furniture of Lutheran commemoration. It only lost its iconic position when, in the nineteenth century, the dream was exploded as a myth.[60]

The dream was so successful because it condensed oral history, Melanchthon's portent, the idea of Hus as the goose, Luther as the swan, and the power of Saxony—and it circulated just when Luther entered material culture, with pottery swans on sale at Luther's house in Eisleben, Luther tiles and tankards, and even Luther book bindings. This was a version of the Reformation centered on the figure of Luther, in partnership with Saxony. It fitted perfectly into the cultural landscape of the late sixteenth century, where the first biographies of Luther were beginning to appear, where Luther's letters and *Table Talk* were beginning to be published, and where the pious Lutheran had to know about Luther's life. That biography had to be defended in the teeth of ardent Catholic polemic presenting Luther as inspired by the Devil.

Dreams, moreover, provided a new kind of legitimation for the Lutheran movement. They offered a prophetic view of Luther's role, authorized by the political power of Saxony itself.[61] Frederick's interlocutors in his dream are his brother John, who would become elector in his place, and the Saxon chancellor; both became leading characters in the Reformation drama, just as the image of the elector would be placed next to that of Luther, stamping the Reformation as a Saxon possession. As the Thirty Years' War loomed a century after these events, Lutherans were becoming ever more inclined to present their hero as a prophet, whose every action was miraculously foretold. Theirs was a movement that required providences to compete against the Calvinists no less than the Catholics.

And so it was ironic that Luther—the man who always mocked dreams, who parted company with Müntzer over the issue of dreams and visions, who derided Zwingli for trusting in dreams to support his interpretation of communion as a memorial, and who laughed at Melanchthon's trust in dreams—became commemorated by a dream. The commemoration was crudely didactic, with none of the ambiguity and complexity of the real dreams the reformers had discussed all those years before. Though Luther insisted that he only submitted to the letter of the Bible, dreams played a powerful role in the Reformation. They also reveal a good deal about his hidden psychology and the wellsprings of his and his collaborators' motivation, no matter how passionately he dismissed them. As historians, we need to interpret our subjects not just through understanding the rationales of their actions, but also by considering their unconscious dimensions, and as we strive to recreate not just individuals but their social networks and their cultural worlds, we need to pay attention to dreams.

# CHAPTER 3

# Manhood and Pugilism

A MOVEMENT THAT CELEBRATES its centenary with a woodcut depicting its hero bearing a giant quill clearly has, shall we say, some issues with masculinity. After all, quills are more than just loosely associated with manhood. There were, for instance, sixteenth century spells for how to control your lover's 'man's feather', and it was perfectly clear what was meant. It was no accident that a quill should have been chosen to represent Luther, one of the most aggressive intellectual combatants of the age. He himself threatened none other than a leading Lutheran prince, the ruler of the territory of Hesse, Philip: 'And I really would not like your grace to get into a quill fight with me'—a bold address indeed for a commoner to a powerful ruler.[1]

It is often said that the Lutheran Reformation owed its success to its alliance with the German princes, who had the political muscle to implement it. Germany was a patchwork of tiny political units, from independent cities through small territories to tiny duchies and bigger princedoms. Luther insisted on obedience to secular authority, and Lutheranism has often been equated with political conformity and respect for authority—indeed, it has even been credited with bequeathing a culture of acquiescence that ultimately paved the way for Nazism.[2] Luther's first biographer, Johannes Mathesius, went out of his way to contrast Luther with the Catholic preacher who, in answer to the question of whether princes could be saved, joked 'Only if they die in the cradle. For once they are big enough to sit on horseback they ride straight to Hell'.[3] Luther, Mathesius insisted, had nothing in common with these old papist clergy who liked nothing better than to give the princes a verbal kicking.[4]

Such conclusions, however, are difficult to square with the conspicuous rudeness with which Luther so often addressed powerful figures. Most theologians take on other theologians, but Luther attacked many German princes as well, even though his Reformation depended on their power and support to be introduced. Luther's enthusiasm for this kind of polemic suggests that more was going on. In this chapter, I will explore Luther's tortuous relationship with secular authority, arguing that what drove it were deep-seated dynamics centrally linked to masculinity.

## ALBRECHT OF MAINZ

Luther used his quill as a weapon from the very beginning of the Reformation when he attacked the selling of indulgences, which were intended to give the purchaser time off purgatory. When he supposedly put up the 95 Theses on the door of the castle church in Wittenberg, he wrote a letter at the same time to the local archbishop, Albrecht of Mainz, enclosing a copy.[5] This letter perhaps more than their posting made certain that the Theses could not be brushed under the carpet. Though Luther probably did not know it, Albrecht was not only supporting the indulgence but using part of the proceeds to service the substantial debt he had incurred with the fabulously wealthy Fuggers in order to secure his (second) archbishopric. Luther abrasively threatened the archbishop that if he did not clean up the preaching of indulgences, then 'someone' would be forced to write against him.[6] From then on, Albrecht of Mainz became one of the figures Luther most liked to attack. He nicknamed him the 'idol of Halle', mocking his famous relics collection, and 'the bride of Halle', impugning his masculinity with no regard for his position as a leading (celibate) churchman and member of the influential noble house of Hohenzollern.[7]

In 1525, Luther wrote an open letter calling on Albrecht, a known womanizer, to enter the married estate. Albrecht's liaison with his mistress was common knowledge and he had even had himself portrayed as St Erasmus alongside his lover as St Ursula.[8] This time Luther proceeded carefully: he sent a copy of his letter to his friend the archbishop's advisor, Johann Rühel, asking him to check with Albrecht in person that he was not displeased by it; only then was Luther happy for it to be circulated and even printed. What is extraordinary about this is that by this point Luther himself was about to marry. If Albrecht should ask why Luther, who urged others to marry, would not do so himself, Rühel was to tell him that Luther always 'feared that he was not capable enough for it' but that he was still determined to marry, even if it should be just an engaged (unconsummated) marriage like Mary and Joseph.[9] There is something in the way Luther imagines himself trotting down the aisle in front of Albrecht ('vorher[zu]traben'), and in the irony of the contrast between Albrecht, who is more than 'capable', and Luther, who wonders whether he is or not, that suggests there was a profound identification with, as well as antagonism to, this most famous opponent of the Reformation.[10]

Not content with attacking Albrecht, Luther soon wrote attacking his brother Joachim, who was the ruler of Brandenburg. He did so by taking up the cudgels on behalf of Wolf Hornung, a minor nobleman whose wife had been seduced—or as he put it, 'robbed'—by Joachim. Luther admitted that Hornung had 'struck her a bit with a blunt knife out of marital enthusiasm', but the contract he had later signed agreeing to leave her alone—and which put her under Joachim's protection—was 'sealed with a Bratwurst', that is, was worthless.[11] So eager was Luther to take on Joachim that he threatened to 'get stuck into the lining of the electoral hat so that your hair really stands on end'.[12] Luther was metaphorically getting stuck into Joachim's potency, in a fight which was essentially over which of them, Joachim or Hornung, owned a woman.[13]

In 1541, Albrecht of Mainz was finally driven out of Halle, and his famous relic collection, redolent of the Catholicism Luther had rejected, was dispersed.[14] Luther could not resist attacking the once mighty archbishop, writing a spoof 'relics list' for him, all of which were strictly biblical: there were, amongst others, 'two feathers and an egg of the Holy Ghost', 'half a wing of St Gabriel, the archangel', and 'a big heavy piece of the shout of the children of Israel that knocked down the walls of Jericho'. Even better, the archbishop had promised to bequeath 'a whole dram of his true pious heart and a whole Loth (ounce) of his true tongue'—all of which would offer complete indulgence from all sins committed up to that hour, against payment of one gulden.[15] He published the brief squib anonymously, but when asked if he had written it, he replied that of course he had.

> This the printers know, the university, the town, so that it is completely unhidden and not secret. Even the bride of Mainz himself must know it. Because I made it so that I would be recognized. And whoever reads it and has ever seen my thoughts or quill will have to say, 'Das ist der Luther'.[16]

It is hard to imagine a more forthright equation of writer, quill, and aggressive manhood.

## HEINRICH OF BRAUNSCHWEIG-WOLFENBÜTTEL

So much for supporting ordained authority, as Luther always insisted he did; Albrecht was not the only man to be driven out of power by Luther's pen. The same fate befell Prince Heinrich of Braunschweig-Wolfenbüttel. Defeated in 1542 by the forces of the Protestant Schmalkaldic League, he not only lost the city of Goslar, which he had attacked the previous year, but forfeited his dukedom as well, even ending up imprisoned in Hesse for a time along with his eldest son. Luther had already weighed in with a pamphlet, *Against Hanswurst*, in 1541. Ostensibly the polemic followed Heinrich's accusation that Luther had shown disrespect to his ruler, Elector John Frederick, nicknaming the elector 'Hans Wurst' or Jack Sausage. Heinrich was an irresistible target: when his liaison with one of his wife's ladies in waiting, Eva von Trott (sixteen years old when the affair began), threatened to become public knowledge, he pretended she had died, held a mock funeral for her and sequestered her away in one of his castles. Heinrich was also suspected of a series of arson attacks that were carried out on Protestant territories, including one which burnt the city of Einbeck to the ground. Luther wrote his attack in a private, not official, capacity, but there was an official response to Duke Heinrich's polemic on the part of Luther's own Saxon elector.

Even Luther's supporters felt that *Against Hans Wurst* was too extreme a response, some considering that there was 'too much insult from a main teacher of our holy gospel'; an opponent thought it contained too much 'satanic raging'; and even the historian of

Lutheranism Johannes Sleidan admitted that Luther's response was very harsh.[17] Luther gets into his stride early, explaining that he did not invent the name Hans Wurst. However, it is a word that he likes to use, especially in sermons, against stupid idiots who want to be clever, but who are not up to it. Be that as it may, Luther goes on, some people think that Duke Heinrich—that is, not Luther— has called the elector 'Hans Wurst' because 'by God's (that is, your enemy's) grace he is strong, plump, and somewhat round. But think what you will, so make in your pants, hang it round your neck, then make a jelly of it and eat it like the vulgar sows and asses you are!'[18] This full-on invective turned his enemies' own weapons against them, transforming 'Jack Sausage' into a potent, full-bodied masculine figure, and slinging excrement at his opponents. The polemic is amongst the most zestful Luther ever wrote. Revealingly, what touched it off was the accusation that Luther did not respect his own ruler—and oddly it gave Luther occasion to put his increasing identification with the Saxon house into words. By this point, Luther himself was, if not strong, then 'plump and somewhat round'. Indeed, at about this time, the Cranach workshop designed a frontispiece to the Luther Bible that was also used in Luther's collected works, showing a solid Luther balancing an equally solid elector, two heavyweights placed either side of a crucifix.

In these 'quill fights', Luther demonstrated all the swagger of male single combat in an age when noblemen had to prove their honour with their bodies, and jousting remained the favorite noble sport. This was after all the era of the codpiece.[19] Authority was expressed through physical prowess and men had to be willing to back their position with their fists. True not only of nobles, Luther had early acquired a similar version of manhood, as he watched his father in the rough mining town of Mansfeld, where physical fights were routine and where economic disaster threatened if your word was not respected.[20]

Indeed, Luther drew power from intellectual combat: his theology was developed in a series of disputations, or staged arguments with other scholars, that were held in public and followed careful rituals. He defended his views first in front of his own Augustinian Order at Heidelberg, then at Leipzig before scholars from all over Germany— tellingly, Luther arrived with a posse of armed students. At Worms

3.1. Title page, Martin Luther's Complete Works. Cranach the Elder, 1558 (re-used). Wolfenbuettel Herzog August Bibliothek.

in 1521, the highlight of the Reformation, Luther stated his position before the emperor and the assembled estates of the empire, including many of the princes he would later attack in print. He showed courage in doing so, and ran the risk of being burnt for heresy.

## DUKE GEORGE

One of the first princely figures Luther attacked was George of Saxony, cousin of Frederick the Wise, and ruler of the other half of Saxony where Luther lived. This was a long-standing enmity, and it reveals much about the limits and dynamics of Luther's political posturing. Critical of the Catholic Church, George had started out as a potential supporter of the Reformation. He hosted the Leipzig Debate in 1519, where Luther and Karlstadt took on the Catholic theologian Johannes Eck. But the debate seems to have convinced George that Luther was indeed a heretic, and he became a staunch and dangerous opponent. For his part, Luther liked to turn George into the personification of the opposition he faced. Straight after his appearance at the Diet of Worms, he wrote to his friend the painter Lucas Cranach that he would rather 'suffer death at the hands of the tyrants, especially those of the furious Duke George of Saxony' but had instead listened to the advice of others.[21] Exhilarated by his escape from Worms alive, and realizing he would not be burnt as a heretic—the martyrdom which he had both longed for and organized to prevent—he half-seriously accused George of being the man who was out to kill him. In fact, Luther could not have been more wrong, for George had been amongst those who insisted that Luther should be given an imperial safe conduct.[22]

Luther, it turned out, was unable to resist any opportunity to beard George; and again, women were often the objects of dispute. In 1523, Luther had arranged for the nuns of Nimbschen in the territory of the elector to escape their convent and come to Wittenberg hidden, so the story had it, in herring barrels. He put the nuns up and eventually married one of them, Katharina von Bora. Two years later, he was 'seizing these spoils of Christ' again (the nuns of another convent) from the 'tyrant', Duke George; he later gave his former student Leonhard Beyer permission to marry one of them, Gertrude von Mylen. Beyer, who had walked over 500 km with Luther to reach Augsburg for the debate with Cajetan in 1518, and had defended theses written by Luther, came close to being an intellectual son.[23] Since convent women prayed for the faithful, they were seen as something of a community possession, their holiness and virginity considered a resource for the whole territory; in a sense, Luther was this time taking George's women. Indeed he had earlier actually termed the man who drove the wagon that carried them, a 'robber', but a 'blessed' one, like Christ robbing the souls from Hell.[24] Nor was Luther above referring to the women collectively as 'my brides'. The affront was only compounded when George's close relative Ursula von Münsterberg fled her convent in Freiberg, ending up in Luther's house in Wittenberg.[25]

Social status formed part of the tussle. When Luther first tried out the secular estate, he did so as Junker Jörg, a nobleman, the disguise he took on when he hid after the Diet of Worms in the Wartburg castle. By marrying Katharina von Bora, a noblewoman and therefore of the same social estate as George himself, Luther could in a sense consider himself his equal. One of Luther's few hobbies was wood turning, a pastime popular amongst nobles, about which Luther was serious enough to order the best supplies from Nuremberg.[26] Conversely, Luther nicknamed Duke George 'der Bauer' (the peasant) when the reformer himself often claimed to be of peasant stock.

Luther and George got into a kind of clinch, publishing vigorously against each other every two years or so.[27] This culminated in Luther's 1531 tract *Wider den Meuchler zu Dresden* (*Against the Meuchler of Dresden*), a shockingly aggressive tract.[28] This particular 'quill fight' began in the wake of the Diet of Augsburg of 1530, when the Lutherans had presented their confession of faith to the emperor. Unable to be there himself, Luther had instead published *Warning to His Dear Germans* and his *Gloss* on the 'antichristian so-called imperial edict', a public attack on the Catholic position written in his usual robust style.[29] Duke George intervened with the Saxon elector, his cousin John, to complain, following a pattern established in many of his previous quarrels with Luther.[30] The elector promptly censured the reformer, and he was summoned for an interview with the Saxon chancellor, Georg Brück, who subsequently wrote to the elector giving the substance of Luther's reply. Having done their duty, the electoral chancellery wrote an anodyne reply to George, who went ahead and published his own attack on Luther, thereby descending to Luther's level. But as an experienced polemicist, Luther stole a march on the duke: George's pamphlet was leaked to Luther, so that by the time it was for sale at the Leipzig Easter Market, Luther's reply was too.[31]

How do two antagonists of entirely different social classes negotiate their social distance to create a conversation? George does so by half-pretending his pamphlet is written by somebody else, the priest Franciscus Arnoldi. He uses the third person throughout, never addressing Luther himself, and is careful not to accord him his doctoral title. He adopts a fairly measured tone as befits a ruler, and although he says Luther is 'of the devil', invective is rather sparse. Luther, by contrast, uses insults in order to create a level playing field, first by addressing the reader and referring to George in the third person, and then slipping offensively into the informal 'you' when he does start to address his antagonist. Right at the outset, Luther makes fun of George for pretending that his tract was written by somebody else—and a priest to boot. The text of George's tract refers to the author's, the 'layman's', view of religion, and Luther makes it plain that he knows perfectly well who the 'layman' is. He threatens to 'beat the donkey in the sack'—if the donkey complains, he can say he is only hitting the sack, not the donkey inside. George's failure to claim authorship licenses Luther to attack him without the respect owed a duke, whilst insinuating that George is a donkey. Luther's greatest insult of all, though, is the title: *Against the Meuchler of Dresden*, that is, the secret, cunning deceiver. Luther never says who the Meuchler is, thus allowing him to attack George without naming him: since he calls him the Meuchler *of Dresden*, however, everyone knew whom he meant. Even Luther knew this went a bit far, and in the *Table Talk* in 1540 he admitted that 'in [choosing] that title I was a rascal'.[32]

Ironically the quarrel raged over George's accusation that Luther preached 'Aufruhr', stirring up revolt and showing disrespect to es- tablished authority, the accusation that would also trigger his reaction to Heinrich of Wolfenbüttel. Luther insisted that this was untrue, though of course his entire tract was designed to destroy George's standing as both a man and a ruler. He concluded by accusing George of slander and perjury, writing that if George can prove that the Lutherans are 'guilty of fomenting revolt' then 'I will consider you to be a man', but George is silent.[33] 'You run away', Luther contin- ued, 'all the while spewing and dirtying the paper with unnecessary words, as if you'd got this new art straight from heaven, you curse us as rebels ('Aufrurer') and you can't make it true and prove it. Do you know what such people are called in German lands? They are called desperate rascals, traitors and dishonourable ruffians, who take the honour of innocent people with their poisonous gobs . . . This is your true name, be you whom you will'.[34] In this passage Luther dramatically turns the insult around: Duke George called him a 'causer of rebellion', but this is a lie and it is therefore George who is actually guilty of perjury, a liar whose word cannot be trusted. He next presents the duke as a slanderer, vomiting over the page, some- one who destroys the honour of upright folk and who himself has no honour: as such, he should be excluded from the political community. Worse still, he hides behind someone else's name. Manhood, one's 'name', and honour are all wrapped up here together (as we will see in the next chapter) and the duke, who ought to be able to contain his fluids, Luther insinuates, voids himself everywhere.[35]

Luther certainly won this round. He escaped a ticking off by the electoral Saxon court and published a far more vitriolic attack on George than George was able to publish against him. But he was sailing very close to the wind, because George was his own ruler's cousin and attacking George's honour was also an affront to the honour of the entire Wettin ruling house. Getting away with it required some quick footwork: Luther apologized on May 8 to the electoral Chancellor Brück for the fact that a copy had reached George in Dresden before it had reached him in Torgau; but he did not apologize for publishing and had not asked Brück's permission to do so.[36] Once again, Luther succeeded. On July 2 the duke and the elector met at Grimma and agreed to a truce, including the condition that Luther cease to polemicise against George, but with the proviso 'in so far as it is possible' and 'not against his conscience and the teaching'. All Luther had to do was not publish the second piece against Duke George that he had threatened in the closing pages of his pamphlet.[37]

3.2a. Friedrich III, the Wise, Elector of Saxony. Cranach the Elder, 1533. Metropolitan Museum of Art.

3.2b. Johann I, the Constant, Elector of Saxony. Cranach the Elder, 1533. Metropolitan Museum of Art.

Just two years later, in 1533, the two resumed their struggle. This time the roles were reversed and it was George—dubbed a perjurer and liar by Luther—who, amongst other things, abused the reformer as a 'meineidig monk' (perjured monk) for having broken his word by breaking his monastic vows.[38] This time Luther got in two replies, and once again taunted the duke about authorship.[39] Rightly guessing that George's tract was actually written by Luther's old enemy Johannes Cochlaeus, he spends pages toying with Cochlaeus's name, calling him 'old snot nose', 'the snail', and so on.[40] Luther also uses the tract to reflect on his life as a monk, and why monasticism was so dreadful, as if the attack by the duke caused him to ponder his own identity and history.[41]

As this example shows, Luther's aggression repeatedly tested the bounds of political tolerance. Far from upholding the dignity of secular authority, he was cocking a snook at George, his own ruler's father's cousin, and making John Frederick complicit in it: he was effectively manipulating both. The same patterns are evident time and again: a ruler complains about Luther to his sovereign, the Saxon elector; Luther is given a light reprimand and is reminded that he is a subject of the elector; this then unleashes a stream of invective and angry posturing as Luther insists on having it out with his antagonist. The themes are not about religious truth, but about who is the man, and whose word can be trusted—a big theme of masculinity in the sixteenth century when oaths were a major guarantor of social peace. Beneath the surface there are several subtexts: who gets the women; who can contain their bodily fluids. Both sides flourish their pens, and the tone on Luther's side is extraordinary for its braggadocio. For all his supposed respect for secular authority, something more complex is at work in Luther's relations with rulers, for it seems he cannot resist testing himself against them.

In 1534, after giving a sermon on All Saints Day, Luther was again called to account by the elector, now John Frederick, for insulting his 'cousin' George and his 'uncle Mainz and Magdeburg'.[42] Always excellently informed, Duke George had complained, and Luther once more received a letter from Chancellor Brück. The reformer's reply to the elector was masterly, admonishing the elector himself by saying that 'I don't like to see you serving [dienen] in this matter'—acting as Duke George's lackey. It was a remark that came pretty close to insulting his own ruler, a man aged just over thirty who had become elector hardly eighteen months before.[43] The whole letter to Brück is wonderfully unbuttoned: 'it is true', he says, 'that I would like to get my hands on Duke George and the bishop', and this letter 'plays right into my hands'. He had indeed preached against the archbishop of Mainz—and the sermon would soon be on sale, he added, hardly designed to set Brück's mind at rest. After the sermon, Luther explained, he had been sitting at table with one of the visiting rulers—we can imagine the jugs of beer—and he had said that the archbishop was of the Devil. He added that he intended to say prayers against the archbishop of Mainz, and that he might perhaps have said the same about the duke too; but if he had not, 'I say it now, even if I have to defend it with my neck', and concluding, 'friend, let them come in God's name'. Here Luther courts a fight, and is explicit about engaging in prayer against both the archbishop of Mainz and Duke George, an extraordinary piece of quasi-magical aggression in a society which routinely prayed for its rulers.[44]

3.3. Portrait of Gregor Brück. Cranach the Elder, 1533. Germanisches Nationalmuseum, on loan from the Federal Republic of Germany.

By this time the old enmity with George had become something of a comfortable routine. In Luther's pamphlet of 1533 there is a wonderful passage where he imagines setting aside the quarrel: 'Ah my dear sir! Let's just drink a little tankard of beer with each other, although you might be stronger and able to drink more little tankards than I in such a case'. This was not to be the last time Luther and his opponent imagine sharing drinks together. And he added, 'this time I'm being so soft that I'm writing with down'. This was the non-phallic Luther, the man with the ticklish 'soft pen'. He was joking, of course.[45]

By the time George died, Luther had almost made his peace with his old enemy, as if he intuited that he had needed him. Passing his own obituary judgment, he remarked that 'Duke George wanted to be neither a Papist nor a Lutheran, but after the Lutherans had been suppressed, to be himself the man who reformed the Church'.[46] The remark revealed Luther's dual identification and competition with Duke George, for if Luther credited himself with anything, it was being the man 'who reformed the Church'. Mathesius, delivering his biographical sermons long after Luther's death, remembered Luther talking about the old duke at table—George had asked Erasmus for advice, and he had given a particularly obscure and twisted answer, to which the infuriated George had replied: 'Dear Erasmus, wash my fur, and mind you don't make it wet, I praise those of Wittenberg, who don't put flour in their mouths, but come out freely and openly with their view'.[47] In the memory of the Reformation, George had become an old buffer: an enemy to be sure, but also a forthright Saxon who shared their hatred of the overly subtle Erasmus.

## Philip of Hesse's Bigamy

We can now understand exactly what Luther was threatening when he warned Philip of Hesse that 'he would rather not have your grace get into a quill fight with me'.[48] This exchange took place in the aftermath of Philip of Hesse's bigamous marriage in 1540. Philip, one of the leading Lutheran princes, was unhappily married, but to a faithful wife whom he could not therefore divorce.[49] Unable to contain himself sexually, but aware that his adultery excluded him from communion, he asked Luther and the other reformers for counsel. When they agreed that a secret second marriage would make his liaison with his concubine Margarethe von der Saale legitimate, Philip secured their signatures on their memorial of advice. He then went ahead and married her in a semi-public wedding. An excited Philip had written to Luther, addressing him as his 'brother-in-law' ('Schwager') since they were now related through his second wife, and sent him a consignment of wine as a present. Not surprisingly, the scandal soon became public and a deep embarrassment to the Reformation. Luther refused to support the Landgrave, insisting that he would simply deny that he had ever suggested bigamy. Philip, however, had the winning card: he could publish the memorial featuring Luther's signature.[50]

It was at this point that Luther made his scarcely veiled threat, and Philip was certainly attuned to its significance. He replied at once that he did not want to get into a 'quill fight' ('Federkampf') with Luther, 'nor to make your feather twitchy, because I well recognize your skill in this, and I am certainly not minded to get into a squabble with you'.[51] The metaphor of the 'Federkampf', and the active, moving quill expressed deliberately the aggression between the two men, with the socially superior man bowing to Luther's polemical power, underlined by the use of 'I' instead of the usual distancing 'we' he used when writing to Luther.[52] Nor are the sexual overtones of the exchange accidental: in the same letters, the Landgrave accuses 'you clerics' of being allowed now to marry whomever they choose, reminding them that the princes agreed not to treat their wives as whores and to recognize their children as legitimate. So (by implication) why not concede the same to him? This was an extraordinary remark, and Philip's outrage betrays just how momentous were the changes wrought by the Reformation. A whole professional class of men who had never expected to marry were now able to marry whom they pleased. Such freedom was enjoyed by few other social groups, especially not the nobility—and it would not be passed on to the next generations of pastors; increasingly, they would find their brides from other parsons' families. As so often, the threat that the two men would fight is immediately followed by an appeal to male bonding, this time on Philip of Hesse's part: 'How I wish that I could spend an hour with you, we'd soon come to an agreement'.[53] Once again, as with

Duke George, the antagonist imagines drinking with the opponent. The full-on aggression was also a kind of closeness.[54]

## MANHOOD AND THE REFORMATION

As the last thirty years of research have made clear, the Reformation certainly accomplished huge changes in what the priest's manhood meant. It abolished celibacy for the priesthood, removed the clergy's immunity from taxation, made priests citizens, and, in the married pastor, created a new model of masculinity.[55] It also did away with monastic communities of men living together. As we saw, Luther's own facial hair made the point, as the pious monk with the tonsure gave way to the hirsute nobleman Junker Jörg, and then to the settled clean-shaven patriarch.[56]

Luther liked to posture as a father figure. He condemned Zwingli for becoming a soldier and getting himself killed on the battlefield at Kappel, insisting that priests should never be soldiers—the pre-Reformation clergy had not been allowed to carry weapons. But when students at Wittenberg smashed the windows of the town judge, so Mathesius tells us, he threatened from the pulpit: 'If such a disturber of the peace came to my house, I'd step out and deal with him with my house spear, and defend the peace of my house and dwelling as a housefather is legally entitled to do. If I stuck my spear into such a rebel, I would stand still and shout "Here God's justice and the emperor's justice, before the two of them I declare self defence".'[57] The housefather with his weapon is ready to skewer anyone who threatens his hearth and home.

But Luther also understood the precariousness of masculinity. By 1545 when his old enemy Heinrich of Wolfenbüttel and his eldest son had been defeated and imprisoned by Philip of Hesse and the elector of Saxony, Luther offered to act as a propagandist on Saxony's behalf. More restrained than *Against Hans Wurst*, the tirade sounds the usual themes: Heinrich must repent his many sins, he is guilty of miserliness ('Geiz') and usury. But it is the ending that particularly interests us here. Luther concludes with two psalms, at the very end of which he movingly explains what the psalmist means by 'schlaff': it is when a man becomes cowardly, and his hands tremble, his legs shake, and his head hangs so that he cannot hold spear or sword, much less fight or defend himself. He just stands there and lets himself be stabbed and hewn as if he were a block of wood. Unable to move, a man's heart is taken away.[58]

There was no obvious need for Luther to supply a gloss on the meaning of this well-known word, but it conveys what had happened to Heinrich, who had been unable to defend himself and had lost his lands. He had lost his 'heart' and his potency. For Luther the heart was strongly connected with courage and the ability to resist, central to his persona since the posting of the 95 Theses. Becoming 'schlaff' was something Luther understood only too well. As he aged, he himself became impotent. In the very last months of his life he wrote to his wife apologising for his incapacity. One senses that as he grew older, Luther's periodic rages gave him back something of the sense of being alive and able to defend himself, enabling him to relive the kind of vitality he had felt when he was under attack at Worms, his life on the line, and in front of the emperor and empire.[59]

Even though Luther said he and the Reformation were subordinate to secular authority, he managed to create a kind of polemical equality that few religious figures would later attain. In a violent, personalized world, Luther's quill fighting helped to establish his masculinity and created a powerful polemical role for him as a prophet who had the right to bewail the state of the nation and speak truths to power. It allowed Luther to irritate the court and poor Chancellor Brück, and to posture as a man who cared nothing for courtly niceties.

And it had a longer legacy too. As Robert von Friedeburg has recently argued, this style of rhetoric was picked up again a century later during the Thirty Years' War, and it legitimated highly personal invective against rulers that broadsided any attempt to see them as divine. Luther has often been viewed as the man who developed the theology of the Two Kingdoms, the kingdom of this world and the heavenly kingdom of Christ, to insist that Christians must obey secular powers.[60] But far from sanctifying political authority, Friedeburg argues, Luther's rhetoric drove a wedge between the all-too-human princes and what would later be conceptualised as the 'state'. In the eighteenth century, therefore, princes gained legitimacy by presenting themselves as guardians of the state, not as identical with it.[61]

This is an ingenious argument, but at least for the sixteenth century, it overstates the effect of Luther's bluster. Luther had no political power in his own right, and he had no institutional church either that could act as a counterweight to a ruler's power. Luther could hold his own in a quill fight against Philip of Hesse or George of Saxony, but only because he was protected by the Saxon electors. There is a libidinal investment in this verbal jousting on Luther's part that suggests there is an element of denial at work.[62] Luther's fulminations could not hide the fact that his Reformation depended in the end on princely power and on the political fragmentation that allowed these colourful characters, like Albrecht of Mainz, Joachim of Brandenburg, or Philip of Hesse, to introduce or scupper religious change.

The enigma that remains is why the princes put up with it. Why did Duke George repeatedly let himself become embroiled in a spat with Luther, which he could only lose? Part of the answer to that lies in the complex machinations between Duke George and the Saxon electors, permanently in competition—and in the end it would be the dukes who won out over the electors, as they sided with the emperor after Luther's death and won the electoral title and lands. Part of the answer lies in the way that, in a fragmented empire with dozens of princes and dukes, politics was very much about showing off. But why did the Saxon electors allow Luther to strut on their stage? Luther was increasingly a cultural icon for electoral Saxony, and though they had constantly to keep a watch on him, he was able to express aggression they could not.[63] The physical resemblance of Luther and the Saxon house on the image that was used on the cover page of Luther's works, Luther and the elector on either side of the crucifix, makes the point: Luther had become a religious authority and a secular property rolled into one. His works were authorised by the Saxon electors, while he vouched for their piety. He was their Saxon.[64]

3.4. Martin Luther and the Wittenberg Reformers. Cranach the Younger, c. 1543. Toledo Museum of Art.

# CHAPTER 4

# Names

MARTIN LUTHER KNEW the value of names. His own name, after all, was an invention. Born with the uncomfortable surname 'Luder', with its connotations of wantonness in German, Luther rid himself of his name around the time he posted the 95 Theses.[1] Playing with different variations, he chose to call himself by the Graeco-Latin name 'Eleutherius', meaning the freed one; over a period of months, he turned that into 'Luther', the name he called himself ever after. From Luder to Luther: in this sense Luther was a self-made man and the progenitor of his own family line.[2]

Signing himself now 'f. [brother] Martinus Luther' in his correspondence, Luther's signature soon acquired a notable visual character.[3] Gradually Luther enlarged the 'R' at the end of the name, balancing the 'm' with an emphatic concluding 'r', a flourish he used irregularly. Corresponding to the name, and invented probably around the same time as his change of name, there was the 'Luther rose' with the cross in a heart at its centre, a design that also came to convey Luther's theology in a simple image.[4] An early version appeared on the cover of the pamphlet published in 1519 that includes the first known portrait of the reformer: even if he is hard to make out under his giant doctor hat and cassock, the logo makes his identity clear (see figure 1.1).[5] He used the rose to seal his letters, so the signature and seal together expressed his identity, guaranteeing that the letter was from his hand. It was also used on printed editions of Luther's works as a guarantor of their authenticity. During the Diet of Augsburg, when Luther's movement finally acquired its own separate identity and confessional document, the Confessio Augustana, Elector John Frederick, presented him with a signet ring with this design. Luther had just a short while earlier gone to the trouble of providing a long description of the rose and its meaning: the cross in the heart 'places the believer into a white, joyous rose, for this faith does not give peace and joy like the world gives'; it should be placed on a blue background representing heaven and hope, and surrounded by a gold ring for eternal blessedness.[6] The elaborate description reveals its importance for him and his insistence that faith was about struggle, not peace.[7]

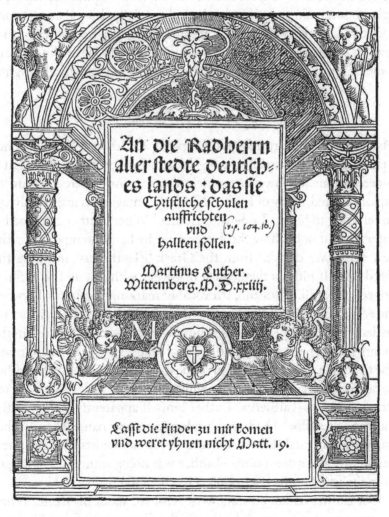

4.1. Title page, *An die Radherrn aller stedte deutsches lands: das sie Christliche schulen auffricht-enn vnd halten sollen.* Martin Luther, 1524. HAB Wolfenbüttel.

How Luther used names can reveal much about his relations with his parents, his father in particular, and with his children. Nicknames and the Latinate names humanists chose for themselves also bound them together, expressing their male camaraderie. And how the new movement of Luther's followers came to name itself has much to tell us about its identity. Naming things was one of Luther's particular intellectual talents, and he was a pitiless inventor of nicknames— a gift that can tell us a great deal about how he thought, and shed some light on some sources of his theological creativity. This talent was connected to his deeper philosophical convictions, because Luther's stance towards language as a system of names of objects lay at the heart of some of his most profound and tenaciously held theological insights.

## Changing Names

Martin became Martinus, but morphing Luder into Latin was not a path open to the serious young Martin Luther, because the Latin 'ludere' means to play, a fact which his antagonists were not slow to exploit. Indeed, many of Luther's Catholic antagonists insisted always on referring to him as Luder, not Luther.[8] When Luther changed his name, he did not follow the patterns set by his contemporaries. The new name was derived from the Greek 'Eleutherius', meaning the 'freed one'. It hid his theological discovery within it and so it functioned rather like a tattoo, irrevocably marking the break between the earlier Luder and the Luther who attacked the papacy, its secret evident only to those who knew him well and who had shared in the months of frenetic spiritual discovery when Luther styled himself 'the freed one'. The final version of the name was emphatically neither Latin nor Greek, but German; whilst some of Luther's followers referred to him as 'Lutherus', Luther himself apparently eschewed the Latinate -us suffix.[9] Deliberately adopting a new name when Luther was already an established academic—most humanists took their new names at a far earlier point—Luther was doing something different from the usual humanist politesse by changing his name.[10]

But Luther remained somewhat sensitive about his name. When Erasmus wanted to attack Luther in the dispute over free will, it was his name that he went for: 'There is also some underlying anger or hidden meaning in the name Luther, which he repeats so often as if it were not correct to name him without an honourable title. If he gets so angry when he is called "Luther", what would he do if I designated him by the titles others have given him, unless perhaps he is pleased when Eck changes "Luther" to "Ludder"?'[11] Johannes Eck, Luther's opponent at the Leipzig debate of 1519 had systematically refused to use the name 'Luther', referring to his antagonist in subsequent polemic as 'Ludder'. As Erasmus well knew, Eck's insistence on calling him by his original name with its pejorative associations grated with the reformer.

Humanists in this period loved to create names, and many celebrated their intellectual identities by inventing Latin or Greek names out of the unpromising material of their workaday surnames. Some simply translated their German names, or took cognates, like the pedestrianly named Philip Black-earth (Schwarzerdt), who became the much more exotic Melanchthon. Some humanists, like Luther's close friend Spalatin, librarian and secretary to Frederick the Wise, took their names from their place of origin; Spalatin came from Spalt near Nuremberg. This was a strategy which allowed an individual to escape the tyranny of their family surname, and since Spalatin may have been illegitimate and raised by a father to whom he was not biologically related, he had good reason to create his own name out of his birthplace.[12]

The name of Justus Jonas, one of Luther's most loyal followers, had quite a career. Christened Jobst Koch, Jonas Latinized his first name, becoming known as 'Jodocus Northusanus', Jodocus of Nordhausen, dispensing with the humdrum 'Koch', or cook, to make himself sound like a classical sage. Koch had started out as a humanist and devotee of Erasmus.[13] Probably when studying law, he turned himself from Jodocus into the Latin 'Justus', 'the just'. Later, perhaps as a gesture to the father whose name he had originally spurned, he adopted his father's Christian name as his own surname, Jonas. Then he encountered Luther, and became as passionate a Martinist—Luther's early followers liked to style themselves after their hero's first name—as he had formerly been an Erasmian. He reworked his name to reflect his religious identity, turning his father's name Jonas into the biblical Jonah. This was why he took the whale as his coat of arms, now using it in its typological sense as referring forward to the resurrection of Christ. Like 'Eleutherius', his new name was an emblem of his rebirth as an evangelical. He used it in the Erfurt book of matriculation: a beautiful miniature illustration shows Jonas in the very mouth of the whale. In the background, the tomb is visible in the cave and the risen Christ stands holding the flag of resurrection, while Jonas, now in academic dress and doctor's cap, kneels at his feet.[14] And in the newly redecorated church at Halle, with its fabulous mannerist balcony, where Jonas was preacher, Jonas's little whale is directly opposite the image of Luther's face, hidden homage to the reformer's influence on his life.[15]

Like Jonas, all the major reformers had emblems of their own, and they represented the Wittenberg 'team' as the movement tried to present itself as a collective effort. By the early 1530s, in book frontispieces from the Wittenberg printer Hans Lufft, the 'famous five' are indicated by their initials and emblems: Luther and his rose, Melanchthon with his serpent (alluding both to his medical training and to the mystery of Salvation), and Jonas with his whale; while Bugenhagen, Luther's pastor and confessor, is represented with the Harp of David, and Caspar Cruciger, another of Luther's trusted followers, as the dove with the olive twig.[16]

Luther employed his name to project his own personal status too, an idiosyncrasy which the shrewd Erasmus had not failed to spot. Surprisingly for someone who had to be persuaded to undertake a doctorate, Luther was very proud of his title, and incorporated it into the initials 'DML', which increasingly stood for him, as though his first name were not Martin but 'Doctor', a habit faithfully preserved in that same image of Luther which decorates the fabulous balcony of the redesigned church at Halle (see figure 5.2). Whereas, as a friar, he had signed himself 'f.', brother, he now often appended 'D' to his signature. He insisted his wife call him by his title 'Herr Doktor', while even Wittenberg followers who were only slightly younger referred to him as their 'father'.[17] Luther's name therefore became a projection of his standing as father of the movement, and incorporated his power and authority.

His rejection of his family name was also a rejection of the mining family in Mansfeld from which he had come. That withdrawal had begun when he had joined the Augustinians and destroyed his

4.2. Jonah and the Whale. Justus Jonas, c. 1517. Universitätsmatrikel in Erfurt.

father's carefully laid plans for his eldest son, in whose education so much had been invested. The family needed someone with legal knowledge, because, as his father Hans Luder saw, the tenure of their

4.3. Title page, *Von den Conciliis und Kirchen*. Martin Luther, 1539. British Museum.

mining leases was uncertain and knowledge of law would give them leverage in negotiations with the counts of Mansfeld, in whose territory the mines lay.[18] Luder turned out to be only too right, for by the

1530s and 1540s the counts of Mansfeld finally dispossessed the mine owners and took over all the leases. Luther came from a small elite of mine-owning families, who all intermarried; every other child of Hans Luder followed this pattern, strengthening their family's precarious position and cementing the ties of alliance and co-operation on which mining depended. It was Luther's younger brother Jacob (or Jacuff as he was known) who, continuing in mining, would carry the family name. Eventually, once the mines had been appropriated by the counts, he would leave Mansfeld altogether for the mines in Braunschweig Wolfenbuettel. By creating the name 'Luther', Martin ceded the family name to his brother, just as he had passed the leading roles in the family mining business to him and to his brother-in-law. Jacuff never changed his name to match that of his famous brother.[19]

On the other hand, Luther's children were emphatically named not for the saint's day on which they were baptised, as Luther had been, but for their connection to their father. There was Hans (Johannes), the eldest, named for Luther's father; next came Martin; and the youngest son was named Paul, reflecting the importance of the apostle Paul to Luther. Thus together the three sons incorporated Luther himself, a heavy burden to bear. The girls, Elisabeth and Margarethe, also bore names that were closely connected to Luther: Elisabeth (of Thuringia) was the thirteenth-century saint who had lived at the Wartburg, where Luther was hidden after the Diet of Worms, and whose glass Luther took from the reliquary collection of Frederick the Wise as a memento. Margarethe was Luther's mother's (and sister's) name, and it is clear that he was especially close to his mother in his devotional life, as Ian Siggins has shown.[20] Only 'Magdalena', the name of Luther's other daughter, apparently came from Katharina von Bora's side of the family: her aunt was named Margaretha, Magdalena, or 'Mume Lehna', and she had been her older female relative in the convent where Katharina was a nun, coming later to live in the Luther household.[21]

The lives Luther planned for them were also linked to himself. Hans was destined for law as if to make good the law career that Luther had never completed, the failure that had so enraged and disappointed old Hans Luder. The boy had a university degree conferred on him at a ridiculously young age, in honour of his father. A letter

Martin wrote to Hans when the boy was not yet eleven years old survives and suggests the tenor of their relationship. Luther writes in simple Latin and exhorts the boy to be obedient to his parents, signing off as his father 'in flesh and spirit'. The letter displays paternal pride as Luther strives to make a connection with his son, its message perhaps somewhat overwhelming to a young boy.[22] Hans was not, it turned out, an academic child and he did not take to the law, changing to study theology. He never, however, managed to hold a preaching post. The second son, Martin, intended for theology, chose law instead but ended up with a sinecure at the Saxon court, offered more out of respect to Luther than because of his own talents. Only Paul, the youngest, aged thirteen when his father died, managed to build a life for himself as a physician and had a family.[23] He alone continued the male family line, while Margarethe also had descendants.[24]

When Luder changed his name to Luther, he was definitively breaking with his father. Luther later repaired the breach and wrote a public letter of apology to his father—prefacing his treatise on Monastic Vows—but his apology went only so far. In it, he recognized that he should give his father 'offspring' and that he had cheated him by entering the celibate life. But he immediately went on to insist that God was his real father, not Hans Luder, and that it was to God he truly owed obedience. Moreover, the 'letter' was a fiction printed for the public: written in Latin, his father could not have read it.[25] When Luther wrote this letter in 1521 he was still some way from being ready to marry: he did not contemplate matrimony for over three more years, long after many of his followers had wed. When he did finally marry and have children, they were Luthers, not Luders. For all that Luther healed the breach with his father, he remained determined to overcome him completely, and create a distinct dynasty with his own distinct name.

Still, he retained a strong tie to Mansfeld and to his family. When his father died in 1530, Luther mused that 'I succeed now in the legacy of the name, and I am almost the oldest Luther in my family', going straight on to reflect on his own mortality: 'Now it is up to me, not only by chance, but also by law, to follow [my father] through death into the kingdom of Christ; may he most graciously bestow this on us'.[26] This is an interesting meditation, because Luther was attracted all his life by martyrdom, which he had both risked in 1521 and planned to avoid; he published accounts of the martyrdom of several other evangelicals, including Leo Kaiser and Heinrich von Zutphen. Luther took his family responsibilities as the oldest of the name seriously. In the late 1530s, he interceded with the counts of Mansfeld, trying to protect the mine owners and arguing that they should not be dispossessed. He even travelled to see the counts about the matter the year before he died, only to find them not at home. Describing himself as a 'Mansfeldian child' and feigning ignorance about the detail of mining leases, he simply insisted that the counts should not take over the heritable leases and that they should let the owners at least honour the contracts made in advance.[27] In 1546, he undertook the perilous winter journey that would eventually kill him, travelling to Eisleben in an attempt to reconcile the counts. Despite having ruined his father's plans for the family, Luther ended up as his family's advocate, in much the same way he might have done had he pursued a career in law, and he always saw himself as a child of Mansfeld.

## Naming the Movement

What name was the new Reformation movement to have? This was not an easy question, for it was not at first clear how far it was simply a movement of criticism of Rome, and how far it was an independent church. In the early years, people called themselves 'Martinists'. Luther referred to 'our people', and soon, to 'the Wittenbergers', a name which identified the cause with the university and the Saxon town, giving it a strong sense of locale. This was the term that dominated during the sixteenth century, and became central to the many commemorations of Luther. Mathesius, who wrote one of the first full-length biographies of Luther, declared himself a 'citizen' of the 'Wittenbergish Church', the earthly institution to whom he owed greatest loyalty.[28] He thanked Jesus who had 'founded and maintained the Christian School at Wittenberg, and had ordained outstanding and miraculous people, whose like had not been seen on earth for many hundreds of years'.[29] A devotional work, the biography began life as a series of sermons, and it made much of Luther's mining connection, closing the work with the 'mining sermon' given in the mining region of Joachimstal. Cyriakus Spangenberg, another early biographer, celebrated Luther's links with mining too, and with Mansfeld, firmly associating the movement with a geographical region. So also, the Frankfurt edition of Luther's *Table Talk*, issued after Luther's death, featured a cover woodcut that showed the reformer with the Wittenberg team, a town hall and not a church in the background. The name 'Wittenberg Church' therefore attempted to link the Church with the university, with Melanchthon, Bugenhagen and the other reformers, and with Saxony.

By contrast, Luther's opponents, including former supporters, *did* use the term 'lutherisch'. In 1533 Georg Witzel, a former Lutheran preacher who returned to the Catholic faith, wrote a denunciation of 'Luterey' and what he termed the 'envious *Luteristen*', whom he condemned as the 'Luterischer sect'.[30] Their sectarianism, he argued, gave birth to yet more sects, unlike the true Roman Church, but 'a sect is a sect and remains a sect, like an ape an ape, dress it up, praise it and defend it as much as you like' (unfortunately Witzel lacked his former idol's rhetorical gifts).[31] By naming their Church after the founder, Witzel could equate it with other historical sects, all rooted in an individual's errors, like Nestorianism or Pelagianism.

For Luther's followers, identifying themselves with a single town was not perhaps good propaganda, though the name did provide a counterweight to Rome. The Sacramentarians, by contrast, did not limit themselves in this way, though Geneva would later play a similar role for Calvin. It took a long time for the term 'Lutheran' to emerge, and even then it did not win out over 'Wittenbergers' for some time. In the 1530s, the Strasbourg reformer Martin Bucer began to refer to 'the Lutherans' in order to distinguish between those who followed his own position of denying the real presence and those who took Luther's line.[32] Indeed, the Church would commonly be known as that of the 'Confessio Augustana' ('your confession', as Luther referred to it in his letters to Melanchthon); it was a name which referred not to its founder but to its founding statement of belief that Melanchthon presented to the emperor at the Augsburg Diet of 1530 while Luther remained holed up in the castle at Coburg. This name gave the movement a strong Saxon identity, and focused on the team, not the individual—ever more important as the movement tried to present the increasingly strained relationship between Melanchthon and Luther as harmonious. But it also restricted the movement geographically and strengthened the tendency to turn Wittenberg into a place of pilgrimage for pious Lutherans, as it remains to this day.

Early on, the movement developed its own mottos and slogans, the most famous of which was VDMIAE, an abbreviation of *Verbum dei manet in aeternum*, 'the word of God endures in eternity' (1 Peter 1:25), worn on the sleeves of those who supported Luther at the Diet of Speyer in 1526. Adopted by Philip of Hesse and Elector John the Constant of Saxony, the sleeve was a propaganda masterstroke which encapsulated Lutheran theology and began the process of publicly pronouncing that there was now a faction which supported Luther and which had political strength. This process led

4.4. Image featuring the sleeve motto, 'Verbum domini manet in Aeternum, 1522'. Gotha Research Library.

in time to the formation of the Schmalkaldic League, and resistance to the emperor, eventually resulting in the ill-fated Schmalkaldic War of 1546–47 after Luther's death, where the Lutherans were defeated.[33]

The motto also offered an irresistible target for jokes by Luther's antagonists. They punned that the slogan should really be 'the word of God *manet im Aermel*'—remains in their sleeves—that is, they hide it up their sleeves, meaning that they twist it to suit themselves.[34] Ironically, the rebel Thomas Müntzer had used it previously, his followers displaying it on their banners in 1524–25. Thus the Lutherans reworked for their own purposes the slogan that was famous at the final Battle of Frankenhausen, incorporating and neutralizing Müntzer's radicalism. One of the interesting features of the Reformation is how it managed to overcome, absorb, and obliterate its own ghosts, of whom Müntzer was perhaps the greatest.

## INSULTS

Names were also weapons of abuse, an art of which Luther was a master. One of his first forays into pamphleteering was directed against the bishop of Meissen who lived at Stolpen and whom he accused of being 'tolpisch', that is, idiotic rather than 'stolpisch'. The humour of this early tract is rather laboured, but it showed Luther using comedy to humiliate his opponents. Writing this kind of polemic in German, not Latin, seems to have unleashed his talent for abstruse flights of fantasy, which would become such a feature of his style. When the papal nuncio Carl Miltitz read it, hot off the press, in the company of the bishop, he could not stop laughing—the bishop however did not take it in good part. Luther's ruler Duke Frederick, whose anticlericalism outweighed his tact, laughed 'as was fitting'.[35]

With his life under threat, Luther's excommunication seems to have brought a new energy and passion to the reformer's writing too. Suddenly he found himself overwhelmed with attacks on and replies to his works, and deciding which ones to answer began to take up much of his time. He devised animal names for his opponents: there was Murner the cat, Augustin von Alfeld the donkey, Emser the goat, and the unbelievably named Hieronymus Dungersheim von Ochsenfahrt. These names gained wide currency, one pamphlet cover depicting the motley crew. He was also merciless in his humour about his antagonist Johannes Cochlaeus, whose name could be mocked as meaning the spoon, the snail, or—even better—the vulva. Luther abused him as a man who should be wearing skirts. Albrecht, the addressee of the 95 Theses, became christened the 'bride of Mainz'. As we saw in the previous chapter, Luther's sexualised invective reached its pitch in his writing against rulers, the most remarkable example of which is 'Wider Hans Wurst' (1541), a name which abused Heinrich of Wolfenbüttel as a carnival figure, a sausage man.

Much of Luther's humour, too, was connected to names. He adored puns, and dubbed the pope's decretals 'dirt-als' ('Dreck' means 'dirt' in German), and published not the legend but the 'Luegend' (lie) of St John Chrysostom, dedicating it to the pope.[36] He loved acrostics and anagrams, and when in 1530, he was forced to stay in the castle at Coburg because he was still under the Imperial ban while the Witten-

4.5. Title page, *Eyn kurtze anred zu allen mißgüstigen Doctor Luthters vnd der Christenlichen freyheit.* Johannes Agricola, 1522. Bavian State Library, Munich.

bergers were at the Diet of Augsburg, he gave his address as Grubok, or Coburg.[37] He invented a parliament of jackdaws dressed all in black to rival the Diet of Augsburg, and punning between German and Latin, insisted that they should not be called 'monedula', that is, thieves (jackdaws are famed as thieves), but 'Mon Edula' meaning 'man Edel', or nobleman. From there he leapt to the fake Latin 'Edelmoni', which he then transformed into 'monedulana', or virtue.[38] The noise the birds made was like that of the sophists, or Cochlaeites, yet another jibe at poor old Cochlaeus, and he took to signing off 'from the empire of the winged jackdaws'.[39] And in 1537, he wrote a spoof of the Council of Mantua, in which, since the Lutherans have been defeated, the assembled clergy turn their minds to the serious question of why in card games the pope card should be so close to the Devil card.[40] The fun comes from transformations, as Luther turns one thing into another and yet another—whether in a joke or a story, Luther always loved to add a final unexpected twist. Such strategies made his antagonists ridiculous and manageable, important for a movement that smashed the reverence underpinning the papist church. And while his opponents stood still, Luther was endlessly jumping forward, from one crazy pun to the next.

This creativity, however, also had its darker side, as we can see by following the logic of one of Luther's last and most infamous works, *Against the Roman Papacy, A Creature of the Devil*. The entire treatise insults Paul III and the papacy as the 'ass-fart pope', a name harking back to the woodcut of the Papal Ass, one of the early pieces of propaganda from 1523, in which Melanchthon had interpreted the monster that had been found in the Tiber in 1496 as prefiguring the end of the papacy.[41] Characteristically Luther plays with transformations in his text, each more disgusting than the last. He brings the Papal Ass to life and imagines him walking gingerly on ice, emitting a fart to which all would say: 'Oh the Devil, how the pope-ass has shat himself',[42] and asks which 'mouth' the pope is speaking out of, the one 'the farts come out of?' or the mouth into which the Corsican wine flows, adding 'may a dog crap in it'.[43] He piles on the excremental imagery in the names with which he addresses the pope.[44] Early on, Luther makes the joke about papal decretals being 'drecketaln', or 'dirt-als',[45] and soon he reaches for the extravagant insult he had used in *Against Hanswurst*: if the papists are angry, then 'let them do it in their pants and hang it around their neck' and they should use this as a pomander.[46] Time and again the humour is about 'doing it in your pants'; but exactly who is doing this switches throughout the treatise: sometimes it is the Lutherans who are imagined doing this in mock fear of the pope's learning; sometimes they are insulting the pope; sometimes the metaphor is reversed and it is the ass-fart pope who is guilty, as Luther puts it 'in good German', of 'dirtying himself in his cleverness'.[47]

The effect is overwhelming. Luther's rhythmic writing assaults the senses—smell, sight, and sound—making it hard to think. The treatise itself is poorly organized and its argument is diffuse and repetitive, so much so that even Luther admits towards the end that it has run away with him and that he has become an old man blathering. What pulls it together, however, is the epithet 'ass-fart pope'. A highly plastic and often contradictory insult, it is repeated throughout and unifies the argument imaginatively, because the greatest stinker is the Devil, and it is by his stink that the Devil's presence is revealed: 'For the Devil just has to do it, so that he leaves a stink behind him, so that you know

4.6. 'Sauritt', *Erklerung der Schendlichen Sünde. . . .* Matthias Flacius, 1550. Herzog August Bibliothek Wolfenbüttel.

he has been there'.[48] That is, the pope farts, stinks, and does it in his pants, and all his power and decrees are actually excremental, so the best way to deal with him is to fart at him in good German style; and the proof that the pope is diabolic is that it is the stench of the Devil that reveals his identity.[49] Luther uses the excremental language to assault learning and argument, so that his own writing lets off a stench.

## The Antichrist

The greatest of Luther's names for his enemies, of course, was his identification of the papacy as the Antichrist. From late 1518 through to the summer of 1520, Luther became convinced the pope was the Antichrist, and he made his views public in such works as the great Reformation treatise of 1520, *On the Babylonian Captivity*, and in his attack on the papal bull that excommunicated him, naming it 'the Antichrist's Bull'.[50] From then on, he rarely referred to the pope without tagging him as the Antichrist, which was in Luther's view his 'true' identity that 'unmasked' him (another metaphor he regularly used). The insult was so effective because it inverted the pope's holiness, suggesting he was the greatest enemy of Christians and imbuing Luther's movement with apocalyptic urgency. It was an identification which worked like a key, transforming the meaning of everything: once you accepted it, you could not accept the Roman Church or monks and priests, because they were linked with Satan. History itself was transformed.

Identifying the pope as the Antichrist enabled the binary thinking that powered the early Reformation propaganda, as we shall see in chapter 5, and it finds its apogee in Melanchthon and Cranach's *Passional of Christ and Antichrist* (1521), where a set of vivid contrasts between the pope and Christ names one lot of practices as true Christian and the other as not only evil but diabolical. It empowers the reader who is shown exactly how they have been duped: what appeared to be good Christian behavior is unmasked as a swindle, practices designed to do nothing more than get money off pious Germans. This, as Luther would often put it, is calling things by their true names.

For their part, Luther's opponents attempted to rename Luther. They insisted that he, not the papacy, was the Antichrist, and produced

4.7. *Passional Christi und Antichristi*. Cranach the Elder and Philipp Melanchthon, 1521. British Library.

images of him with horns or in conversation with devils, but for the most part they did not at first develop this very far. Writing in 1534, Petrus Sylvius, for example, averred 'that Luther is not a simple heretic, but is actually the long-prophesied Antichrist'[51]—and attempted to prove this by demonstrating that his biblical interpretations were incorrect. Others, more cautiously, dubbed him merely the Antichrist's 'forerunner'.[52] Luther, however, had long since stolen their thunder, and his insult against the papacy stuck.

## NAMES AND BINARY THINKING

The place of names in Luther's humour is revealing, because Luther's intellectual talents had a good deal to do with naming. He was a magnificent simplifier. The 95 Theses famously begins with a question about language and its meaning: 'When our Lord and Master Jesus Christ said "repent", he willed the entire life of believers to be one of repentance'. That is, 'this word cannot be understood as referring to the sacrament of penance, that is, confession and satisfaction, as administered by the clergy.'[53] Or, as he goes on to explain, it does not

99

mean 'buy indulgences', a brilliant insight that was easy to grasp; and that opened up a whole new way of understanding what the devotional life might encompass.

Typically Luther's written works made great use of contrast and of grouping things together, tactics that enabled him to cut through complex theological debates and get to the heart of the issue. Luther's theology itself could be grasped in terms of a few key concepts and their opposites: Law and Gospel, grace and good works, scripture and human accretion, Christ and the Devil. The rest of the 95 Theses play constantly with contrasts, between the prophets who cry 'peace, peace', and there is no peace, and who are to be rejected; and the blessed prophets who say 'cross, cross', and there is no cross.[54]

The rhetoric of contrasts did more, however, than simply bifurcate the world. In *On the Babylonian Captivity* of 1520, Luther sets out the three 'walls' that have defended the papacy: the idea that spiritual power is superior to temporal power, the principle that only the pope can interpret scripture, and 'their story . . . that no-one may summon a Council but the pope'.[55] He follows this straight up with a lovely reversal—'In this way they have cunningly stolen our three rods from us, that they may go unpunished. They have ensconced themselves within the safe stronghold of these three walls so that they can practice all the knavery and wickedness which we see today'.[56] Here he uses a single unforgettable image, that of walls, to name and place a whole variety of practices together, making sense of them and showing that their only function is to preserve the papacy from attack; and then he imagines the papacy as a naughty schoolboy, puncturing its pomp. Or, in *The Freedom of a Christian*, he uses the word 'freedom' repeatedly to name a spiritual state and an attitude towards the Church—employing a word with enormous resonance, which was deliberately ambiguous between secular and religious freedom. No wonder the peasants drew on Lutheran terms in their assault on the foundations of feudalism, proclaiming that all Christians were free. Here the name took theological insights into the social and political arena, allowing others to do things with concepts Luther had invented.

The technique of naming could also be employed with devastating effect against those who disagreed with him, one of Luther's less pleasant characteristics. If in 1517 Luther had castigated the prophets who call 'peace, peace' when there is no peace, by 1524, as the Peasants' War loomed, he was mocking his opponents like Thomas Müntzer and Andreas Karlstadt as 'heavenly prophets', a brilliant epithet which ridiculed their insistence that they were divinely inspired. As he warned the town of Mühlhausen, they should steer clear of the 'prophet' Müntzer, and if he says that 'God and his Spirit sent him like the apostles, let him prove it with signs and miracles—or stop him preaching!'. He himself, Luther continued, was—unlike Müntzer— a properly instituted preacher and 'I cannot boast that God sent me straight from Heaven, as they do'.[57] Indeed, Luther titled his major polemic against them 'Against the Heavenly Prophets', ensuring that the name stuck. The words elevated the struggle against them to an apocalyptic battle: they were like the biblical 'false prophets', whose presence proved the Last Days were at hand. Müntzer and his ilk, he repeatedly insisted, were 'murderous and blood-thirsty prophets'; the Devil was using these 'rebellious spirits and murderous prophets' as his instruments in these 'dreadful times'; the 'bloodthirsty peasants and murder prophets' were on the loose, and therefore, he thundered in his infamous *Against the Robbing and Murdering Hordes of Peasants*, it was a Christian work to 'smite, slay, and stab' them, words, which, as we saw, echoed Müntzer's own bloodthirsty rhetoric.[58] Throughout the bitter months of the Peasants' War and its aftermath, Luther used the name 'prophet' to devastating effect. Those prophets who claimed authority through divine inspiration, overturning the established authorities of this world, were rebels and disturbers of order and peace. Now Luther, who had begun by insisting, as the Gospel of Matthew said, that Christ did not come to bring peace but a sword, was supporting peace and secular rulers.

The defeat of the peasants was a watershed in the Reformation. Yet just as the Lutherans had re-appropriated Müntzer's slogan 'May the Word of God endure forever', so also, once the war was over, the Lutherans gradually found themselves renaming Luther as the 'German prophet'. Being a prophet gave Luther the right to criticize the actions of secular rulers as the Old Testament prophets did. Luther himself took an interest in prophecies about him and his own prophetic role: in 1529 his friend Friedrich Myconius reminded him of the monk Johannes Hilten, who had died in Eisenach, a victim of the cruel monks, and who had prophesied that a monk would attack the papacy in 1516. By 1529 the Turks were at the gates of Vienna, and apocalyptic prophecies had sudden salience: Luther, it seemed, was the prophet Hilten foretold. In 1530, when Melanchthon wrote the Apology for the Augsburg Confession of Faith, he began the section on Monastic Vows with the story of Hilten.[59] By 1537, medals were being struck commemorating Luther as the 'Propheta Germaniae';[60] and the wheel would come full circle with his death, when Luther was finally commemorated as a 'prophet' as his followers mourned him as their lost Elijah.[61] They incorporated for themselves the power of the name Luther had used so devastatingly against his enemies.

At around this time too, Luther devised the term 'Schwärmer', or swarmers, the enthusiasts or crazies, to group his opponents together despite the extreme differences in their positions.[62] They were like bees, swarming and buzzing uselessly together. Lumping Karlstadt together with the revolutionary Thomas Müntzer and even with the Swiss Sacramentarians—with whom Müntzer had nothing in common—was a masterstroke. It put Karlstadt on the defensive, forcing him to prove that he did not share Müntzer's revolutionary views. It obliterated Luther's and Karlstadt's common theological past in Wittenberg and their shared formation in the values of Gelassenheit (relaxedness), which had been the watch word of Johannes Staupitz, Luther's confessor. It vilified them all as people who similarly fell for their emotions, who followed dreams, and who were not rational.

It also meant that Luther did not have to engage with their arguments—and as Amy Burnett has shown, Luther almost certainly did not read all Karlstadt's Eucharistic pamphlets, but rested content with his *Dialogue*.[63] Because he already knew it all, Luther had no need to read it. Worse, it meant that he did not engage with the Swiss, or with Bucer, who was trying to broker unity. Luther's intransigence and bitterness would make it very difficult for the Reformation to unite. By presenting himself as rational and his opponents as dreamers, Luther also denigrated emotionality in devotion, a legacy that would not be overcome until the Pietists returned to the wellsprings of early evangelicalism and rediscovered Luther's Augustinian confessor, Staupitz, and the German mystical tradition of the *Theologia Deutsch*.

## NAMES AND THEOLOGY

Names were important to Luther at an even deeper level, connected to his most firmly held values. Not for nothing did he describe himself as a 'nominalist', or 'terminist'.[64] In the disputes over the direction in which intellectual life should go, Luther rejected the Aristotelian account of abstracts and particulars, denying that collective nouns referred to an inherent, universal quality: abstract collectives just referred to lots of particular things. This abstruse debate mattered because it coloured how Luther grasped fundamental theological issues, determining both the stance he took on the Eucharist and the line he took on baptism, the two most important issues of the Reformation.[65] In relation to the Eucharist, Luther could not accept the standard account of the miracle of the mass. This held that the accidents of the bread and wine—taste, smell, and appearance—remained the same, while the essence was transformed into the body of Christ. For Luther, who did not accept the idea of accidents and essences, this made no sense. He used the image of red hot iron, which is at one and the same time iron and fire, to explain how the bread could simultaneously be both the body of Christ and bread. A name referred plainly to an object, and the fact that Christ's real presence could not be grasped by human reason was central to Luther's understanding of the Eucharist. Nothing would induce him to give up this position. For Karlstadt and the Swiss, however, the Eucharist did not contain the real body and blood of Christ; it functioned, rather, as a memorial, and should not therefore be honoured, elevated at the moment of consecration, or carried about in procession. The philosophical accounts of the Sacramentarian theologians who denied the real presence varied, but for them the bread represented rather than was in actuality Christ's body, and the Scriptural 'this is' did not refer to the bread. Their understanding of how words mean was more complex, whereas for Luther there simply was no argument: a word referred to a thing, and this was what the words meant, even if it did not make sense to 'the whore', as he called it, human reason. As the words attributed to him at Marburg in 1529 put it, when he broke so emphatically with Zwingli: 'The word says that Christ has a body. This I believe. The word says that the body of Christ ascended into heaven and sits on the right hand of God. This

103

I also believe. The word says that this same body is in the Supper, and I believe this. Why should I discuss whether it is outside of a place or in a place? This is a mathematical argument. The word of God is above it, for God created mathematics and everything. He commands us to have faith in this matter'.[66] Language simply named reality; words were names. This was why the meaning of scripture could be, in Luther's view, absolutely transparent, requiring no interpretation through the tradition of the Church—though of course he also held that properly educated clergy were the ones who had to preach that biblical truth.

Baptism, the other sacrament which Luther retained, is fundamentally about names, for it is the ritual during which the infant acquires a name and enters the community as an individual. It may seem ironic that Luther, who famously placed such value on the authority of scripture alone, insisted on retaining infant baptism. After all, the gospel says that those who believe should be baptised, and babies cannot profess belief. This was the reason why Anabaptists rejected infant baptism and maintained that only adults who believed should be baptised. To their argument that infant baptism had no Scriptural warrant, Luther replied that it was up to those who rejected infant baptism to prove that scripture explicitly condemned it: 'they can produce no statement which says, "You are to baptise adults but not children"'; since there was no clear condemnation, it must be permitted even if scripture did not say so. Children, he argued, could believe, even if we could not understand how. Addressing an imaginary Anabaptist interlocutor, he wrote, 'Now it is up to you to bring forth a single scripture verse which proves that children cannot believe in baptism. . . . I grant that we do not understand how they do believe, or how faith is created. But that is not the point here'. This was a tortuous argument that depended on a Scriptural absence; it hardly looked like 'sola scriptura'.

For Luther, baptism was hugely important. It was the sacrament which accompanies us throughout life and gives us confidence in God's promise to us. He liked to tell the story about the learned doctor who sees a Christian wrestle with the Devil and subdue him through the power of baptism; when the doctor, impressed with this feat, tries to copy him, he fails because he is too clever to trust in as simple a promise as his own baptism.[67] Luther's radical Augustinianism led him to see baptism as God's gift to us, not something that can be merited by having faith. This was also vitally important in terms of his own experience, because Luther's 'Anfechtungen' (temptations, struggles) seem to circle around his own deep-rooted doubts concerning faith itself. Baptism had therefore to be freely given by God, and did not turn on the believer having to demonstrate faith—which is why the memory of his own baptism provided solace to Luther when he felt most despairing. One's given name, one's identity, was therefore tied to God's promise. And once again, his Catholic antagonists intuited its importance. Johannes Nas mocked Luther's boasting about his own baptism: 'Dear friend, what need is there to praise Luther because of his baptism? Has no-one been baptised but he?', and he went on to imagine Luther's mother exclaiming that he had 'gededelt' (peed) in the priest's hand when he was baptised, just as he would go on to sully the priesthood itself.[68]

Luther at first reformed baptism to only a limited degree and he kept perhaps the least scriptural part, the institution of godparents, the adults who make the profession of faith on behalf of the infant. He made great use of godparents to tie his family into social networks: he acted as godfather for Cranach's son and he in turn acted as godfather for Luther's. Nor was he above exploiting social connections: from 1533, his son Paul boasted the electoral Saxon Marshal Hans Loeser and the elector's younger brother, Duke John Ernest himself, as godfathers. Back in 1526, at the birth of his first son, he had asked the Mansfeld Chancellor Caspar Mueller with irresistible self-mockery to stand godfather for 'a child born of a monk and a nun'—Luther's requests to act as godparents were always highly personal, humorous, and direct.[69] He also drew extensively on the other Lutheran clergy in Wittenberg, Jonas, Amsdorf, and Melanchthon. As a result, the Wittenberg clergy were tied to one another through a vast web of godparental relationships, creating a new kind of professional belonging that had not been possible amongst the Catholic clergy, who had no legitimate children. In short, Luther used the naming ritual of baptism as a means of creating social cohesion amongst the Wittenberg pastorate and as a route to integrate the clergy into the ruling elite.

There was another important reason why Luther so ardently rejected a believer's baptism. Baptizing all infants at birth meant that the religious and secular communities were the same—whereas Anabaptists were a minority who soon found themselves in opposition to secular authority as they tried to implement scriptural values in daily life. Retaining infant baptism helped to guarantee Luther's political role and influence because almost all inhabitants of Wittenberg were members of the same Church. The ritual of naming thus incorporated everyone into the Church and into the political community in the wider sense at the same time. Baptism, then, was also fundamental to Luther's view of politics. This was what allowed him and the Wittenbergers to formulate religious policy for the Saxon elector, and permitted him to assume the mantle of troublesome prophet, slinging mud at Albrecht of Mainz, Heinrich of Wolfenbuettel, or George of Saxony.

How do all these different uses of names cohere? My argument here has been that understanding the nature of Luther's humour, creativity, psychology, and narcissism can give us a deeper understanding of his theology. In other words, I am arguing that an individual's psyche can illuminate their intellectual life so that we can arrive at a fuller comprehension of their ideas and their limitations. Names were deeply significant to Luther, and he loved to play with them. His own name was carefully crafted to reveal central features of his identity, and his choice of names for his children reveals a stubborn preoccupation with himself. Luther's creativity had much to do with his ability to group things together and provide a name for them that made sense, and that others could take up and use; it could also fire some of his worst and most destructive rhetoric. But names were also central to his deepest theological convictions about baptism and the Eucharist. These were the questions over which the Reformation would fragment and over which Luther could simply not negotiate, because they were part of his psychic and theological identity.

Names are great identifiers, and Luther's followers also used their names to bond with one another. They wrote in one another's autograph books, picking quotations to characterize themselves or their friendships. To secure an autograph from Luther was of course a great honour, and Luther was an assiduous autograph-giver, creating, as Ulinka Rublack has argued, a whole new kind of 'grapho-relic'.[70]

Just how important names were to the Reformation can be seen in the Wittenberg parish church itself, which contains the most extraordinary grapho-relic of all. Cranach's remarkable altarpiece of 1547 completed the year after the reformer's death depicts Luther and his followers administering the sacraments; Bugenhagen hears confession, Melanchthon administers baptism, while Luther preaches on the predella in the presence of his wife and children. Most astonishing of all is the back of the altar. On the reverse of the predella the souls of the damned are depicted in Stygian gloom, while above on the bright central panel, the risen Christ stands in triumph on top of the dragon who sports a papal-esque crown. Below, amongst the damned, generations of Lutheran students have etched their names into the dark paint, ruining Cranach's artwork. In the church most central to Lutheranism, on the back of the image of their leader preaching, Lutheran students have made themselves eternal. By adding their names, these students testify that they are, like Luther, the worst of sinners; and by making their mark, they literally wrote themselves into the 'Wittenberg church', behind the altar itself.

4.8. Details of the Saved and the Damned (verso), Altar of the Sacraments or Wittenberg Altarpiece. Cranach the Younger, 1547. JMP Agency.

# CHAPTER 5

# 'Living I Was Your Plague'

'LIVING I WAS your plague, O Pope, dead, I will be your death'. According to his personal doctor, Johannes Ratzeberger, Luther wrote these words in chalk on the wall the night before he died.[1] He was in a good mood and he shared this remark with his friends and co-workers Justus Jonas and Michael Coelius, who would also be with him when he died. The bitter saying—known as Luther's motto—was repeated in the funeral sermons for the reformer given by Johannes Bugenhagen, where it forms the powerful conclusion pronounced in Latin and then translated into German: 'Pope, Pope, while I lived I was your pestilence, when I die, I will be your bitter death'.[2] It can be found on countless memorial images of the Reformer, and even stood outside the house in Eisleben where Luther was born, like a tavern sign. When the house was rebuilt after a fire burnt it to the ground in 1689, the image, with its imprecation, miraculously survived unscathed.[3]

Luther's comment was neither a joke nor a chance remark.[4] Ten years earlier, back in 1537, Luther had been suffering from urine retention at Schmalkalden, in the midst of important negotiations. He was in great pain, swollen, and had experienced a euphoria caused by the infection. Realising just how ill he was, and convinced he was on his deathbed, he made the same remark, prefacing it with the words: 'My epitaph shall remain true'.[5] Ten years before that, in 1527, when Luther had experienced a complete collapse and expected to die, he had compared himself to John, the author of the Book of Revelation, who had also 'written a good strong book against the pope'.[6]

Ratzeberger is hardly a neutral witness, but the story certainly captures something that was at work in his deathbed scene. Luther had

5.1. Unburned Luther. Anonymous, 1583. Luther Memorial Foundation of Saxony-Anhalt.

travelled to Eisleben, the town where he was born, to settle a dispute between the counts of Mansfeld, fully aware that this might be his last journey. He was taken ill there and, as it became clear that he was dying, his followers recorded his every prayer, along with his movements to and from the bed as he prayed in Latin in the words of Psalm 30, echoing Christ's own words: 'Into your hands I commend my spirit; you have redeemed me Lord God of truth'. According to the official account of Luther's death, he shook hands with each of his companions, wished them good night, and admonished them to 'pray for our Lord God and his Gospel, that it go well with him, for the Council of Trent and the vexatious pope are struggling hard with him'.[7] That is, even the official account records that one of his last prayers was an appeal to pray for God and his gospel because of the attacks they faced from the forthcoming Council of Trent and the pope.

True or not, therefore, Ratzeberger's legend was correct about the deep emotional connection between Luther's dying and his hatred of the papacy. Indeed, Johannes Bugenhagen's funeral sermon—concluding with Luther's motto—and the account of the reformer's death were printed together in a slim memorial volume, prefaced with a moving image of the Luther's face in a roundel, with his trademark wayward curl and far-seeing, deep-set eyes.[8] He wears the clerical uniform of doctor's hat, academic gown, and high shirt that he invented; and the uncharacteristic gentleness of his expression almost seems to convey the sense that he is no longer with us.[9] Luther's rage against the papacy was undimmed, even at the end; and for its part, at the moment of greatest loss, when the movement mourned its founder, it too expressed undying fury and hatred of the pope. So much a part of Lutheran culture was the motto that one owner of the book transcribed it in their own hand on the page facing the title.

The motto was in a sense a 'name', acting as a title for the memorial portraits of the man whose face was so recognizable that no name was needed. A double portrait of Luther bearing the date of 1537 has the imprecation painted on it, linking it to his near-death experience at Schmalkalden in that year. After his actual death, its use made anti-papalism inseparable from the memorial culture of the man himself. For example, it adorned the relief tombstone of 1571 that was intended for Wittenberg but ended up at Jena. The original wooden model for the tomb was made in Erfurt, and similarly included the motto. It can also be found on the image of Luther with the swan in St. Peter's Church in Hamburg,[10] or in the roundel relief image of Luther's head that dominates the beautiful balcony adorning the Marktkirche in Halle, and was frequently copied.[11] It decorated the copper gilt image of Luther in the Hildesheim town hall, and a similar one was to be found at Jena.[12] It appeared extensively in print too, in lettering running around the frames of many of the printed memorial images of the

5.2. Medallion relief of Luther, Marktkirche Halle. Jobst Kammerer, 1553. © Photo: akg-images.

reformer, or prominently placed near his head. It graced the final scene of seventeenth-century didactic broadsheet pictures of the reformer's life that showed his funeral procession (though the Catholic version showed the coffin sliding out of the door of the Wittenberg monastery straight into the fires of Hell)[13] (see figure 1.12). During Luther's own lifetime, the motto was placed underneath an autograph book sketch of the reformer by one of his students, and when the reformer died, Melanchthon added it to the last sketch of Luther drawn in 1546.[14] It is to be found on a woodcut stuck onto the page of a manuscript with the inscription underneath, together with the date of his death, 1546, a reverent devotional image.[15] Ghoulishly, it even appeared on a portrait of Luther on his death bed.[16]

5.3. Prophecy of the Reverend Mr Doctor Martin Luther. Anonymous, 1546. British National Archives.

The words associated the reformer's death with the fulfillment of his great wish, the destruction of the papacy. The Lutheran faithful who saw the slogan would have recalled Luther's biography: his collapse in 1527, his near death in 1537 at Schmalkalden, and his actual death in 1546. From the start, the reformer's various illnesses and

5.4. Portrait of Martin Luther in Melanththon's notebook. Philipp Melanchthon. Getty.

Anfechtungen featured in his hagiography, presenting a suffering, wounded hero whose tribulations formed the closest thing to martyrdom. Invoking these moments, therefore, yoked that tragic vulnerability to anti-papalism. And it guaranteed the truth of Luther's message, because the imprecation was a kind of prophecy. Writing in

5.5. Martin Luther on his deathbed with motto, not infrared. Cranach the Elder, 1546. © bpk Bilda-
gentur / Staatliche Kunsthalle, Karlsruhe, Germany / Art Resource, NY.

the 1560s, his early biographer Mathesius listed it as one of Luther's many prophecies, dating it to 1530 and linking it to the Diet of Augsburg. He claimed that the prophecy had been fulfilled, 'for since that day the papacy has daily declined'.[17]

The saying was also tied to the establishment of the Lutheran Church. At the Diet of Augsburg in 1530, Melanchthon had presented the Augsburg Confession to Charles V, the founding statement of the new church's beliefs. It was said that Luther had devised the anti-papal verse in his friend Spalatin's house in Altenburg on 8 or 9 October 1530, after the Diet of Augsburg had definitively failed to achieve a compromise with the Catholics. This was only partly true, because he had used it earlier in the Diet too, in his tub-thumping *Exhortation to All Clergy Assembled at Augsburg*. In a passage defending Lutheran marriage against the false chastity of the bishops, he had proclaimed, 'For as long as you will not let our marriage alone, you shall also not have much pleasure and honour from your harlotry and anti-Christian "bishopry".' He had added, 'If I die for it, there are others who can do it better'. Then followed the words 'If I live, I shall be your plague. If I die, I shall be your death'.[18] The words stood for what separated the Lutherans from the Catholics: clerical marriage, no bishops, and Luther himself.

Hostility to the papacy was thus closely woven into Lutheran devotional culture and idolization of the man himself. Medals that mocked the pope were circulating from the 1530s, and there was a rich material culture of anti-papalism, including picture puzzles, plates, and anti-papal tankards for use in the home.[19] Historians of the English Reformation have shown how important hatred of the pope was to English religious culture in the seventeenth century, even arguing that anti-papalism was the glue that held together the fissiparous English Reformation.[20] Decades ago, Bob Scribner demonstrated how Reformation visual propaganda made great capital out of hostile images of the pope, plundering popular culture and images of the Devil.[21] But the extent to which aggressive anti-papalism coloured Lutheran devotion even at its most emotional moments of sadness and loss can shock modern viewers, attuned to hate speech and its consequences.[22] The propaganda's folksy populism can make it easy to overlook its nastiness. Indeed, the imprecation can even be difficult for modern viewers to see—literally so in some cases, because the owners have simply painted out the embarrassing words.[23]

What are these words doing? Like a verbal gargoyle, the motto wards off the power of the Devil and the pope at precisely the same time as it invoked the presence of Luther himself. Both a prophecy and a curse, it represents Luther as a 'pestilence', more powerful in death, even, than in life. The cursing of the pope was thus indissolubly linked with Luther's death, with the foundation of his church, and with his claim to be a prophet; and it was in particular often attached to images, especially to post-mortem portraits of the man whose face was so familiar that he needed no label. At its core, then, Lutheran memory enshrined bitter vituperation and unrelenting hatred.

This was the shadow side of Luther's flamboyant, masculine pugilism. Luther was no iconoclast and very aware of the power of images. He was also directly involved in the making of some of the most hostile ones, just as it was he himself who invented the motto 'Pestis ero vivens, moriens ero mors tua, Papa'. It exemplifies the bond between word and image, which was fundamental to Lutheran culture and in particular to its memorialization of its founder. This was a religion which knew how to represent its doctrine visually. To understand the emotional punch of anti-papalism in that visual culture, we need to return to its beginnings.

## KARLSTADT'S WAGON

The story starts with the first visual propaganda for the Reformation, Karlstadt's *Fuhrwagen*, produced by the artist Lucas Cranach in early 1519, before there were even any portraits of Luther in circulation. Ironically, it was created by Luther's supporter Andreas Karlstadt, the man from whom he would later separate on very bad terms. It was Karlstadt, not Luther, who first forged the partnership with the local artist Lucas Cranach, and who first saw the possibilities of using images to convey the Reformation message.[24]

This broadside is, however, a complete failure as propaganda, since the viewer cannot immediately grasp the message. The text utterly overwhelms the image, ruining Cranach's finely observed landscapes and even slicing off the head of God the Father. Only the German

5.6. Karlstadt's Fuhrwagen, Cranach the Elder, 1515–1519. Hamburg Art Gallery.

version survives complete, but the fragment which has survived of the original Latin is also swimming in words. The broadsheet's key message is that one should leave one's own will behind and surrender oneself to Christ, but this is tucked away in the top left of the image behind the cross where the words—'G'lass willen vnd dich' ('leave will and you')—are written side on and border on the incomprehensible. Karlstadt simply had not left himself enough space to cram in the words he needed. Suspicious of the ambiguity of images, Karlstadt could not abide anything without a label. No wonder his supporters in Nuremberg told him they could not understand the woodcut. Ever the intellectual, Karlstadt responded with a fifty-page treatise explaining the image, but even with all those words he only managed to interpret the top row.[25]

One could argue that this broadsheet was a brilliant experiment that went wrong. Cranach's workmanship is of much higher quality than much of his later propaganda for the Reformation: the bodies of the horses are rounded, each stone has its own beautifully observed shadow, just like the stones that later set off his famous Venuses of the 1530s. The movement of the horses is visually ambitious, and the image is crammed with a fantastic array of tiny impish devil figures, each one clamouring for the viewer's attention: one attempts to hold the wheels of the upper row, another greases the wheels of the cart.

The broadsheet was produced in the lead-up to the Leipzig Disputation, the most public event of the Reformation to that point. Angered by Johannes Eck's refutation of Luther's 95 Theses, Karlstadt challenged the theologian to a debate, devising a massive 406 Theses against him. At stake was the issue of the role of human will in salvation: can man do any good work to merit grace?[26] The broadsheet, which was produced in German as well as Latin, was the first work Karlstadt had ever published in the vernacular, and it marked the start of the Reformation's engagement with a public outside theology faculties. On the top line, three figures, the Christian sinner, St Paul, and St Augustine process towards the Cross; on the lower, a line of riders trot to Hell. On the bottom row, a man whose features are individualized enough to suggest it is a portrait, sits in a cart mischievously labeled 'own will'. This ambiguously summarized the position of those like Eck who insisted on the role of the individual will in the path towards salvation, and insulted the man in the cart as 'self-willed'. Karlstadt was coy about admitting who this was meant to be, but there is no doubt that it was Johannes Eck himself. Eck was furious, and complained to Luther's ruler, the Elector Frederick the Wise, about the image.[27] A second figure is less easy to identify, but may have been intended to represent Pope Leo X. If so, the anti-papalism which would become such a feature of later Reformation propaganda would be there from the start. But, well aware of the dangers of making such an extreme statement, Karlstadt carefully did not explain the identity of any of the figures on the bottom line. Text and pictures are at war in this image as Karlstadt pushes the possibilities of both to the limit.

By a fine irony, Karlstadt, the man who was the first to use images in the service of the Reformation's message, would soon become its initial iconoclast. When Luther was in exile in the Wartburg, it was Karlstadt who set about removing images from the Wittenberg churches. As he put it, 'Our eyes make love to [images] and court them. The truth is that all who honour images, seek their help, and worship them, are whores and adulterers'. Images took hold of the heart, where they seduced the viewer to love and worship them: 'my heart has been trained since my youth to give honour and respect to images and such a dreadful fear has been instilled in me of which I would gladly rid myself, but cannot. Thus I am afraid to burn a single idol'.[28] Exiled from Wittenberg, he had moved to the rural church at Orlamünde and did the same there, removing the statues and pictures from the church, and weaning his flock off their attachment to idols. Karlstadt's *Fuhrwagen* might be seen as a product of a collaboration between a theologian who never trusted images because of their indeterminacy and emotional power, and an artist who would never again let his images be ruined by a profusion of printed words.

But there is another way of looking at this printed image. Instead of viewing it as a failure because of the profusion of words, it could be seen as the precursor of the comic, where text and image are equal partners and one is not subordinated to the other. The image is, after all, a narrative. Indeed, the line that the viewer's eye is meant to follow is slightly different for text and image. Visually, the procession should be read from right to left along the top, and from left to right along the bottom. Yet when Karlstadt came to explain how his broadsheet was to be understood, he started with the key idea placed in the top left-hand corner, that one should leave oneself behind and follow Christ. This message was the classic theology of Gelassenheit, the idea that the Christian must give up attachment to all earthly things and all human relationships in order to make his or her will conform to the divine. Hidden behind the cross, this is not the point from which the eye would naturally start. But Karlstadt's way of viewing his text was circular, and did not simply follow the line of the procession; rather, the viewer is meant to meditate on the cross and on his or her relationship with Christ.

This interpretation suggests that two modes of viewing are in tension in this early image. One is linear, simple, and propagandist: the bad ride to Hell while the good travel to Christ and the cross. The other requires more immersive, repeated viewing. Like the visual clues, the doggerel of the German rhymes helps the viewer to memorize and so meditate on central religious truths. Karlstadt is trying to convey the profound mystical experience of Gelassenheit in pictorial terms, but it is an experience which simply cannot be expressed visually—nor does he manage to communicate it in the barely intelligible slogan 'G'lass willen vnd dich'. Unable to convey his meaning, he turned instead to writing theological tracts in language that became increasingly abstract and difficult to follow. Both modes of viewing, however, would persist in Reformation art, even though a man like Karlstadt proved unable to cope with the painful contradictions they set up.[29]

## LAW AND GOSPEL

By 1521, Luther had written his three great Reformation treatises, his break with the Church of Rome was definitive, and he was about to be summoned to defend his views in front of representatives of the entire Holy Roman Empire at the Diet of Worms. Luther was now convinced that the pope was the Antichrist. Cranach again became involved in propaganda for the Reformation, this time not just providing portraits of Luther but illustrating a set of paired images that would become famous as the *Passional of Christ and Antichrist*. This told the story of Christ's passion, with words provided by Johann Schwertfeger and Philip Melanchthon, Luther's new helper and the man who had displaced Karlstadt. The first edition of the *Passional* appeared in February 1521; Luther arrived at the Diet in April.[30] This piece was a far more effective piece of propaganda. The format and design of the *Passional* shows just how much Cranach had learnt from Karlstadt's *Fuhrwagen*. Instead of the horizontal right to left, left to right lines of the *Wagen*, which cannot be taken in at a single glance, each double page has a simple vertical contrast, much easier and faster for the eye to absorb. On the left is a familiar scene from Christ's passion, on the right, a matching scene where the pope does the opposite. So we see, for example, Christ on the left clearing the temple of the moneylenders while on the right the pope sells indulgences.[31] Good is contrasted with bad. The identities of the characters are unambiguous, the point, devastatingly simple. Words no longer overwhelm the image but have been banished to outside the picture space altogether, and there are many fewer of them. The images themselves are less artistically ambitious; there is no play with three-dimensionality, as with the rounded shading of the horses' rumps in the *Wagen*, or the stones with their shadows. Even the format is more conventional, and the *Passional* is in the shape of a standard booklet, not a giant poster.

It might seem as if the *Passional* created the format that Reformation propaganda would subsequently follow, with its simplified lines and powerful vertical contrasts. But in fact many of the *Wagen*'s techniques remained in much of the painted visual culture of the Reformation, particularly in the visual representations of Law and Gospel, one of the key slogans of the Reformation, because it encapsulated the idea that the believer needs the Law to recognize his or her own sin, so that the Gospel may then bring grace and salvation. This iconography, which became such a trope of Reformation devotional imagery, was invented by the Cranach workshop and became used from the late 1520s on, through to mid-century and beyond. Amongst others, Hans Holbein picked the subject up and produced his own version. Cranach's pictures mixed words and image, a possibility which fascinated him: time and again, he would include painted text in his images, imitating the technology of print with the brush, just as he would also create images put together out of endlessly re-used pieces of visual kit. Gripped by the possibilities of multiplying images, whether in print or in the production line of a workshop, Cranach

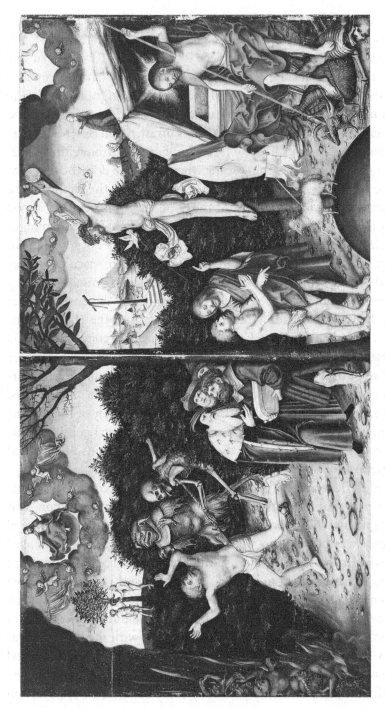

5.7. Law and Gospel. Cranach the Elder, c. 1535–40. Germanisches Nationalmuseum, Nuremberg.

himself owned a printing press for a time. As part of this wider enterprise he created a new, didactic form of standardized iconography for the Reformation. Most of the Law and Gospel images were painted panels, though there were woodcut versions produced too.[32] They are instantly recognizable, like the workshop's Luther portraits, and the pieces were reassembled in different patterns: so, for example, one version shows the serpent and the tents *in the right* background, while another shows it *in the left*. The iconography follows a set recipe, just as Luther's theology increasingly followed the familiar forms of words Luther had first articulated in 1520. Both stuck to formulae.

Like Karlstadt's *Fuhrwagen*, these images operate with powerful contrasts of good and evil, like Reformation written propaganda. The Old Testament promise is aligned with obedience to the Law, legalism, and the dead 'letter'; the Gospel means grace and salvation. But both are required, for without recognition of his or her sin, which the Christian receives through the Law, there can be no grace. In keeping with this, the images require non-linear, contemplative viewing; the viewer has to move from one part of the iconography to another, and the path taken is not necessarily sequential. Instead of one simple, single overall message, there are several different messages, and each section works like a mini-narrative, just as the *Wagen* does. Pictures such as this invite the viewer to meditate on a theological truth, to incorporate it mentally and emotionally, and to 'grasp' it. In other words, it creates a story out of a series of narrative scenes, rather like an illustrated comic book.[33] It asks more of the viewer than a simple binary contrast does, and conveys a positive theological insight, not just a polemic against enemies.

## DEATH, THE DEVIL, AND POPERY

In 1545, Luther truly was dying. Earlier that year he had delightedly mocked a papist obituary: he was, he insisted, very much alive; and he prefaced the pamphlet with his motto in an extended verse form, threatening that his death would most assuredly also be that of the pope.[34] Luther had cheated death once again that time, but he knew he did not have long left, and the verse advertised the fact. Meanwhile, the Catholic Church was summoning a Church Council. Luther had fought so long for this, but he was to be excluded, and so he railed from the sidelines. Convinced that the Council was yet another papist trick, and outraged by the tone of Paul III's letter castigating Charles V for his concessions to the Lutherans, he wrote his bitterest tract against the papacy, *Against the Roman Papacy, A Creature of the Devil*.[35] In it he defamed the pope as a sodomite and hermaphrodite, a creature both woman and man, denouncing Paul as 'Virgin Paula the third'.[36] It is a strange text, that reflects his state of mind as he recognized his own physical weakness and impending death: early on he writes that 'my head is weak' and that he cannot write all that he wants to say 'before my strength gives out completely'.[37] Screwing himself up for one final polemical assault, he writes of how papal decrees are 'sealed with the devil's own dirt, and written with the ass-pope's farts',[38] and that the Roman Church is nothing but the 'devil's synagogue'.[39] This is the treatise where, as we have seen, he castigates the pope as an ass, an ass-fart pope, who stinks like the Devil.[40] The treatise is intended to cover three points, but after a long introduction Luther spends most of his time on just the first, as he gets lost in the mire of his own invective.[41]

The invective is both monotonous and full of flights of extravagant fancy. Luther imagines the pope as a donkey trotting gingerly on the ice, who lets out a fart;[42] and he concludes this part with the even more bizarre image of the pope and all his retinue along with their keys and decretals being dunked in the bath at Ostia to wash away their filth. Filth ties the work together: all the pope's power and decrees are excremental, and the best way to be rid of the Devil is to turn his own weapons against him and fart at him in good German style. Filth even unifies the argument: the pope must be diabolical because he stinks, dirtying himself in his cleverness, and 'Because the Devil simply has to do it, that he leaves a stink behind him, so that one knows, he was there'.[43] As we have seen, the brilliance of the epithet 'ass-fart pope' is that it condenses all these associations, stories, and connected images into one unforgettable name that demolishes any reverence for the papacy.[44]

It also goes back to the Papal Ass, one of the very first propaganda successes of the Reformation: a monstrous ass had been found dead in the Tiber, and back in 1523 Melanchthon had interpreted this as an emblem of the papacy.[45] Indeed, the work contains a lot of reminiscence.[46] Luther recalls that nearly thirty years have passed since he first attacked the papacy, and he returns to the arguments that he first made when he began to suggest that the existence of the Greek Patriarch proved that the pope had never been head of all Christendom.[47] The fear that his church is at stake partly drives the aggression: Pope Paul's summoning of the Council and Luther's exclusion from the Council marked the final break with Rome, and consequently Luther had to define what he meant by the Church. Key to this was his interpretation of Matthew 16: when Christ said 'on this rock I will build my Church', he did not mean Peter, still less, his successors; he meant himself, Christ, and he was talking about faith.[48] In the tract, therefore, Luther had to grapple with the issue of authority. He had rejected the idea that the pope or church tradition should determine what scripture meant; rather, Christ's word alone in scripture was self-evidently clear to the believer. This conclusion did not answer what to do if there were different views of what scripture meant, and it also left open what structures the new church should have, and what would happen to it once its charismatic founder, Luther, was dead.

These existential issues perhaps explain why this tract is so foul-mouthed and excessive. Luther was determined to throw dirt at the papal church and destroy it because he knew his existence and that of his own church were on the line. This is what he meant by 'Living I was your plague; dead I will be your death, O Pope'. In fact, Luther's death would *not* be the death of the pope; quite the reverse. Whilst the Council of Trent gradually introduced a new phase of recovery for the Catholic Church, the Lutheran Reformation, robbed of its leader, began to splinter between Lutheran loyalists and the followers of Melanchthon. When he insisted that his own death prophesied the death of the pope, he was engaging in a kind of magical thinking, in which Luther's followers joined together in mourning, united in trouncing the pope. It gave meaning to his death, as if his whole life was nothing but his long battle with the pope. Luther ends the treatise by threatening to write another treatise, but 'If I should die meanwhile, may God grant that someone else make it a thousand times worse, for this devilish popery is the last misfortune on earth, nearest to that which all the devils can do with all their might'.[49]

While Luther wrote the treatise, he also commissioned what he called his 'Testament', a set of images to accompany the text.[50] Now, however, the image stood in a different relationship to the text, for only the cover picture was part of the treatise itself. It showed a magnificent set of jaws of Hell, with tiny devils flying in to feed the maw with monks, priests, popes, and cardinals. This was the very same motif as the mouth of Hell in Karlstadt's *Fuhrwagen*, and even the devils owe a visual debt to the devils on the final page of the *Passional*, who drag the pope down to Hell. The other images clearly function as illustrations for the treatise even though they never appear to have been published as part of it; apparently they were sold separately for reasons that are not clear. One series of images took up key Reformation visuals and ideas and recycled them in a new context, with verses and titles supplied by Luther himself.[51] It is hard now to be certain exactly what the full set consisted in and which images were included, since the surviving collections vary.[52] One, for example, shows the pope's tongue nailed to the gallows, a precise reference to Luther's treatise; another is clearly the 'ass-fart Pope'. There is an image of the pope riding a sow, of German mercenaries farting at the pope, and of mercenaries defecating in the papal tiara that sits atop the papal arms. There is even the hoary old Reformation image, the Papal Ass,[53] first used in the early 1520s; its re-use here twenty years later suggests that, as Luther's life neared its end, the Reformation was also pondering its own history and the tradition its image-making had created—just as the text of *Against the Roman Papacy* does. These images would go on to enjoy a long life, and in this sense they were indeed Luther's 'testament'. Republished and reworked, they appeared in versions throughout the sixteenth century and right into the seventeenth, their iconography of hatred unaltered.[54]

One pair of Cranach's images from this time is worthy of particular attention. They are rather different from the rest, of higher artistic quality. Although they did not form part of the series, they are perhaps even more closely connected with the text of *Against the Roman Papacy* than others.[55] We know that Luther knew of these images in their design stage, and that he called Cranach a 'crude painter' for how he depicted the pope: he said that 'He could have spared the female sex for the sake of God's creation and our mothers'.[56] It has usually

# Wider das Bapstum zu
## Rom vom Teuffel geſtifft/
### Mart. Luther D.

### Wittemberg/1545.
#### durch Hans Lufft.

5.8. *Wider der Bapstum zu Rom vom Teuffel gestifft*, Martin Luther, 1545. Newberry Digital Collections, Newberry Library.

# HIC OSCVLA PEDIBVS PAPAE FI-
# GVNTVR.

PAPA LOQVITVR.

Sententiæ nostræ etiam iniu-
stæ metuendæ sunt.

Responsio.
maledetta.

Aspice nudatas gens furiosa nates.
Ecco qui Papa el mio bel vedere.

5.9. The Papal Belvedere, image 1. Cranach the Elder, 1545. British Museum.

# ADORATVR PAPA DEVS TERRENVS.

5.10. The Papal Belvedere, image 2. Cranach the Elder, 1545. British Museum.

been thought that Luther found the pictures' explicit nudity shocking and believed women would be offended. But such tender concern for female sensibility does not ring true for the period, and besides, the two woodcuts are full of explicit male genitalia, so why should he have worried about female modesty?

Luther, no prude, was saying something different. If we look closely at the image *The Origins of the Antichrist*, we see that the pope has a prominent vagina. What Luther meant was not that Cranach was a lewd painter, but that the pope's vagina was an insult to the female sex, which was exactly the point he himself made in the text of *Against the Roman Papacy*. The daisy chain only underlines the point—it conceals nothing.

The first image of the pair shows *The Origins of the Monks*. A female she-devil sits on a gallows and defecates monks. They fall upside down to the ground, their legs apart, their genitals exposed: the testicles, penis, and anus of the monk front right are clearly visible, next to the naked foot of his comrade. This is a world turned upside down where monks are robbed of their dignity and shown to be nothing but randy males underneath their cassocks, all atumble and covered in excrement from their unusual birth. The gallows were the most dishonourable place imaginable, polluting all who came into contact with them. In the background is the pope's citadel, Castel S. Angelo, crudely depicted just the way it always had been on Lutheran images, linking the monks with the power of Rome. The phantasmagoric devils are fully realized, three-dimensional figures with foolscaps, hideous nostrils, and fantastic claws; and each sports a single horn; the one on the right has a toothless grin, sagging breasts, and a rounded stomach; that on the left has thicker limbs and seems to be male. The message is clear, as the German text set apart from the image proclaims: 'Where monks come from'. There is a lot of invention in this image and it requires immersive viewing to get the jokes: feet and hands are shown at all kinds of angles, one pointing out onto the gallows space, the soles of the feet drawn with care. The rounded tonsured heads are disconcertingly penis-like, underlining the lasciviousness of the monks. Their presence also, of course, mobilizes fears of castration: back in 1522, Luther had equated celibates with eunuchs.

5.11. The Origins of the Antichrist. Cranach the Elder. British Library.

5.12. The Origins of the Monks, Cranach the Elder. British Library.

The matching image 'On the Origin of the Antichrist' shows the same monk figure, again upside down revealing his genitals, and devils with similar horns and claws. If the message of the first image is that monks are the offspring of the Devil and under the sway of Rome, this one reveals the pope to be a hideous female, breathed into by two devils. He is the Antichrist. On the right-hand side there is an inversion of the image of Christ in the winepress, with two devils pressing a giant mortar which looks like a key, perhaps a papal key, onto a tub of monks. Rather than Christ putting himself in the wine press to create the wine of Communion for us, here devils manufacture the juice of the Antichrist, damnation. The matching tonsured heads of the monks are again carefully drawn and shown at all kinds of angles, but now we see more of their faces: many of them sport long, exaggerated noses. In sixteenth century Germany, noses could be a sign for the penis, but they can also represent Jews, and indeed the head to the right wears a black hat above his extended nose, probably intended to be a rabbi's hat—he has no tonsure. A turd lies in the foreground while the two devils attempt to animate the monstrous pope, clearly shown with a vagina. Other flying devils supply monks of different orders to be brought to the giant mortar—petrified with fright, they void their guts.

Luther's Testament, as he called it, marks his final, unrelenting conviction that the pope is the Antichrist and his henchmen, the monks, are the Devil's spawn. Shortly before he died, he remarked: 'With those naughty pictures I really made the pope very angry. Oh how the sow will twitch its rump, and even if they kill me, they will eat the dirt which the pope has in his hand'.[57] He was thinking of the image of the pope riding a sow and reaching out one arm in blessing while carrying steaming excrement in the other, which the sow is eagerly sniffing. The remark brings together so many of the themes of Luther's conscious and unconscious thought explored throughout this book. Luther, for whom the pig was so important, equated the sow with the Jewish Sow but also with the Germans themselves.[58] Once again he linked his death with the trashing of the pope, and implicitly, the Jews, and thus with his other 'Testament', Living I was your plague, dead I will be your death, O Pope.

But Luther's Testament is also not seriously intended; and we need to look at these images through the eyes of contemporaries, many of whom would have found them funny. The image is bursting with visual jokes: the trunk of one of the two devils who wield the pestle is actually a face. The devils with their coxcombs, assorted breasts, and wings are comic creations. After all, Luther did not believe that monks were produced by diabolic defecation, nor did he believe that Pope Paul III truly was a hermaphrodite. Rather, he deflated the holiness of the pope with laughter, slinging mud at him and mobilizing the energy of play. The artist, whoever he was, is equally at home in this kind of activity, piling on the visual jokes and mocking the clergy by showing them from every conceivable immodest angle, the sense of space, flight, disorder, and falling mirroring the upside-down world the text itself conveys.

Text and image have now gone their separate ways: they even had to be purchased separately. The 'Bb' marked on the mortar is an interesting touch, for as it happens, the Wittenberg edition of the text runs to folio Aaiii verso; the next sheet therefore would have been Bb, perhaps one final visual joke.[59] Luther liked to declare 'I am the Pope's louse, I torment him, and he keeps me, and I live off his goods',[60] and this was perhaps truer than he knew. Much of the Reformation's energy and invention came from its relentless corporeality and its zesty anti-papalism.

But this was not just a joke, as the centuries of religious conflict that would follow revealed. The aggression of Luther's motto remained part of his legacy, woven into the deathbed images, and central to how his followers mourned his loss. It was part of his church's foundational identity, built on honouring marriage in the teeth of bishops and pope. Luther's 'testament' was his final anti-papal polemic along with its illustrations; it was also his bitter curse against the pope. Luther himself was a great hater, unrelenting in his hostility to the papacy. His polemic genius, his talent for naming, and his capacity for aggressive hate would also be put at the service of his anti-Semitism, the subject of the next chapter.

# CHAPTER 6

# Luther the Anti-Semite

I N 2015 PLAYMOBIL released their best-selling figure ever: Martin Luther, with quill, cassock, and doctor's hat. A year later, with over a million of them sold, it had to be pointed out that this lovable toy was actually anti-Semitic, because the left-hand page of the Bible in Luther's hand bears the legend 'Old Testament: END'. The quirky figure was proclaiming that the Old Testament and with it, the Jews, had reached their end, now superseded by Luther and the New Testament. The words were taken from the original nineteenth-century statue on the Wittenberg marketplace, on which the figure is modelled. Playmobil responded at once, releasing a Spring edition for the jubilee year 2017 that deleted the word 'END' so that the Bible now simply shows the Old and New Testaments side by side, removing the anti-Semitic implication. Why was it possible to make such an embarrassing mistake in the most successful piece of Luther kitsch ever, and why did it take so long for the anti-Semitism to be recognized?[1]

The answer to this question reveals how difficult Lutheranism has found the issue of its own anti-Semitism, and how profoundly it has affected its history.

6.1. Playmobil Luther figure. Photo by John Cairns.

In the literature, Luther's anti-Semitism is often relativized as a product of the time in which he lived, related to his theological understanding of Christ as the Messiah, or treated as a metaphorical hatred directed against those whose theological mistake was to insist that salvation depended on fulfilling the Law. Heiko Oberman, for one, argued that Luther's later anti-Semitism must be understood in relation to his conviction that he was living in the last days, when the Antichrist would mount an all-out attack on Christians. His anti-Semitism was thus indissolubly linked with his hatred of papists and the Turks. Oberman goes so far as to argue that even the concept of his anti-Semitism is a postwar invention: '"Luther and the Jews" thus becomes a separate issue only in virtue of the historical developments that postdate Luther'.[2] Others claim that the absence of a theory of 'race' in the early modern period meant that his anti-Semitism was merely an intellectual stance of anti-Judaism, not a species of racial hatred. It was part of his apocalyptic thinking, and he became angered because the Jews refused to convert.[3] Yet others see his anti-Semitism as a regrettable lapse, a blot on an otherwise heroic figure, or a product of his increasing tetchiness as he aged and as his various physical ailments darkened his mood. Such analyses make his anti-Semitism seem unfortunate but incidental. In the years after the Second World War and the Holocaust, Lutherans were at pains to insist that there was no direct line leading from Luther's views to the Holocaust. However, Thomas Kaufmann's study of Luther and the Jews marks a genuine confrontation with Luther's anti-Semitism by the leading interpreter of Luther of our time, and who considers its legacy within Lutheranism.[4] This chapter is my own attempt to come to terms with Luther's anti-Semitism.

## LUTHER'S ANTI-SEMITISM

It can be easy to forget just how raw Luther's anti-Semitic ranting could be. The text *Vom Schem Hamphoras*, for instance, is hardly mentioned in most recent studies of his anti-Semitism, and was not included in the postwar American translated edition of his Works. In it, Luther imagines Jews worshipping excrement: 'the Devil has . . . emptied his stomach again and again, that is a true relic, which the

Jews, and those who want to be a Jew, kiss, eat, drink and worship'. And he goes on to describe how the Devil fills the mouth, nose, and ears of the Jews with filth: 'He stuffs and squirts them so full, that it overflows and swims out of every place, pure Devil's filth, yes, it tastes so good to their hearts, and they guzzle it like sows'.[5] Here Luther conjures up an extravagant image of Jews gorging themselves on diabolic ordure, a picture designed to elicit profound revulsion.

The reformer rarely but periodically wrote works containing rhetoric of this kind, and when Luther is off the leash, pigs, excrement, and bodily fluids tend to feature. Similar passages, not directed against the Jews, can be found in his early sermon of 1516, in parts of *Against Hans Wurst*, and in *Against the Roman Papacy, a Creature of the Devil*. But his anti-Semitic outpourings are more extreme and have none of the humour that leavens his assault on the papacy, or his diatribes against individuals, like poor Heinrich of Wolfenbüttel. Moreover, such writing was not part of the normal currency of anti-Semitism which tended to claim, by contrast, that it was rather the *Jews* who believed Christians to be unclean and disgusting, so that Christians must therefore reject their contempt.[6] Luther's version of anti-Semitism flipped this around, projected these ideas onto the Jews themselves and amplified them.

Fantasies this disturbing and deep belong to the kind of material I encountered when working on the witch craze.[7] They suggest that Luther's anti-Semitism was linked to deep phobias buried in the unconscious, and go back to early infancy, connected to ideas about eating, the boundaries of the body, excrement, and to fears of dissolution. But to derive Luther's anti-Semitism from his first experiences with his mother would offer a reductive and individualistic explanation of what was a far more significant social phenomenon, and one which had a lasting legacy. Nonetheless, the extreme and phobic nature of some of Luther's writing on the Jews offers a challenge to intellectual history. Luther willingly lets his emotions develop his thought. How then was Luther's anti-Semitism related to his epistemic drives?

Luther's anti-Semitism was not a single phenomenon, but rather suffused different areas of his thought and feeling. It encompassed both gut instinct and carefully worked out argument, and as a case study, it can illuminate Luther's mind. For a man whose thought followed his intuitive reactions, and whose ideas were unusually closely linked to his bodily experiences, Luther's anti-Semitism bears all the hallmarks of his characteristic intellectual processes; it exemplifies both his brilliance and his flaws. To explore it, I have therefore drawn eclectically not only from Luther's theological treatises, but also his letters, the early biographies, and the *Table Talk*, the informal dinner conversations he held at table that were noted by his students and, though not intended for publication, were published after his death and quickly became part of popular Lutheran culture. The two questions that have confronted me are how Luther's unusually virulent anti-Semitism might be connected to other currents within his thought, and how integral, therefore, anti-Semitism might be to Lutheranism.

## Luther and Jews

What were Luther's contacts with actual Jews and what did he know of Jewish history in Wittenberg? David Nirenberg has ingeniously argued that since Luther did not personally know any Jews, his anti-Semitism was anti-Judaism and a prism through which he attacked the Catholics, accusing them of being, in effect, Jewish. This is why, for example, he attacks the Roman Church in *Against the Roman Papacy* as a 'devil's synagogue'; and why one illustration to this work shows the pope carrying excrement and riding on a sow, an image which reproduced exactly the linkages in Luther's own rhetorical arsenal between the papacy and the Jewish sow (see figures 4.6 and 5.11). Luther's anti-Semitism, Nirenberg argues, derived from his fundamental distinction between the Law and Gospel and from his way of reading the Old Testament, especially the Psalms, so that it referred forward to Christ and was drained of Jewish content: 'His "Jewish problem" was the product of his theory of how biblical language works and how it should be interpreted—in other words, of hermeneutics, not of sociology'.[8] Luther's anti-Semitism, in Nirenberg's view, was at root a cypher for his anti-papalism, which then became directed in policies against real Jews.

However, Luther's rhetoric against the papacy—whilst laced with sexual and anal insult—lacks the disgust and bitter physicality of his outbursts against the Jews, suggesting that the anti-Semitism did not spring from his anti-papalism. Nor does the crudeness of Luther's anti-Semitism seem to derive from his intellectual stance on the Law and Gospel. Nirenberg's interpretation makes Luther's anti-Semitism appear cerebral, and though it is surely right to relate it to other currents in his theology, it avoids confronting its vileness and emotional punch.

Moreover, it is true that Luther did not know many Jews, but we now know from Thomas Kaufmann that he had in fact met some.[9] He also believed that Jews had targeted him personally. In a rude letter to Rabbi Josel of 1537 he refused to see him or to intercede with the Saxon elector for safe passage for the Jews. The missive includes several classic anti-Semitic tropes, accusing the Jews of blaspheming against Christians, and wanting 'to rob from [Christians] all that they own and are'. With crude irony he pretends to adopt the Jews' perspective, and refers to himself and Christians as 'heathens'—a dig at the Jews for what Luther sees as their 'Verstockung', their 'blockedness', and their insufferable pride in their own faith. Luther concludes the letter by styling himself as a 'heathen prophet', a further insult to the Jews.[10]

Luther started to learn Hebrew using a Hebrew grammar while he was still in Erfurt; we know that he and his old friend and fellow Augustinian Johannes Lang worked on their Hebrew together there. Johann Oldecop mentions that Luther learnt Hebrew from a Jewish doctor in Rome; but Oldecop was an antagonist of Luther,[11] and Luther himself does not mention a Jewish teacher. So far as we know he did not learn Hebrew on a long-term basis from a Jew—unlike, for example, his contemporary Andreas Osiander, the reformer of Nuremberg. When Luther himself described how he learnt the language, he mentioned using grammars and learning in particular by comparing one passage with another, which would have made learning the language an extremely tough proposition.[12] Throughout his life Luther was modest about his abilities in Hebrew, exclaiming in the 1530s that 'if I were younger, I would want to learn this language'.[13] And although Luther loved biblical Hebrew, he was withering about its modern version: he claimed that it had become irredeemably corrupt since the Babylonian Captivity, 'mixed and impure, like the Italians speak Latin', a conviction which allowed him to dismiss the help of modern Jews.[14] Indeed, the history of the

Chair in Hebrew at Wittenberg (one of the appointments in which Luther was actively engaged) betrays at best an ambivalence towards Jews: the first occupant, Johannes Boeschenstein, was rumoured to be of Jewish parentage, which he denied; he stayed only three months, and Mathias Adrianus, his successor, a Spanish Jew, lasted less than a year. They were replaced by Matthaeus Aurogallus, who was already at Wittenberg and shared Luther's view of the study of Hebrew in a Christian context; he stayed until his death in 1543.[15] Luther did not apparently ask Jews for advice on Hebrew when he translated the Old Testament, and he criticised Sebastian Muenster's later translation for having relied on the Jews too much.

Some have argued that Luther was concerned not with the Jews as an ethnic group, but as a religious challenge, whose conversion was required before the Last Days could arrive. By the 1530s, however, Luther was not interested in converting the Jews—if he ever had been, for as Thomas Kaufmann has pointed out, he certainly never made a serious effort to evangelise them. Indeed, he opens his 1543 treatise *On the Jews and Their Lies* insisting 'Much less do I propose to convert the Jews, for that is impossible'.[16] And *Vom Schem Hamphoras* too begins by explaining that he has no interest in converting the Jews because converting them 'is as little possible as converting the Devil' and a 'Jewish heart is as stock, stone, iron, Devil hard that it is not to be moved in any way'—only to end the work by insisting that he would have 'nothing more to do with the Jews'. If any do wish to convert, he writes, 'may God give them his grace, that they (even some) might recognize and praise God the Father, our creator, together with our Lord Jesus Christ and the Holy Spirit forever, Amen'. They must become, in a sense, true 'Jews', because as Luther states in the previous paragraph, the Jews of today do not know Moses and the Bible, 'so shamefully have they dirtied him with their Judas piss', an insult to which we will return.[17] In fact, converted Jews were a byword for perfidiousness with Luther. Time and again in the *Table Talk* he and his companions told stories about Jews who apparently converted but then apostasized, and he even joked that 'If I get another pious Jew to baptise, I'll take him to the Elbe bridge and hang a stone around his neck and throw him in the river' so that he might die before relinquishing Christianity.[18]

This suspicion coloured Luther's response to pastoral cases. So, when the widowed sister of Hartmut von Kronberg claimed to have married a Jew who left her pregnant with their child in Wittenberg and then turned out to have more than one wife, Luther's sympathies lay entirely with the abandoned mother; he raised no objection when her relatives took the law into their own hands and ambushed and murdered her husband, and even became godfather to her child.[19] Subscribing to the anti-Semitic clichés of his day, Luther saw Jews as unreliable, prone to break their word, and insincere, an ethnic type-casting that outweighed any inclination he might have had to convert them. They were guilty of the sins of 'Ruhm und Halsstarrigkeit', of obstinacy and pride that made conversion impossible; and he repeatedly uses the term 'verstockt' to describe them, a powerful word which implies that they are not just stubborn but blocked, lacking the flow of normal emotions.[20] Indeed, rather than wanting to convert Jews, the rumours that Jews were converting Christians provoked his ire in *On the Sabbatarians*, while *Vom Schem Hamphoras* opens with a long diatribe against Christians who convert to Judaism.

As so often with Luther, personal 'experience' cemented prejudice. He believed that Jews had been sent to kill him, and from early on, a series of lurid assassination attempts became part of Lutheran folklore, one supposedly plotted by a Roman nun who planned to 'turn a knife in him', and several attributed to Jews.[21] One concerned a Jewish doctor with light-coloured hair about whom Luther had been warned in 1525. The Jew had supposedly been paid a thousand gulden to engage Luther in a game of chess, during which he was to place a poisoned 'Bisenkopf' (pomander) into Luther's glass.[22] Luther, however, was forewarned, and when a second Jew also appeared, with dark instead of light hair as foretold, the man was sent to the barber-surgeon to have the colour investigated. Both were clapped into prison. Something of the ambivalence towards Jews which pervaded Wittenberg can be glimpsed in an anecdote about a supposedly likeable Jew who visited several of the reformers in the early 1530s and discussed scripture with them. When Luther went on a journey he became convinced that the genial Jew answered the description of the man sent to kill him many years before. At once the Wittenbergers became suspicious, but the man had already fled. When Mathesius tells the story in his biography of Luther, he presents it as a miraculous delivery from a perfidious Jew. However, the story also betrays Wittenberg paranoia, for if the university men were at first curious to learn from this stranger who knew several languages, it took no more than Luther's sudden change of heart once away from Wittenberg to convince them all—without any apparent evidence or investigation—that the man was a dangerous assassin. The predicted light-haired Jewish assassin remained a bugbear, and in 1540, a man by the name of Michel von Posen appeared, wishing to convert from Judaism. Luther, addressing him as 'du' (the informal form of 'you', rude in this context), told him that although he had been warned that a man like him would attempt to kill him, 'you look too simple'.[23]

It is hard to know what to make of these assassination stories, or of Luther's reaction. Though Luther and his followers anticipated such attacks throughout his life, and took care to check the medicines he was offered in his final illness,[24] these fears seem not to have driven their anti-Semitism, even if they remained part of the hinterland of Lutheran presuppositions about Jews as dangerous.

In Luther's day, Wittenberg no longer had any Jews—they had been expelled in 1304, just as they had been in many German towns—but when he walked through the town in which he spent most of his adult life he could not but be reminded of their former presence. Whether treading the streets to the castle, to the printer's, or to Cranach's studio, Luther passed by the Jüdenstraße and through the so-called 'Jewish quarter', one of the administrative districts into which the town was divided. In the wider region, he was well aware that, as he put it, 'there are so many Jews Streets that this shows how common the Jews once were', and when he pondered on how many of them there must have been in tiny Judea, he imagined a hundred of them squashed into a house the size of 'Magister Ambrosi's' on the Wittenberg marketplace, probably a reference to his friend Ambrosius Reutter's house: his measure of Jewish overcrowding was translated into his local, daily experience.[25] Every time Luther mounted 'his' pulpit to preach in the city church, St Mary's, he did so in a church which had a Jewish sow on its exterior, high on the outside wall. This fourteenth-century sculpture shows a sow suckling three Jews, whilst a rabbi lifts the sow's tail and looks into its backside.[26] It is labelled

'Schem Hamphoras' in writing which has been added later, the name a mangled version of the name of God, which Jews regard as holy and which should not be written down or uttered. The statue itself is an insult to the Jews as a people and mocks their God by putting his name in letters. Depictions of Jews and pigs were to be found on the outside of many German churches in the late Middle Ages, and Wittenberg's is particularly vicious. In 1543, Luther wrote a tract in which he praised this sculpture as the work of a 'learned honourable man' who was the 'enemy of the disgusting lies of the Jews'.[27]

To understand Luther's anti-Semitism, therefore, we need to track not only the theological works dedicated to it, but a range of sources and materials that are less usual for intellectual history. We also need to relate it to Luther's psychology, for an intellectual history that misses this irrational component would not do justice to a figure like Luther. The contradictory themes of Luther's anti-Semitism need to be teased out, a difficult task because they arouse a pitch of disgust that makes it difficult for the reader to think. The comments of the contemporary Zürich church on Luther's writings make it clear that I am not alone in this. They wrote that 'no-one has ever written worse, more coarsely and more unfittingly against Christian discipline and modesty than Luther', and they named two of his writings against the Jews, along with the 'swinish, dirty Schemhamphorasch book'.[28] They were referring to the work he wrote in 1543 about the sculpture, the second of three anti-Semitic tracts he wrote that year.

Anti-Semitism is not simply of one kind, and the kinds of fear and prejudice it mobilises could, and have, varied historically. Luther's anti-Semitism was not identical with late medieval anti-Semitism, though it was of course formed by the world in which he grew up. More extreme in some respects, it was milder in others: ferocious though it was, Luther did not call for the Jews to be exterminated. Nor did Luther condemn the Jews as Christ-killers in emotive language.[29] He did not focus on the sufferings of Christ on the cross, nor attempt to whip up anti-Semitic hysteria by exploiting believers' emotional identification with Christ. He avoided the tales of Jewish ritual murder, in which Jews were believed to steal and kill Christian children in order to use their blood in secret ceremonies; and he did not accuse them of poisoning wells or causing plagues, though he did believe that Jews wished Christians harm, and, in the coda to his final set of sermons published shortly before his death, he accused them of knowing how to poison someone, 'from which they must die in an hour a month, a year, in ten or twenty years'.[30] As a theologian who insisted that Mary was not a mediator and should not be worshipped as queen of Heaven, Luther did not share the passionate Marianism which could drive such hatred and spur medieval attacks on Jewish communities. Luther did not call for the Jews to be slaughtered. But he did advocate the destruction of Jewish books, the burning of synagogues, the razing of the Jews' houses, and forcing them to live 'under roof or stall' like the gypsies. He did wish to drive them off the roads, ban them from practising usury, and force them to labour; and he did call for the Jews to be driven out of Saxony.[31]

## THAT JESUS CHRIST WAS BORN A JEW

Luther's attitude to the Jews certainly changed over the years. In 1523, he wrote the remarkable book *That Jesus Christ Was Born a Jew*, a work that has often been praised for its open, tolerant approach to the Jews. Luther points out that Christian policies have forced Jews into usury, 'when we forbid them to labour and do business and have any human fellowship with us', and he blames Christians for 'treat[ing] them like dogs'.[32] As Luther puts it: 'Our fools, the popes, bishops, sophists, and monks—the crude asses' heads—have hitherto so treated the Jews that anyone who wished to be a good Christian would almost have had to become a Jew. If I had been a Jew and had seen such dolts and blockheads govern and teach the Christian faith, I would sooner have become a hog than a Christian'.[33] He suggests that if Jews are properly treated, they will 'turn again to the faith of their fathers, the prophets and patriarchs. They will only be frightened further away from it if their Judaism is so utterly rejected that nothing is allowed to remain, and they are treated only with arrogance and scorn'.[34] He jokes that the Catholics will soon be denouncing him as a Jew.

Yet the opening of the work is peculiar, for it starts with a long discussion of the role and status of Mary, as Luther exclaims, 'A new lie is being circulated about me'; namely, first, that he believes that Mary was not a virgin but conceived Christ through Joseph and had other children after the birth of Jesus; and second, that Christ was the seed of Abraham through Joseph. As we saw in chapter 4, 'lies' about him were deeply offensive to Luther, and to 'lie' was to be both dishonourable and unmanly. The first half of the tract is devoted to roundly refuting the rabbis who argue that Mary was an 'alma', a young girl or maiden, and not a 'bethulah', virgin. Because the Old Testament Fathers followed Genesis, they can be said to have believed too that God would raise up from woman's seed one who would tread the serpent's head, that is, they believed in the Messiah born of a virgin and are therefore 'true Christians like ourselves'.[35] Why should the issue of the status of the Jews call forth Luther's defence of the virginity of Mary?

Miri Rubin has shown that there is a long and deep-seated connection between anti-Semitism and Marianism. On the outside of many churches, the synagogue is frequently represented as a blind, erring maiden in contrast to the serene female figure who represents Mary and the True Church: the two are twinned.[36] Because they did not accept Jesus as the Messiah, Jews were believed to be rejecting Mary as the mother of God and insulting her status as theotokos. They were believed to deny Mary's virginity and to regard Jesus as a 'whoreson' and his mother a whore. In the doublethink characteristic of this kind of anti-Semitism, Christians could focus on the imagined assault on the status of Mary, endowing their anti-Semitism with all the fury of a counterattack to protect their mother figure, who ironically embodied mercy and intercession. Defending Mary therefore required eliminating Jews. Churches dedicated to Mary were frequently erected on the sites of former synagogues, and the Judensau in Wittenberg is on the church of St Mary.[37] Indeed, in 1519, just four years before Luther wrote *That Jesus Christ Was Born a Jew*, there had been a pilgrimage to Mary in Regensburg after a pogrom; a contemporary woodcut depiction of the pious procession shows the ruins of Jewish settlement still visible beside the lofty new pilgrimage church.[38] Conversely, any effort to dethrone Mary from her powerful position in late medieval Christianity opened one up to accusations of philo-Semitism and of questioning Mary's virginity. This was exactly the attack Luther now met, accused of arguing that Jesus had been born of Joseph's seed, and of denying that Mary was a virgin for the rest of her life. These allegations against him were being peddled by senior princes in the empire, including Archduke Ferdinand.[39]

Luther was therefore walking a tightrope in his tract of 1523. On the one hand, he too was minimizing the role of Mary, the mother of the Messiah, and so was not susceptible to one of the major forces contributing to medieval anti-Semitism, Marianism. On the one hand, he insists that 'the perverse lauders of the mother of God . . . do nothing more than to glorify only the mother of God; they extol her for her virginity and practically make a false deity of her'.[40] On the other, Luther did not reject Mary, and he upheld her virginity. Despite the philo-semitic language, Luther goes to some lengths to attack contemporary rabbis, establish himself as the better interpreter of scripture, and recruit the Old Testament Jews to his side, arguing that they are 'true Christians like ourselves'. They do not have a separate genealogy; instead, Luther lays claim to the Old Testament. Indeed, there is an undercurrent of threat that runs through the pamphlet. If the Jews do not convert at first, Luther argues, 'Let them first be suckled with milk, and begin by recognizing this man Jesus as the true Messiah; after that they may drink wine, and learn also that he is true God'.[41]

As we shall see, these arguments, including those over the interpretation of Hebrew, were exactly the ones he would make in later texts that were anti-Semitic. One might argue, therefore, that rather than presenting a philo-Semitic case here, Luther was developing what would become a new variant of anti-Semitism. Though he maintained Mary's virginity against what he too took to be a Jewish attack, he did not do this by exalting Mary and invoking her as an imperilled maternal figure whose honour must be defended. Instead he turned his fire on the rabbis: he repudiated rabbinic learning, claimed Old Testament traditions and figures as 'Christian', and offered Jews acceptance in German society if they would convert.

It might seem to matter little whether Luther's anti-Semitism circled around the status of Mary or around the respect due to rabbis, but it is extremely significant. Psychologically, one might speculate, one deep wellspring of much medieval anti-Semitism was a set of fantasies to do with idealised femininity and motherhood. To protect Mary as the mother of Christ, an ideal woman, the Jews, who denied her that status, must be destroyed. The more her purity was lauded, the more vicious the assault on the Jews. This would place the unconscious roots of medieval anti-Semitism in issues to do with the relationship to the mother, with individuation, and with separation, the kinds of psychological issue that are also connected to envy. In the first six months of life, so the psychoanalyst Melanie Klein argues, the infant's primary relationship is with the mother's breast, and the infant copes with the terrors of abandonment by creating an image of a 'bad breast' which does not comfort, and a 'good breast', a kind of splitting that can eventually lead to polarised views of womanhood, and over-idealisations of particular women. In most cases these fears are resolved and the infant moves towards reparation, and starts to integrate the good and the bad. If they are not, there can be potential for unleashing deep and irrational feelings; to splitting people into good and bad; and to projecting one's own aggression onto others, especially the inadmissible aggression one might feel towards the mother. These are the issues about which Klein has written so penetratingly, and that also cast light on the psychological dynamics of the witch hunt. Irrational fears that mobilise fantasies of this deep kind can lead people to undertake violent acts, projecting their own unacknowledged negative feelings onto others, in this case, the Jews. The threat Jews were imagined to pose to Christendom was therefore felt as an assault on Mary the mother of Christ and the mother of all Christians. Added to jealous fears about the economic power of Jews, and envy about their imagined easy lives, it could lead Christians to slaughter people who lived in their own communities, drive them out of their cities and towns, and destroy their synagogues and temples. This was *not* the variety of anti-Semitism that Luther espoused.

## CIRCUMCISION

By the 1530s, however, Luther's tone had dramatically changed, moving far away from the kinds of sentiment he had expressed in 1523. Why did a man who started out as someone the Jews believed would support them then become such a dedicated anti-Semite? The 1530s were precisely the years when Luther was becoming increasingly preoccupied with creating an identity for the new Lutheran Church; this was his overriding concern in the years after the formulation of the Augsburg Confession, as it became clear that there would be no reconciliation with the Catholics. The future of his Church after he died haunted Luther from the time of the Diet of Augsburg in 1530 onward, when negotiations with the Catholics failed and as he also faced his own increasing physical frailty and the ailments he believed were caused by the Devil. Anti-Semitism for Luther was therefore bound up with his understanding of his own role in salvation and church history, and of the genealogy of his Church. It was also inseparable from his recognition of his mortality. In short, it was about his legacy.

At the same time, Charles V was pursuing a more tolerant policy towards the Jews. Though he was intolerant of the Jews in Spain and supported their exclusion, in his German lands his policy was different, and he protected the Jews as Maximilian had done, reaffirming his policy at the Diet of Augsburg in 1530 (the same Diet where the Lutheran Confession of Faith was presented and Lutheranism became effectively a separate Church) and repeating this in 1532 at the urging of Josel of Rosheim. By 1544 at the Diet of Speyer and in Regensburg in 1546, Charles extended the policy further, guaranteeing freedom of movement and trade, confirming that synagogues could not be destroyed without his approval, and banning the expulsion of Jews from anywhere they had been living at the start of his reign (counter to the 1540 ban on Jews in Saxony). Blood libel cases could only be decided by the emperor and it was forbidden to spread rumours about such cases. In the 1530s Moravian Jews were expelled, and Luther feared there would be an influx of Jews; he feared, too, that a more militant Judaism was developing which was converting Christians. Luther was therefore developing a more openly anti-Semitic line at a time when Imperial policy towards the Jews was becoming more liberal.[42]

Moreover, the kind of anti-Semitism Luther articulated was distinctive. In particular, he obsessed about circumcision. This is a major theme in Paul, who so profoundly influenced Luther's theology; but this does not entirely explain Luther's preoccupation with it. When he thought of Jews converting Christians in his 1538 tract *Against the Sabbatarians*, he immediately thought of circumcision: 'the Jews are making inroads at various places throughout the country with their venom and their doctrine, and . . . they have already induced some

Christians to let themselves be circumcised.'[43] This tract came just a year after his rejection of Rabbi Josel's plea for his intercession to secure the Jews' safe passage in Saxony. Back in 1522 when Karlstadt first established his own independent congregation and it was rumoured that he had allowed a bigamous marriage, Luther had joked 'they will be introducing circumcision next'—a jibe which made fun of Karlstadt's previous lecture series on the Old Testament at Wittenberg, and mocked him as a crude biblical literalist. Luther made the same joke in his Lectures on Genesis, when he remarked that the Sabbatarians in Moravia were insisting on celebrating the Sabbath as the Jews did, so 'Perhaps they will insist on circumcision too, for a like reason'.[44]

Jewish circumcision represented the covenant between God and the Jews, marking them out as God's Chosen People. *Against the Sabbatarians* continues by condemning the Jews because of their history and arguing that God has deserted them, as the destruction of the Temple proves. If the Jews argue that they are being punished because of their sins, Luther rhetorically insists, then they must name a sin that would justify God withholding the Messiah from them, and if they are able to do so, 'Then I, old fool and miserable Christian that I am, will immediately have a stone knife made and become a Jew. And I will not only circumcise that one member but also my nose and my ears'.[45] Luther's leaden humour is laced with insult because slitting a nose was a revenge mutilation connected with cuckolding and slit ears were a judicial punishment. It is remarkable that he should imagine himself as a Jew in this treatise, which, as he says at the end in what almost sounds like an unconscious double entendre, simply 'grew under my hand', so quickly did the quill run.[46]

In 1543 Luther produced three major treatises against the Jews, the worst of his anti-Semitic outpourings. The first of these, *On the Jews and their Lies*, argues that the Jews are no longer the Chosen People. Here again, Luther writes about circumcision, linking it with the Jews' pride in their race. Drawing on the descriptions of Jewish practices by the converted Jew Anton Margaritha, Luther now evokes the experience of circumcision, and argues that Jewish practice has added a 'devilish supplement' because 'in addition to cutting off the foreskin of a male child, the Jews force the skin back on the little penis and tear it open with sharp fingernails, as one reads in their books. Thus they cause extraordinary pain to the child, without and against the command of God, so that the father, who should really be happy over the circumcision, stands there and weeps as his child's cries pierce his heart'.[47] Again this is followed by heavy-handed irony as Luther repeats Moses's injunction about circumcising the heart, and imagines the Jews rejecting Moses because of their pride in their own circumcision.

The issue of circumcision is also closely allied to what kind of group the Jews are, and here Luther's stance is ambiguous. In *Vom Schem Hamphoras*, for example, the second of the three tracts of 1543, he begins by denying the Jews any special racial status because we are all children of Abraham and of Adam. This looks like a strong rejection of racial arguments of any kind since all humans, Luther insists, have the same ancestors. But he then undercuts this position, attacking the Jews for pride in their race, recounting their history as a 'people', and implicitly separating them from the German society. They are outsiders whose rights in the empire need to be circumscribed. This argument is another striking instance of doublethink, because Luther knew that the Jews had been settled in German lands for centuries. He was fascinated by thieves' cant, or Rottwelsch, and republished the *Liber vagatorum* with a dictionary, discussing the language which, he argued, came from the Jews, because it borrowed many Hebrew words.[48] Having therefore started by insisting that we are all of one race, Luther has it both ways, arguing that the Jews both are and are not a race. And for good measure he goes on to insult the Jews as members of a watery race, a people like gypsies, a people whose blood has become weakened, and who have little in common with the Jews of the Old Testament. So he writes: 'And these dreary dregs, this stinking scum, this dried-up froth, this moldy leaven and boggy morass of Jewry should merit, on the strength of their repentance and righteousness, the empires of the whole world—that is, the Messiah and the fulfilment of the prophecies—though they possess none of the aforementioned items and are nothing but rotten, stinking, rejected dregs of their fathers' lineage!'[49] Thus he can insist that there are no 'races', and deny the Jews any special status as a chosen people—a status he claims for Christians—while still defining the Jews as a people set apart.

Luther next turned his attention back to Jewish history to argue that the Jews as a people had been punished by God. This is why the Temple had been destroyed and why Jews now led such miserable lives as a lost, wandering people. Luther had rehearsed these ideas in his Lectures on Genesis, written sometime after 1535, arguing, 'Thus the Jews must confess that they are no longer the people of God for if they were the people of God, they would have that land'.[50] This premise ran through *Against the Sabbatarians*, of 1538, as Luther harps on Jewish history, as a people deserted by God. That the throne of David has been destroyed for 1,500 years shows that either the Messiah has come and now sits on that throne, or else God is a liar, an argument Luther insists is conclusive.[51] He follows with his habitual insults, writing of the Jews' 'foul and worthless lies and idle chatter' and of how 'they are given to babbling and lying'.[52] This opposition of 'Jews' and 'Germans' underlies his demands in 1543 that they should not be allowed to use the highways, that their synagogues should be burnt, their writings destroyed, their dwellings demolished, and that they should be put into reservations where they should be forced to work.[53]

These kind of arguments tap straight into ethnic caricaturing of the Jews. So whilst Luther in 1523 rejected allegations that the Jews poison wells or spread plague, his treatise on usury four years earlier frequently featured a caricature of a Jew on the cover, implying, of course, that Jews are usurious moneylenders, out to fleece Christians. As Thomas Kaufmann has pointed out, some of the editions of this treatise came from Wittenberg, where Luther could surely have intervened to prevent this association.[54] Instead, the reformer absorbed anti-Semitic stereotypes of Jews as money-grubbing, untrustworthy, and work-shy, and repeated them in *On the Jews and Their Lies* of 1543, where he explicitly called for the Jews to be forced to work. In a passage that is as nastily comic as it is memorable, he castigated them as people who 'sit behind the stove, idle away the time, fart, and roast pears'; that is, layabouts who corner the warmth of the heater and eat delicacies, refusing to work.[55] We know that he once recited the rhyme at table 'don't believe a wolf on the wild heath / also no Jew on his oath / believe no pope on his conscience / or else you'll be shat on by all three'.[56] In the same vein he claimed that the Jews were unreliable, and he told the story of the Jew who offered Duke Albrecht of Saxony a magic bauble ('knopf') with strange characters on it that would protect the wearer from cold iron: the duke hung it around the Jew's neck and stabbed him through with a sword, because thus it would have gone with him had he trusted the Jew. Luther continued straight on to muse: 'If I were the lords of Frankfurt'—a byword for Luther for big Jewish populations—'I would summon all the Jews and ask them why they call Christ a whoreson and his mother a whore . . . and a shithouse'; if they can prove it I would give them a thousand gulden but if not, 'I would rip their tongues from their throats'.[57]

In contrast to medieval anti-Semitism, Luther's was linked to a set of fantasies surrounding circumcision and the Jews as the Chosen People. Psychologically, in Freudian terms, such fears would be connected with the Oedipal stage and with castration, and not with the early infant stages about which Klein has written so powerfully, where relations with the mother are primary. The infant feels rivalry towards the father, and fears that the father will take revenge on him by castrating him. Jews, so the irrational fear would run, have undergone a kind of symbolic castration by having the foreskin removed as a sign of the covenant with a paternal God. The circumcised Jew would therefore function as a nightmare vision of what might happen to oneself. Anti-Semitism would consequently be connected to issues about sexual difference, power, and parents. It would be fundamentally concerned with identity.[58]

Intellectually, the issue of the identity of the new Church and of Luther himself was becoming particularly urgent for him after 1530, as it became clear that there would be no reconciliation with the Catholics and that the Lutherans were becoming a separate church, with their own confession, formulated at the Diet of Augsburg. A church, however, required a history, and Lutherans needed a genealogy that presented them as the true church. This was an issue of life and death for Luther; and as the Catholic Church began to move towards holding a Council from which Luther would be excluded, his anti-papalism became ever more shrill, as we saw in chapter 5. Increasingly Luther began to see the Lutheran Church as the true Chosen People, and himself as a prophet. As he did so, he denied that the Jews were the elect of God, attacking their exegetical ability and their status as a race.

6.2. *Eyn Sermon von dem Wucher*. Martin Luther, 1519. Lutherhalle Wittenberg. (The speech bubble reads: 'Pay up, or give interest!')

As he had done back in 1523, Luther also attacked rabbinical tradition, and he duly set about mocking the wisdom of the Jews in a reprise of his insistence on scripture alone and his rejection of papal authority. The Jews, he claimed, were just like the authoritarian papists who insisted on reading scripture in particular ways. This subject was close to Luther's heart, because from the 1520s onward he was translating the Old Testament from Hebrew, an enterprise which involved a large team of Wittenberg theologians and which he would continue to perfect for the rest of his life. God had chosen the Lutherans as the true interpreters of scripture; Bernhard Ziegler of Frankfurt, Luther claims, is a better Hebraist than any Jew.[59] Ziegler, who owed his position to Luther and Melanchthon's patronage, came from the lower nobility, and was impeccably German and Christian. He had learnt his Hebrew from the converted Jew and author of anti-Semitic tracts on the Jews Antonius Margaritha.

It was one of Margaritha's notoriously anti-Semitic tracts from which Luther drew when writing *On the Jews and Their Lies*, quoting large parts of it verbatim. In this tract, Luther returns to the argument about the meanings of 'bethulah' and 'alma' that he had set out in 1523, parading again his own knowledge of Hebrew and of the Old Testament. One might wonder here whether Luther is trying to out-rabbi the rabbis, and whether part of his indignation against the Jews and the Talmud springs from his desire to be the sole interpreter of scripture—after all, he composed exegetical prefaces to each book of the Bible explaining how they should be read. He, and not the rabbis, should have the power to interpret scripture. We see this, for example, in the lectures he gave on Genesis sometime after 1535. Luther reads the story of Jacob's ladder as referring to Christ and, in line with late medieval commentators, argues that the ladder is Christ. He then interprets the three stones which become one pillow as foreshadowing the Trinity, and attacks the rabbis for their refusal to recognize this. The ground on which Jacob slept, Luther argues, was not the site of the Temple but elsewhere—and thus, by implication, he rejects a reading which sees the passage as bestowing the land of Israel on the Jews. He then speculates that the land may have been the stone where Jesus was buried, though he grants that this cannot be proved. Here Luther systematically replaces Jewish readings with Christian ones that delegitimise Jewish claims, while also insulting the rabbis for their pigheadedness.[60] So far does this rhetorical pattern extend that by the time he ends the tract *Vom Schem Hamphoras*, Luther comes full circle. Having begun by denying that Jews could ever convert, he concludes by imagining Jews who *might* convert, but they would do so through joining the 'true' Jews, that is, the Christians—an argument he had also made back in 1523.[61]

One interesting incident reveals Luther's thought, and how memory can shift. Luther did engage in debate with three rabbis at some point before 1526, an exchange which he referred to in his sermon on the 25th Sunday after Trinity 1526. He explained that they had refused to accept his biblical proofs relating to Christ and had just insisted on following the Talmud. He apparently referred to the same episode years later, in his *Table Talk* of 1540, but now the memory had become transformed so that the Jews had become much more aggressive. The *Table Talk* passage begins with the assertion that the Jews call Christ 'hanged highwayman', that is, they mock the crucifixion as the death of a criminal; and that they call Maria 'Haria', which Luther explains means 'latrinam' (lavatory). Luther then recollects his meeting with the three Jews, who, he says, had explained that their rabbis claimed that 'alma' does not always mean virgin—the passage which Luther discussed in his tract of 1523, and to which he would return in 1543. In 1540, according to Luther, the Jews commented that since the Lutherans were reading Hebrew and the books of the Bible, they would soon become Jews; Luther retorted it would be the other way around. In 1543 he told the story a third time in *On the Jews and Their Lies*. As Luther tells it this time, he was instructing the Jews rather than arguing with them, and when they gave him their interpretations, he 'forced them back to the text'; they still insisted on following their rabbis. Luther 'took pity on them' and interceded for them with the authorities, but he later discovered that they had insulted Christ as a 'hanged highwayman'—that is, the statement that had originally introduced the anecdote now became incorporated as the story's climax.[62] 'Therefore I do not wish to have anything more to do with any Jew . . . they are consigned to wrath; the more one tries to help them the baser and more stubborn they become'.

Luther's 'recollection' therefore developed over time, and it concerned a key issue of textual interpretation about Mary's virginity. It appears indirectly a fourth time, in *Vom Schem Hamphoras*, as Luther lengthily ridicules the rabbis for refusing to accept that 'alma' means virgin.[63] The rabbis are now no longer mentioned, but the story has become a general truth. Whatever the three rabbis did or did not say, the memory clearly had a powerful but shifting—and intensifying—significance for Luther, moving from being an encounter with no particular point beyond the authority of the rabbis, to becoming a story about how the Jews besmirch the name of Mary, insist on following their rabbis, insult Jesus, and are not to be trusted. They deliberately distort scripture, and Luther is a better reader of Hebrew than they are. They turn on Christians who want to help them. In this form, experience itself—as re-remembered—becomes the guarantor of truth. In 1576, long after Luther's death, Nikolas Selnecker retold the episode and placed it at Worms in 1521 as Luther defended his works before the emperor and the estates of the empire; he included the story just before the famous tale of Luther's encounter with the man who would become his anti-biographer, Johannes Cochlaeus. Cochlaeus, who had originally been a sympathiser, insisted on meeting with Luther in the hope of persuading him to return to the Church with the killer argument that if an interpretation of scripture was contested, how could the matter ever be settled if not through the authority of the Roman Church? By placing these stories in this sequence, Selnecker presents the Jews as offering a similar kind of temptation to that offered by the Catholics: instead, Luther sticks to scripture alone.[64]

Not only, however, does Luther deny that the Jews can truly read scripture: Luther's own most prized identity was that of professor of Holy Scripture, his job description at Wittenberg and the only formal position he held in relation to the Lutheran Church. He was effectively the rabbi of the Lutherans, deriving his authority from his ability to teach, and not from his rank in the Church. Conversely, in some of the worst passages of *Vom Schem Hamphoras*, Luther attacks the Jews as deriving such clever glosses on scripture from their consumption of 'Judas piss'. He argued that they guzzled up the contents of Judas's guts when he was hanged, 'nourishment' which gave them such 'sharp sight'. Luther bolsters his intellectual authority by denigrating the Jews, repeatedly referring to their interpretations in shorthand as 'Judas piss' insights. Luther certainly liked to dirty his antagonists, but the nastiness of the insult is unusual even for Luther. Interestingly too, he implicitly links his authority here with his masculinity, constantly presenting himself as the aggressive disputant with the Jews and aligning himself with Elijah, a powerful patriarch. By reading the Old Testament as pointing towards the New, Luther aimed to create an unbroken genealogy between the prophets and the Lutherans as God's Chosen People, a powerful biblicism that would usurp the Jews themselves.

This understanding of Jewish destiny became part of the identity of early Lutheranism, which is why it is not just a matter of Luther's personal peculiarities. Increasingly his followers liked to stylise him as Elijah; and indeed, by 1537, medals were being produced showing Luther's face and titling him 'Prophet of Germany'.[65] In his address to the students of Wittenberg University when Luther died, Melanchthon concluded movingly that 'the charioteer and the chariot Israel died', a reference to Elijah's ascent to heaven witnessed by Elisha.[66] Metaphorically, Melanchthon was equating Wittenberg and Lutheranism with the true Israel, just as the Wittenbergers liked to equate their city with the true Jerusalem, and as Calvinists did for Geneva. But there was yet more to this, for Elijah is the prophet who will prepare the way for the Messiah. By claiming his identity, Lutherans were insisting, in contradiction to the Jews, that the Messiah had already come. Interestingly, Elijah is specifically invoked in the Jewish ceremony of circumcision, to which Luther devoted fascinated attention.

By identifying Luther with Elijah they implicitly linked Luther to anti-Semitism. The Jews were not God's Chosen People; Lutheran history instead cast Luther as the true Elijah leading the Chosen People to the Messiah and ascending to Heaven. Circumcision, Luther had argued, was irrelevant; it did not guarantee the Jewish status as a chosen people. The identity of the Lutheran Church, as Luther first began to understand it, depended on usurping the position of the Jews.

In the very last months of his life in 1546, Luther's final printed sermons, given at Eisleben, the town of his birth, included a postscript calling for a campaign against the Jews.[67] Reminding his audience that 'perhaps I might not be able to preach to you again', he exhorted them to 'remain firmly with the Word', and told them that their lords 'should not suffer the Jews, but drive them out' if they would not convert, lest they become party to the Jews' sins. He repeated the old allegations: the Jews call the Virgin a whore, Christ a whoreson, and call us Christians 'changelings', 'and if they could kill us all, they happily would'. They pass themselves off as doctors, and so poison people. Luther's followers should not doubt that anyone who refuses to convert is a 'wicked Jew, who will not stop blaspheming against Christ, sucking you out, and, if he can, killing you'.[68] Luther's hatred of the Jews had all the force of a deathbed injunction. In 1559, when Georg Walther compiled a collection of Luther's prophecies, the first concerned the Jews and their 'vberdrus' or sloth, which was preventing them from converting to the true word of God, while Nikolas Selnecker included the stories of Jews out to attack Luther in his brief biography, and Mathesius recounted such stories in his long series of biographical sermons.[69] And in 1566, when Luther's *Table Talk* was published after his death, his sayings were grouped by topic, so that his remarks on the Jews were easy to find.[70] In 1617, when the first anniversary of the posting of the 95 Theses and the beginning of the Reformation was held, Luther's treatises on the Jews were republished, and the editor added a series of unpleasant anecdotes about Jews in the Preface.[71] Not all of Luther's followers commended his anti-Semitism; the Nuremberg Lutheran preacher Andreas Osiander found his work appalling.[72] Nevertheless, Luther's anti-Semitism featured in the picture of the reformer that his followers transmitted, and became part of his legacy, albeit often in muted form.

## *VOM SCHEM HAMPHORAS*

The final strand of Luther's anti-Semitism concerns physical disgust for Jews. The Zurich congregational representatives almost certainly had these in mind when they accused him of writing dirty books. Luther's writing in this vein is mostly confined to *Vom Schem Hamphoras* (*On the Unknowable Name of God*). *On the Jews and Their Lies* is an ostensibly rational treatise, and though it rambles and Luther repeats his seven-point plan of action after it has already been set out, it does have a recognisable shape and argument. *Vom Schem Hamphoras*, by contrast, is a shapeless, irrational piece which has the quality of nightmare. It is as if it were the unconscious underpinnings of *On the Jews and Their Lies*, the fantasies that legitimate Luther's programme of cultural destruction of the Jews.[73]

It is here that Luther writes about the sculpture on the outside of the Wittenberg church and praises its makers, though it takes a good third of the treatise before he actually gets on to the ostensible subject. As he often does, he associates the Jews with pigs: Jews do not eat pork because they are akin to pigs. The Jewish sow is therefore a vicious insult to the Jews, and using the rabbinic name for the ineffable name of God in the title of the treatise is provocatively blasphemous to the Jews because God's name cannot be uttered. Worse, Luther then goes through a series of the verbal transformations and puns of which he was a master, reversing *Schem Hamphoras* to read '*Scham Haperes*', which means, according to Luther, 'here dirt, not the dirt that lies on the street, but which comes from the stomach; "Scham" means: here or there, "Peres" means that which is in the intestines of the sow and all animals'. In other words, Luther converts the unutterable name of God into sow ordure.[74]

The pig has a long pedigree in Luther. In his 1523 treatise, *That Jesus Christ Was Born a Jew*, Luther had joked that if he had seen 'such dolts and blockheads govern and teach the Christian faith', then he would sooner be a 'hog than a Christian'.[75] As we know from archaeology undertaken on Luther's childhood house, the family liked to eat suckling pig and ate more pork than was probably usual for the period.[76] Yet Luther could also associate the pig with the diabolic, and Mathesius tells us that he once saw the Devil in his garden 'as a wild black sow'.[77] *On the Jews and Their Lies* repeatedly uses the metaphor of the sow, which runs like a leitmotif throughout the treatise. But the role it plays is contradictory, as Luther compares the Jews to 'filthy sows' who 'fall into the trough, defaming and reviling what they refuse to acknowledge and to understand'; he calls for sow dung to be thrown at Jews who utter the name of God; and he insults the Jews as misreading the Bible, worthy only to read 'the bible that is found under the sow's tail, and eat and drink the letters that drop from there'—a direct reference to the Wittenberg church sculpture.[78] Here the sow is associated with defecation, and is equated with the

Jews. Later, however, he accuses the Jews of insulting Christians and not treating them as human: 'For the stupidity which they ascribe to us I could not assign to any sow, which, as we know covers itself with mire from head to foot and does not eat anything much cleaner', the rhetorical mirror image of what Luther has been saying about Jews. Finally, Luther returns to his comparison of 1523, rhetorically averring that he would 'much, much rather be a sow than a human being' if the Jewish Messiah were to be what God promised. He goes on to say: 'For a sow lies down on her featherbed, on the street, or on a dung heap; she rests securely, snores gently, sleeps sweetly, fears neither king nor lord, neither death nor Hell, neither the devil nor God's wrath, and lives entirely without care so long as she has her bran'; indeed, she does not even feel death if the butcher does his job right.[79]

The language here is poetic and evocative, the words of a man who has truly pondered pigs.[80] The mention of dirt and manure is not so much disgusting as indulgent as Luther talks about what was for him one of the deepest mysteries of faith: if God is indeed a God of the Old Testament, not of the New, and if the Messiah has not yet come, then he would wish to be a sow, that is, a Jew. The pig was in this sense a totemic animal for Luther, representing both the foul Jew and Luther himself, if it should turn out that God is not God.[81] Luther only ever refers to the female pig, the sow, in *On the Jews and Their Lies*, perhaps because sexual inversion is simply another of the extravagant hyperboles of this text, or because his imagination was already preoccupied with the sculpture on the outside of Wittenberg's St Mary's Church—where the Jews suckle the hanging teats of the sow.

He turned his full attention to this sculpture as he wrote *Vom Schem Hamphoras*. Two passages in particular evoke physical disgust for Jews. The first comes after Luther has reprinted and translated a slab of the anti-Semitic work by Porchetus. A diatribe against Christians who convert to Judaism, this section is a lengthy account of what those who become Jews have to believe. At the end of it, Luther changes gear and, using his own voice, describes the disgusting people such apostates are joining. He calls on them to come and kiss the Devil, for he has emptied his stomach which 'is a true relic, that the Jews, and whoever wants to be a Jew, should kiss, eat, drink and pray to.

And similarly the Devil should also eat and drink that which those his disciples vomit up and void above and below', going on to imagine Satan sucking up the Jews' vomit and excrement with his trunk, as if it were a delicacy on which he could feed like a 'sow'.[82] In sharp contrast to the measured tone of the proceeding section, this passage is written with verve and gusto, as Luther piles on the onomatopoetic verbs and works up a shrill rhythm imagining the body of the Jew stuffed to bursting with diabolic excrement. Its placement here allows a letting out of breath, a zestful break from the litany of what the Jews must believe; and the filth might be regarded as a prophylactic piece of mudslinging against the faith of the Jews, just as Luther prescribed excrement as the surest protection against the Devil. When Luther does this, he is often playful—so, for example, he praised 'Dr Pommer' for his recipe against witches who attacked butter: Bugenhagen ('Dr Pommer') advised defecating in the churn, but whilst such a remedy might be effective, the joke is that one would hardly then eat the butter.[83] There is no such lightness of tone in *Vom Schem Hamphoras*, however, despite the text's ludic qualities. Instead of the Devil being blown out of the infant in the exorcisms at baptism, here the Devil's filth is poured in. Luther lingers on the bodily fluids so that the image of the sow has become fully repellent, with none of the folksiness of *On the Jews and Their Lies*.

The second point comes after a long passage in which Luther has been attacking the Jews' interpretation of the word for virgin. At stake is the issue of Mary's virginity: first, Luther claims that the Jews argue that Mary cannot be the mother of the Messiah because scripture says that the Messiah will be of the line of David. The New Testament says only that Joseph was of the line of David, and does not refer to Mary; since Joseph was not involved in Jesus's conception, Jesus is not of the House of David. Luther presents several responses to this, including to say that the fact that Joseph was of the line of David does not prove that Mary was not. But he also makes a much more daring argument, namely, that since Jesus *is* the Messiah, Mary *must* have been of David's line. Here he deliberately argues in reverse, twitting the Jews by taking Jesus's status as axiomatic, and deriving Mary's status from the assertion that Jesus is the Messiah. This is one of those irrational proofs of belief, the theology of 'reason as the whore' and faith as something that defies reason, that Luther so loved. He makes a similar claim for the nature of Christ's presence in the Eucharist, where the host is at one and the same time both bread and the body of Christ, which must be experienced as a mystery of faith, not argued with rationality. So also, Luther did not think it wise to dwell too much on the consequences that there was, as he claimed, no free will and that everything was predetermined: here, thought stopped.

It is in this paragraph that Luther pours scorn on the Jewish exegetes and castigates them for getting their sharp sight from 'Judas piss'. 'I, accursed Goy, cannot understand where they get such a superior art [of exegesis] from, unless I believe that when Judas Iscariot hanged himself, so that his intestines burst, and as happens to the hanged, his bladder burst, that the Jews perhaps had their servants there with gold jugs and silver bowls so as to catch the Judas piss (as it is called) together with the other relics, and then ate and drank the dung (Merde) together, and so got such sharp sight' to interpret scripture; or else, Luther continues, 'they looked in the behind of their God and in this gas hole they found it written'.[84] Luther tars the Jews with filth at precisely the point where his own argument, as he knows, escapes rational moorings and becomes what he would regard as a mystery of faith. Its sheer excess of revulsion stops thought. Later in the text too, Luther refers to rabbinical interpretations as 'Judas pisse' and 'Judasschweis', the 'sweat' of the Jews, likely to be a euphemism for 'scheis' or 'shit'. This is not a word Luther ordinarily uses, and its repetition here works as shorthand for the disgusting visions he has just invoked—so that the reader is constantly reminded of the vision of the Jews gobbling up the contents of Judas's guts even when Luther does not refer to it directly.

The perception of Jews here was not, however, confined merely to flights of rhetoric, but coloured Luther's interactions with Jews, as is clear from some throwaway comments in Luther's letters to his wife. On his last journey to Eisleben, for instance, Luther imagines that he has been made ill by the magical assaults of Jews. As he frequently did, he ventriloquizes Katharina to express what he is not willing to say directly himself, writing to her that 'Had you been here, however, you would have said that it was the fault of the Jews or their god' and going on to explain that they had travelled through a village in which many

6.3. The Judensau from Wittenberg. Einblattdruck mit Darstellung der Wittenberger Judensau, 1596. Wikimedia—ref. German Wikipedia.

Jews lived, 'and perhaps they blew on me so hard'. He then trumpets his next duty: 'I have to start expelling the Jews'.[85] These same letters discuss his own impotence, as if thoughts about his masculinity were linked with thoughts about Jews.

Luther is a thinker whose mental processes often mirror digestion, and there seems to be a digestive logic here as well. On the one hand, Luther wants to usurp the position of the Jews, to claim their status as God's Chosen People and be a better Hebraist and exegete than the rabbis. He wants to incorporate them, to take them in and gain all the things which give them strength. He wants to arrogate their history for himself and his own church, and his stylisation as Elijah makes good that promise. Like a rabbi, his standing derives from his position as interpreter of the Bible, and so he reserves his full scorn of the Jews as 'piss eaters' for their (in)ability to interpret scripture; this is his right, not theirs. There is a sense in which he wants to take for himself everything that is the Jews', to ingest it, and make it his own; to become a sow and 'roll in muck'. By accusing the Jews of coprophagia, he can then imaginatively equate them with excrement, and vomit them up or void them from the body. This double process of ingestion and emetic defecation reflects what is most puzzling about Luther's anti-Semitism, because it is animated by a deep recognition and identification, at the same time as it heaps dirt upon them.

## PLAYMOBIL LUTHER

Luther's anti-Semitism is difficult to explain, and I do not think that I have satisfactorily explained it here. Part of it probably sprang from Luther's unconscious recognition of how close his theology was to Judaism in many respects. As in Judaism, there was no female divine figure in Luther's religion. Mary was an exemplar of humility for all Christians, but she was not queen of Heaven and she should not be invoked or prayed to. Like the Jews, too, Luther had little to say about the afterlife. He did not laud celibacy, but preached a theology that was remarkably positive about human sexuality. And he insisted on the value of scripture and learning, his own religious authority deriving not from his position in a church hierarchy but as professor of the Bible, as if he were himself a rabbi.

Luther wanted to claim the status of the Chosen People for himself and his Church, placing his Church as the 'true' one and garnering its history for the Lutherans. This tactic goes back at least to Luther's first pamphlet on the Jews from 1523. Later, he insisted that the Lutherans were the better Hebraists, who understood scripture better than the Jews, and he was vicious in his denunciation of the rabbis. His anti-Semitism was bound up with his conception of the Church and of Lutheran identity, which is why Lutherans were later able to recuperate this part of his legacy as they created a Lutheran culture. Luther liked to style himself as Elijah, the prophet who foretells the Messiah. He did not just take

6.4. Portrait of Martin Luther. Cranach the Younger, 1562. Staatsbibliothek zu Berlin.

on a Jewish identity but actually took it over: he is the true Elijah who knows that the Messiah has come. In translating the Old Testament with his Wittenberg colleagues, the project that occupied him for the rest of his life, Luther deliberately sought to create a German Bible that was definitively Lutheran and not Jewish.[86]

So how did the anti-Semitic Bible which the Playmobil figure holds come to be created? It was not lifted from a sixteenth-century Cranach design but, rather, from the monumental nineteenth-century statue of Luther which stands, twinned with a statue of Melanchthon, in the Wittenberg marketplace. Its origins, that is, lie not in the Reformation era but in the nineteenth-century historicist creation of Luther as German hero. The Bible held by that statue displays the words 'Old Testament: End', taken from the closing page of the Old Testament of Luther's 1534 German Bible. But Luther's original printed Bible does not have the anti-Semitic tone of the Playmobil figure. After the

6.5. Statue of Martin Luther in Wittenberg. Wikimedia Commons (photographer released, OTFW, Berlin).

closing words of the Old Testament, Luther's Bible reads 'Ende der bucher des alten Testaments' (End of the books of the Old Testament). These words come at the bottom of the page below scripture, but they do not face the opening page of the New Testament as on the Playmobil figure's Bible, and 'Ende' is not in block capitals, nor does it come at the end of the line.[87] Luther's original 1534 Bible, as printed by Hans Lufft, simply does not have the same anti-Semitic typographic effect.

The nineteenth-century statue *does* place the Old and New Testament pages side by side, and 'ENDE' is written in block capitals at the end of the line. The Bible which this Luther holds, however, also includes some words from the Old Testament. These are partly covered by Luther's fingers, but the overall effect is far less negative towards the Old Testament because the only scripture that can be seen are Old Testament verses.

Where, then, did the anti-Semitic Playmobil Luther come from? It seems that the simplified design was actually taken not from the nineteenth-century statue direct, but from the twenty-first century artist Otto Hörl's kitsch plastic version of that statue. This was made for an art installation in 2010 when the nineteenth-century statue was taken away for cleaning, and hundreds of gnome-size red, green, and blue plastic Luthers dotted Wittenberg in serried rows. Even so, the contrast between the Old and New Testaments is much less extreme in Otto Hörl's version because Luther's hand obscures the words. The Playmobil figure was a simplification of a simplification of a nineteenth-century iconic statue, and as the simplifications became ever cruder, so the anti-Semitic message—implicit in Luther's actual anti-Semitism—became visible. For Luther, the Old Testament had to be read in the light of the New, and the Old Testament was at an end, its people now accursed by God. The Lutherans were now the Chosen People. Unfortunately the original Playmobil figure reproduced this feature of Lutheran thought unintentionally but completely accurately.

The Jewish Sow of *Vom Schem Hamphoras* still stands on the outside of St Mary's Church in Wittenberg. The Nazis held a rally underneath it, and the plaque that is there today draws attention to this fact. In 2017 the Jewish sow became the target of weekly vigils calling for its removal. Even the pastor today finds it uncomfortable to preach

6.6. Plastic figure of Martin Luther. 'Martin Luther', 2010. www.ottmarhoerl.de. Photo from Ottmar Hörl Archive. © Ottmar Hörl.

in a church which, as he explains, insults another religion. There is a commemorative sculpture in the pavement, calling on people to remember the six million murdered Jews; but it is in the shape of an equilateral cross. Just as the Playmobil figure subsumes Jewish religion under Christian, so also the memorial cross that commemorates the holocaust here, however well-intentioned, hints that Jewish suffering can now be subsumed under a quasi-Christian religious symbol. Once again, Jewish history is being appropriated by Christians.

Toys and pavement memorials, it might be objected, are not serious matters, and everyone can make a mistake. But the error in the Playmobil figure has something of the character of a Freudian slip, an unintended 'mistake' that suddenly lifts the lid on a set of unacknowledged anti-Semitic prejudices. Luther's anti-Semitism, I have argued, was connected with his theology of the Church, and this is very much a live issue. Luther did believe that the Lutherans had

6.7. Group of plastic figures of Martin Luther. Scuptural installation, 'Martin Luther—Hier Stehe Ich', Wittenberg, 2010. www.ottmarhoerl.de. Photo by Werner Scheuermann. © Ottmar Hörl.

become the true Chosen People, displacing the Jews. His doublethink about the Jews—representing them as a people who are outsiders in German society while denying them the status of a worthy race—shows some of the confusions that still surround attitudes to Jews in Germany today. So much of the engagement with the Nazi era still focuses on the Germans and German guilt, so that there is little room for Jews to define their own history. Any serious consideration of Luther's anti-Semitism must confront its extreme irrationality, its use of bodily imagery and its mobilisation of revulsion. It has to recognize that Luther's anti-Semitism went further than that of many of his contemporaries, and was not merely the expression of the age. Luther is a thinker who was unusually alive to the role of emotions and remarkably unbuttoned about bodily processes. Here I have tried to show how these very qualities coloured his thinking, how they shaped his peculiar variety of anti-Semitism, and how they leached into different areas of his theology and into the legacies of his Church.

# CHAPTER 7

# Luther Kitsch

I N 2017, LUTHER was national news. He stared out at us from the cover of *Die Zeit's* supplement (Germany's leading weekly broadsheet), was regularly featured on television, and he even hit the front page of *Der Spiegel*. Celebrated as the 'first modern man', Luther's commemoration, in a Germany united between West and East, confronted Germans with the question of what German identity and culture now meant. It posed this question at a time when a right-wing party was growing in power especially in the old Lutheran heartlands and as the integration of a wave of refugees, admitted by Angela Merkel in 2015, was headline news. And even a generation after reunification, as any casual traveller can see, the former East Germany remains markedly different from the West, noticeably less prosperous. At the same time Britain's vote to leave the European Union left Germany more culturally dominant within Europe, and this meant that a united Germany needed to present an open and peaceful image within Europe, an understanding of itself that would be less dominated by the legacy of the Nazi era.

Commemorations are statements about group identity. Whether consciously or not, they entail choices. They evoke significant dates and people, and they blot out others; they enact rituals in which groups represent themselves to each other. They involve claims to public space: frequently they include the erection of monuments and involve celebration at salient places such as buildings, townscapes, or landscapes. They can bring people together; they can also divide them, resulting in what Philippe Buc termed 'failed rituals', in which the ritual goes wrong in some way, and so fails to instantiate national or religious unity.[1]

In 2017 a great deal was at stake. It might have seemed that celebrating Luther could unite West with East, as the region where
Luther lived and had his greatest influence, and that Luther might
provide an example of a good, heroic German who shaped the German language through his translation of the Bible. The stage was the
newly spruced-up Wittenberg, with its first Western-style shopping
mall and its main street now looking like a film set. Its centrepieces
were the recently restored castle of Fredrick the Wise and the Luther
house, and during the summer its city walls hosted a carnival of religious stalls and installations, from 'Experience Baptism' and a 'light
church' to a Bavarian beer tent. There was even a Luther Garden, a giant
manure heap from which sprouted exotic, vividly coloured flowers—
an appropriate tribute to the man with such a taste for scatological
rhetoric. Thousands of people made the pilgrimage to Wittenberg,
while the surrounding area of Thuringia and Saxony offered a host
of exhibitions to tempt tourists into the lands of the former East.[2]

Luther casts a long shadow in German history, literally so because
nineteenth-century statues of the reformer decorate so many town
squares throughout Germany. Heavy and monumental, his forbidding
presence gazes down at us in Wittenberg, Magdeburg, Dresden, Hannover, Berlin, Worms, Hamburg, and a host of other towns.[3] These
statues present him as a colossus, an archetypal German. In 1894, a
gigantic statue of Luther was incorporated into the Berliner Dom,
alongside sixteenth-century German political heroes like Fredrick the
Wise and Philip of Hesse, the new church a temple of Prussianism
in a newly united Germany with its capital Berlin. Bronze friezes at
the entrance to the Dom narrated the drama of the Diet of Worms
on the left and the presentation of the Confession of Augsburg in
1530 on the right, the two dramatic occasions where religion met
politics, as they do in the Dom itself. In World War I, Luther and his
hammer embodied the spirit of the strong German: a postcard for
the Front from 1917 showed three 'oaks': Luther, the 'German oak',
and Bismarck in a Pickelhaube.[4] Just how Luther could be put into
the service of politics is evident in the Luther memorial church in
Mariendorf, Berlin, built in 1933–35. There swastikas (now chiselled
out) sit alongside Christian symbols including the Luther rose, where
the pulpit shows a Hitler youth alongside a Brownshirt, and where

7.1. Berliner Dom Luther statue. Anonymous. Wikimedia Commons (photographer released, Ziko).

7.2. Mural at Martin Luther Gedächtniskirche, Mariendorf, Berlin. Details of the triumphal arch of the Martin-Luther-Gedächtniskirche, Berlin. © Konstantin Manthey.

the light fittings are in the shape of the iron cross. Celebrating Luther, therefore, has regularly raised issues of national identity, and often in troubling ways.[5]

For church historians and theologians too, the 500th anniversary celebrations of Luther's life posed dilemmas but of a different kind. Of the 74 million Lutherans worldwide in the Lutheran Church Federation in 2017, only 34 million live in Europe, only 12 million of them in Germany where Protestants (21.9 million in 2016) are now—just—outnumbered by Catholics (23.6 million). There are 23 million Lutherans in Africa, 12 million in Asia, and 3 million in the USA. A celebration of Luther as 'German' therefore risked alienating the majority of its members.[6] At the same time, the experience of those in what used to be the heartlands of Lutheranism in the former East Germany has led to indifference and alienation from religion, where the church now worries about its future; indeed, in Luther's own Wittenberg, only 12% of the population are Lutheran; 4% are Catholic and the rest have no religion at all. Sachsen-Anhalt, the cradle of the Reformation, has the lowest proportion of Lutherans of any of the German states. The Lutheran Church felt that it needed to use the celebrations as a way of connecting with people it had lost. But what was the best way to do that? And how was Luther to be celebrated? On the one hand, Luther's personality—though it attracted media attention and his human story appeals—loomed so large that he threatened to overwhelm any serious narrative of the Reformation as a complex event produced by the actions of many. On the other, how does a movement that set out to destroy the cult of the saints and insist that there were no mediators between God and man deal with a figure whose charisma has always risked making him a figure for whom relics are collected and Wittenberg a place to which pilgrimages are made?

Perhaps surprisingly, the most ubiquitous monument to Luther in 2017 turned out to be the Playmobil Luther we discussed in the last chapter. With over a million sold since its appearance in April 2015, it was easily the best-selling figure Playmobil ever produced. There is a wonderful irony here, for if the nineteenth century celebrated Luther in monumental statues cast by leading sculptors, 2017 was dominated by the plastic mini-Luther you could assemble yourself. This chapter explores the historical roots of the invention of Luther as a character with a biography, why and how Luther entered material and visual culture so early and so pervasively, and what the phenomenon of Luther kitsch in 2017 can tell us about rituals, commemoration, and identity.[7]

## LUTHER'S LIFE

The outlines of Luther's life were set in stone soon after he died, and virtually every biographer provides the same heroic account of the reformer's life; so much so that the challenge for any biographer of Luther is finding something new to say. The story has a clear narrative arc: it begins with the 95 Theses, proceeds through Luther's meeting with Cardinal Cajetan at Augsburg and refusal to recant, moves to the Leipzig Debate, and the burning of the bull of excommunication, until our hero arrives at Worms and defends his works at the Imperial Diet in front of the Emperor Charles V and the assembled estates of the empire. This is the climax, a tale of remarkable courage and defiance. Luther is then spirited away to the Wartburg and kept in safety, only to return to Wittenberg nine months later, in contradiction of his ruler's orders, to restore order and take command of the Reformation. In 1525, the Peasants' War breaks out and Luther's antagonist Thomas Müntzer leads the peasants in revolution. Luther sides with the princes; order is re-established and the rebellion bloodily suppressed. From then on, the focus shifts from drama to consolidation. Luther's church develops at Wittenberg. There are attempts to unite with the Swiss at the Colloquy at Marburg in 1529, and at the Reichstag of Augsburg in 1530 (the other moment depicted on the Berlin cathedral frieze) the Lutherans present their Confession of Faith to the emperor and Lutheranism becomes a separate church. Not much happens after that as Luther becomes increasingly grumpy, ages, and finally dies in 1546.

With few variations, this narrative structure is followed by almost every modern biographer. The challenge it poses first is structural: how to deal with the downside of the narrative arc, what happened after the dramatic climax of Luther's appearance at Worms. And it presents the complex drama of the Reformation as a story of an individual, personalising the narrative so that the intricate events of the Peasants' War that mobilised thousands, attacked serfdom, and produced so many ideas are reduced to a theological struggle between two individuals, Luther and the revolutionary Thomas Müntzer.

Modern biographers did not invent this narrative. It was already becoming ossified when Luther died, and from the outset it found its way into visual and material culture. In 1557, Ludwig Rabus' life of Luther provided a set of illustrations for the key events of Luther's life, their seeming vividness only partly dented by the fact that many of them are re-used: the illustration of the Diet of Worms does double duty as the image for the Colloquy of Marburg, and so on.[8] Beautifully hand-coloured in many copies, they gave rise to a series of visual representations of Luther's life for pious Lutherans, and by the seventeenth century these were produced in broadsheet form, with a picture for each of the iconic moments, ending with Luther in his coffin. One eighteenth-century hand-painted series is made up of tiny roundel scenes of the reformer's life. Made in Augsburg, and about the size of a communion wafer, it could be folded up into a round wooden box and carried like a sacred relic or used for meditation.[9]

7.3. *Historien*—Luther and Cajetan. Ludwig Rabus, 1557. © Photo: akg-images.

7.4. *Historien*—Luther burns the Bannandrohungsbulle. Ludwig Rabus, 1557. © Photo: akg-images.

*Intitulentur libri*

*Hie steh ich Ich kan nicht anders, Got helffe mir Amen.*

7.5. *Historien*—Here I stand, I cannot do otherwise, God help me, Amen. Ludwig Rabus, 1557. © Photo: akg-images.

7.6. Luther's life. Lutherhalle Wittenberg. © Luther Memorial Foundation in Saxony-Anhalt.

7.7. Hand-painted series of roundel scenes. Lutherhalle Wittenberg. © Luther Memorial Foundation in Saxony-Anhalt.

As in any commemoration, who is not shown is as significant as who is: Karlstadt, Luther's first co-worker, the man who gave him his doctorate and from whom he split so painfully in the early 1520s, is air-brushed out of the early Reformation, and Müntzer and those whom Luther termed the 'swarmers' are not on view. The narrative also omits some interesting events. First, and most famously, there is the posting of the 95 Theses themselves. Luther was certain that the Reformation had begun in 1517 on the date when the Theses were posted, and he toasted it with his friend Justas Jonas on its tenth anniversary.[10] But when he told his life story in the Preface to his Collected Works in Latin he did not mention specifically what he had done that day.[11] There are no sixteenth-century visual representations of the posting of the Theses whatsoever, no images of Luther swinging the hammer. These had to wait for the seventeenth-century centenary in 1617, and even then, the first depictions are, as we saw in chapter 2, part of the broadside entitled 'The Dream of Frederick the Wise'. Here Luther writes up the 95 Theses to be sure, but not in real life. This is an episode in Frederick the Wise's prophetic dream, and the popularity of the myth owes a good deal to the fact that there was no usable sixteenth-century image of the posting of the Theses.[12]

Second, the visual narrative does not mention Luther's marriage in 1525, an omission from contemporary written Lutheran accounts too: Luther's contemporaries Georg Spalatin and Rabus do not mention it in their narratives, and Johannes Mathesius refers to it only briefly.[13] Luther's contemporary and opponent Johannes Cochlaeus, who wrote the first 'biography'—an anti-biography, in fact—does mention it, condemning it as a double sacrilege since it was the marriage of a monk and a nun, both of whom broke their vows: 'A nun married to a monk; a damned woman to a damned man; an infamous woman to an infamous man; clearly so that this might be a work worth the trouble of performing, and equal might be easily joined to equal, and St Paul might lie when he said "They have damnation, because they have made their first faith void".'[14] The innuendo about 'work' was surely intentional; he later wrote a salacious play satirising the sexual behaviour of the Lutheran preachers, presenting Luther as a super-stud and Katharina as a nagging wanton.[15] Catholic polemicists repeatedly attacked the wedding and the marriage, and Johannes

Hasenberg issued a mock appeal to Katharina to return to the convent, with another pamphlet depicting Luther under Katharina's thumb.[16]

The wedding is not included in the broadsheet picture lives either; but significantly, it *is* depicted in an eighteenth-century visual anti-biography which shows Luther as inspired by the Devil. By basing itself so closely on the seventeenth-century Lutheran broadsheet biographies, this Catholic one pays tribute to their popularity. It depicts the reformer's scandalous wedding below a scene of him leading the nuns astray—and for good measure, it satirises the scene of his death as well, showing Luther's coffin tumbling out of the monastery into the fires of Hell—an inversion of the death scene's imprecation which we discussed in chapter 5, 'Living I was your plague, Dead I will be your Death, O Pope!'

Luther himself skips over his marriage in the autobiographical reflections he penned at the beginnings of the collected editions of his German and then Latin works. In the funeral sermons, neither his long-term co-worker Melanchthon nor Bugenhagen, the parish priest of Wittenberg and Luther's confessor, referred to it, even though Katharina was sitting in the congregation, and despite the fact that double portraits of the two of them had been produced by the Cranach workshop to send out as propaganda from 1525 to 1530. Its omission suggests just how awkward the reformers still found Luther's marriage and his positive attitude towards sexuality. Even though so many of Luther's generation of monks had gone through the shock of giving up a life of celibacy in an all-male institution where everything was provided for, and had entered into marriage with all its attendant household insecurities and life with women, they did not apparently feel comfortable enough to include this amongst the reformer's other epochal deeds. It was not until the nineteenth century that the reformer could be depicted as the lute-strumming founder of the Protestant parsonage, his children singing along; and it was not until modern times that Wittenberg celebrated 'Luther's Wedding', a popular carnival, now a tourist attraction, involving the whole town dressing up in sixteenth-century clothes and cheering on 'Martin and Käthe'.[17]

Thirdly, the standard narrative did not date a clear 'moment' at which Luther saw the light. Luther himself had described how he

7.8. Luther playing the lute to his family. Gustav Spangenberg, 1866. Lutherhalle Wittenberg. ©
Luther Memorial Foundation in Saxony-Anhalt.

meditated on Romans and then had a sudden understanding of the
grace of God: 'And this is the meaning: the righteousness of God is
revealed by the Gospel, namely, the passive righteousness with which
the merciful God justifies us by faith, as it is written, "He who through
faith is righteous shall live". Here I felt that I was altogether born
again and had entered paradise itself through open gates'.[18] But he
dated this to 1519, long after the composition of the 95 Theses. Melanchthon described it as an intellectual process that happened as Luther commented on Romans and he placed it where it should logically
have happened: in 1515–16, before the 95 Theses were even thought of.[19]

In his table conversations, Luther described his 'Reformation discovery' as happening in the 'cloaca', the tower in the monastery where
the privy was situated and where Luther's study was; but he did not
date it. None of the early visual Luther biographies represent the
'discovery' moment either; certainly none depict Luther in the privy.
Much of the early-twentieth-century Luther scholarship therefore
devoted huge attention to pinpointing exactly when Luther made his
discovery about Romans. What is significant here, however, is their
fixation on identifying a single, emotional experience, a 'conversion

Arthur Kampf

Der Thesenanschlag zu Wittenberg 1517

7.9. Luther posting his Theses in Wittenberg, Der Thesenanschlag zu Wittenberg. Arthur Kampf, 1936. Lutherhalle Wittenberg. © Luther Memorial Foundation in Saxony-Anhalt.

moment' of the kind that had become so important to later Protestant identity. Luther himself was surely modelling his own account of his experience on Augustine's story of his conversion, and in turn, on that of Paul. And yet this was not the primary way of understanding the religious experience for Luther. For him, as we saw in chapter 2, the religious life was not a once-and-for-all conversion experience, but a struggle with God that lasted one's whole life; and up until his final years he suffered from Anfechtungen, even spending a sleepless night when he thought he had misunderstood a key scriptural passage; he would have to be set straight by his confessor, Bugenhagen, or 'Dr Pommer' as he liked to nickname him.[20]

The modern Luther story is heir to the Lutheran parsonage and to evangelical ideas of 'conversion'. Requiring a dramatic hammer-wielding hero, it has thus improved on the original story. The seventeenth century added Luther the family man, who by the nineteenth century had become a lute-strumming, hymn-singing paterfamilias, sitting with his children by the fireside, the inventor of Christmas.[21] By the early twentieth century, Luther's act of revolution was the posting of the 95 Theses, not so much his appearance at Worms: the hammer, after all, makes a more dramatic and less crowded picture.[22]

## LUTHER'S BIBLE IN 2017

In 2017, the tradition of regarding Luther's life story as part of what every Lutheran needs to know reached its apotheosis with the publication of the revised Luther Bible. The culmination of decades of world-class biblical scholarship, it was issued by the Lutheran Church as its official Bible. It has a sixty-page supplement on Luther's life stitched into it, as if (it might perhaps be unkindly said) Luther's life were part of Holy Writ, a fact which has raised eyebrows in Catholic circles. This too reflects a feature of Luther himself who prefaced each book of the Bible with an introduction in the same style and typeface as scripture, explaining how it was to be read; from its very inception, the Lutheran Bible incorporated Lutheran interpretation and exegesis, as well as Luther's sometimes idiosyncratic renditions of the text. In spite of the strongly ecumenical instincts of so much of the 500th anniversary celebrations, the new Bible was aggressively denominational: non-Lutherans can hardly use a Bible and the wealth of scholarship it contains when it treats Luther—a heretic according to the Catholic Church—as part of scripture. The edition of 2017, with its colour supplements on the history of Lutheranism and the life of its hero, was a Bible for Lutherans only. Tellingly, perhaps, future editions will not include these sections on Luther's life, creating a more confessionally open Bible that is usable by non-Lutherans too.[23]

From early on, Lutherans worried that their man would become a miracle-working saint. They dealt with it by increasingly presenting Luther as a prophet, whose actions were miraculously foretold, and whose life presaged the end of the papacy, as we saw in chapter 5.[24] Luther himself, who had once castigated his antagonists in the Peasants' War as 'heavenly prophets', later became interested in prophecies connected to him, such as that of the monk Johannes Hilten concerning someone who would arise in 1516 and preach against the monks, and in his funeral oration of 1546 Melanchthon explicitly identified Luther as a second Elijah.[25] This only strengthened the extent to which Luther and his life became set apart from his historical context, a man out of time. Such a perspective does little to help us understand either the society in which he worked or the kind of man he was, a trap in which the celebrations of the 'Luther Decade' that culminated in 2017 still found themselves. The Luther quincentenary offered historians of the German Reformation a public platform which they will never have again, and yet its focus on the biography of the hero may also have resulted in concealing a rich and diverse historiographical tradition of Reformation scholarship, in both East and West, on the Peasants' War and on the Reformation at local levels, a far more patchy, theologically diverse, and messy phenomenon than the progress of the ideas of a single 'modern man'.

## COMMEMORATING LUTHER IN 2017

Looking back after the year was over, pundits in Germany generally concurred that the *Lutherjahr* had not been a success. Visitor figures in Wittenberg and at the various exhibitions were lower than had been hoped, and Lutheranism in the former East had not been re-awakened; instead, the Church in some parts of the former East was facing a financial crisis, with membership figures so low that they may simply be unable to support the number of historic churches for which they are responsible. Still, Lutheran pastors have lamented since time immemorial that the people had failed to convert inwardly or reform their godless behaviour, so such gloomy assessments are nothing new, nor do they show that the celebrations accomplished nothing.

How can we understand the commemorations if we consider them in relation to the literature on rituals and memorialisation? The celebrations followed a long ritual cycle of preparation—indeed, in a sense they had begun a decade earlier with the proclamation of the Luther Decade as money was poured into conserving Wittenberg. There were three primary types of commemoration which one might distinguish: the museum visit, the church service, and the tourist pilgrimage to Wittenberg itself.

First, the museum visit. It is hard to imagine any figure or event for which exhibitions have been so numerous in Germany since the War. Indeed, visiting an exhibition was the primary way of consuming Luther culturally: not restricted to Wittenberg, Luther exhibitions of different sizes were held in a remarkable series of places throughout Germany, including in the central national space of the Berlin Martin-Gropius-Bau, a highly innovative and unexpected exhibition which presented Luther in international context. Large exhibitions in places like Torgau or smaller ones in Altenburg or Schmalkalden off the regular tourist trail attempted to interest outsiders in travelling to see these towns unfamiliar to those brought up in the former West. They were matched by blockbuster exhibitions in the USA, which involved close collaboration with West Germany's central postwar ally and reflected the degree of common purpose between these two powers since 1945.[26] The exhibitions also generated a vast amount of scholarship, as generously illustrated catalogues were published for so many of them. Indeed, one might mischievously suggest that the academic conference became the ritual of choice associated with the exhibition, with local dignitaries and political figures invited, keynote lectures by major academics in gigantic halls, and audiences of other academics and 'public'. These followed standard patterns, beginning with joint sessions where part of the experience was noticing the numbers of those present and being part of the crowd, moving through the coffee breaks where less formalised interactions could take place, and culminating in the conference banquet and conference concert. Just about every major town had at least its own commemorative lecture, and some conferences—including outside Germany—hosted political figures and even royalty.

They were also, in Philippe Buc's sense, often 'failed' rituals. The blockbuster international exhibition in Berlin did not quite come off, and though it was imaginative, the sections on South Korea, the USA, Africa, and Sweden did not contain enough objects to recreate fully the Lutheran cultures they aimed to represent.[27] The sheer number of exhibitions also meant that their contents were somewhat predictable. The Luther portraits discussed in chapter 1, for example, were taken out of storage for many of them, and the fact that the double portraits of Katharina von Bora and Luther are more attractive because they feature a woman may have misled us into overestimating their importance; as we saw, after their brief heyday between 1525 and 1529, the wedding portraits were replaced by double portraits of Luther and Melanchthon, and these remained the abiding double-portrait format well into the eighteenth century.

Indeed, the Luther Exhibition has also become a genre, to such an extent that the Wolfenbüttel Library deliberately attempted to subvert it with an exhibition on the form itself: *Luthermania*.[28] That exhibition, too, faced the fundamental difficulty for any such show: the key exhibits are Luther's printed books, but books in a dimly lit glass case, where only one open double page can be shown, are not in themselves visually interesting, nor can they convey the excitement of reading. They inculcate a sense of reverence for the book as a material object, and display it spotlit as a kind of relic. Yet this is not how cheap print was used, the pages roughly handled, the arguments engaged with, and the text annotated.

Exhibitions generate media coverage, design, and—in the museum shop and café—consumption, but that consumption happens individually, not collectively. Museum audio guides might attempt to choreograph the visitor's progress, but each person visits along their own time line, at their own pace. And though exhibitions can create a powerful presence in the town or museum where they are held, the ritual space is temporary. That said, they do allow individuals to share a common experience and to navigate their way through a narrative which has been carefully constructed, as they pass from room to room.

The second form of engagement was the commemorative religious service, and many were held, all over Germany and the world, throughout the year; yet their overall timing was somewhat awkward. The anniversary itself falls on 31 October, when schools and universities are back for the autumn term and when the weather is likely to rain off any parade. So the celebrations were planned to culminate in a giant midsummer sleepover outside the walls of Wittenberg, followed by a mass celebratory church service the next morning. This had the unfortunate consequence that it looked as if the town—in the former East Germany and now only 12 per cent Lutheran—was besieged by an army of Lutherans outside.

Closely related was the third type of event, the tourist visit to Wittenberg. Because Wittenberg has few hotels, the Wittenberg 'pilgrimage' had to fit into a single day, and it centered on a single street: starting from the station, the visitor strolled through an avenue to the Lutherhaus, down to the townhall and central square, and on to the Schloss, all of which had been renovated.[29] The events, services, and exhibitions were mostly held in the summer. It was during the summer months, too, that the massive carnival of stalls and stands in the walls around the town, the giant Bible tower that was a mock-up of the new confessional *Lutherbibel*, and the concerts and art exhibitions were all open. What was refreshing about this profusion of events was their anarchic nature, reflecting the Lutheran Church's own lack of hierarchy and its devolved nature within Germany as a series of regional churches, or 'Landeskirchen', in communion with churches outside Germany too. But it meant that there was no single 'ritual meaning' to which all could subscribe. Every pilgrim to Wittenberg perforce created their own Luther experience.

## KITSCH

Above all, the Luther 500th anniversary festival was characterised by kitsch. In 2017, Luther kitsch was ubiquitous. Every second shop in Wittenberg's main street seemed to be selling it; every museum shop had its own selection. There were the Luther socks saying, 'Here I stand',[30] the Luther beer bottle opener based on a Cranach design, and the Luther Duck, which comes both with and without a clerical uniform and is perfectly designed for the annual 'plastic duck races' that are such a feature of life in German university towns.[31] There were odder ones too: the 'Luther tomato'—Luther could never have encountered one because they had not yet been imported from the New World[32]—and the Tübingen chocolate Luther, which combined chocolate art with an ironic reference to the now surely passé compact disc.[33] The most disturbing were the 'Luther-nudeln', pastas in the shape of Luther's head which I could not bring myself to cook. And everywhere, there was the Playmobil Luther, in its anti-Semitic and improved versions.

The largest piece of kitsch was the Wittenberg Panorama—at €4 million, it was also the most expensive monument of the Luther quincentenary. A gigantic walk-through exhibit in Wittenberg that allowed the visitor to 'experience' the Reformation mood, it was full of accurate historical references but did not purport to be 'wie es eigentlich gewesen' ('how things actually were', as the nineteenth century historian Leopold von Ranke liked to think of the task of the histo-

7.10. Luther marzipan, pasta, duck, Playmobil figure, socks, snowglobe, and cookie cutter. Photo by John Cairns.

rian). Rather, it sought to recreate the deeper emotional significance of the events. Housed in a tall red conical building, it was the first stop on the tourist trail from the Luther-Wittenberg train station. If you timed it right, you passed through the turnstile and entered the Panorama as the dawn rose on a sleepy Wittenberg where indulgence preachers sold their wares, the town brothel in the background (its position is historically accurate). From there you passed by the outside of the massive Schlosskirche, where no-one was posting up theses, but where a monk—Luther himself, though he is not signposted as such—was expostulating to passers-by.

The Wittenberg Panorama is a tried and tested formula, and its creator, the artist Yadegar Asisi, has made panoramas of the Dresden Bombing, the Berlin Wall, Mount Everest, the Great Barrier Reef, and even the Titanic. His format evokes the vanished nineteenth-century panorama, a form of popular entertainment which was the forerunner of film. Deliberately anachronistic in the age of digital animation, it provides less rather than more realism, presenting linked frozen narrative frames rather than a moving film, around which viewers can walk at their own speed, while a soundscape and lightshow provide an overall progression. Rather than simulate the sixteenth century directly, it evokes the nineteenth, the era which gave us the monumental Luther; but it does so using present-day actors, with a series of photographs that tease us by translating the past into present-day snapshots. These are modern individuals, Photoshopped and dressed in sixteenth-century attire—and they convey the idea that we are watching a distinctively German history, with German characters. Indeed, Luther, always depicted with dark hair by Cranach, was played by a blonde Aryan.[34]

The panorama's moment of greatest drama is also a historical invention. Luther and Müntzer struggle on a bridge, as Luther tries to stop the revolutionary stabbing the elector, and if you stand in front of the scene, you can hear Luther shout: 'Clear off Müntzer, clear off!'. This fictitious fight is meant to represent Luther's support for secular authority and his opposition to Thomas Müntzer the villain (Karlstadt has been omitted from the Panorama). In the background a storm begins to rumble, lightning flashes, the lights dim, and the fires of the Peasants' War can be seen; these are the forces of darkness which stand in the way of Luther's Reformation.[35]

The Panorama is also a commentary on another monument, Werner Tübke's magnificent GDR Peasant War Panorama in Frankenhausen, which was built on the site of the rout of the peasant forces led by Müntzer to mark its 450th anniversary. Instead of celebrating the Reformation, this East German mural commemorates the defeat of the peasants, and Müntzer, not Luther, is its tragic hero. Probably the biggest painting in the world, it is 14 meters high, and 123 meters long; and it was the largest artistic commission ever made by the East German government. With cruel historic irony, it opened in September 1989, weeks before the fall of the Berlin Wall and the end of the regime which had commissioned it. Asisi's Panorama quotes from Tübke's images and echoes his design: it, too, is almost entirely circular and requires the viewer to walk along it; and it plagiarises Tübke's monstrous printing-press-cum-mine and his depiction of the artists Dürer and Cranach, reversing its heroes and villains. In Asisi's work, Müntzer and the peasants are now the ones who must be overcome if German Lutheranism is to fulfil its destiny; and Luther is the hero.

Asisi's is an arch piece of popular entertainment, aiming to create the Reformation 'experience'; Tübke's is a complex work of art, crammed with quotations from the sixteenth-century visual corpus. In one corner of Tübke's Panorama, a man based on one of Brueghel's peasants is bent double under the weight of a Bible; in another, the artist himself is shown exhausted beside the flood of lost souls (the work took him over a decade to complete after years of design); in the centre, Müntzer preaches near a version of a sixteenth-century printed prognostication, wrapped in a mysterious egg-shaped cracked bubble—each detail has the depth of reflection and the richness of inventive irony that comes from knowing the the images and artists of the sixteenth century inside out.[36] Tübke's monument is far from being a celebration of the East German regime which paid for it: Müntzer is shown at the moment of defeat, his banner is lowered, and the monument's circular progression follows the cycle of the seasons, intimating that history is not about progress. The Wittenberg Panorama, by contrast, thumbs its nose at the Frankenhausen masterpiece, as it conveys a Reformation 'experience' of a new dawn. It feels as if it is stamping on the ruins of the East German past, and whatever one may feel about the DDR regime and its policies towards its citizens,

Tübke's work of art was not a piece of pro-regime propaganda. It does not deserve this mean-spirited riposte.[37]

If the nineteenth century commemorated Luther in permanent monuments, the twenty-first seems determined to celebrate Luther in transient kitsch. The gigantic mock-up Bible that the tourist could climb has been taken down already. Even the outsize Wittenberg Panorama is a temporary monument that will only last a further five years. In terms of physical space, the Luther celebrations will leave few dedicated monuments behind.

And yet Luther kitsch is itself a significant cultural phenomenon. After all, it has historic roots. Eisleben, the place where Luther was born and ironically also died, probably sold pottery swans to Luther tourists as early as the sixteenth century;[38] and Luther beer mugs, Luther tiles, and Luther book bindings were part of popular culture from at least 1550 on.[39] Framed prints were on sale in the nineteenth century for Luther tourists to remember Wittenberg,[40] and Lutheran preachers were early complaining about the use of 'Luther splinters' against tooth ache,[41] while Luther's ring, worn piously by Elector John George I until on his deathbed in 1656, became a treasured part of the Dresden Green Vault collection.[42] Most ghoulish of all was a life-size wax Luther in St Mary's Church in Halle, dressed in academic gown and doctor's hat and sitting at his desk, his hands and face supposedly modelled from the plaster casts made from his corpse in 1546: probably destroyed in the 1930s, now only the death mask and casts of the hands remain, decorously displayed in a side room at the back of the church.[43]

No other Protestant sect has generated a material culture approaching the historical richness of Lutheranism,[44] and of no other sixteenth-century reformer do we have the same number of portraits. As chapter 1 showed, Cranach's workshop made Luther's face well known from the outset, and one important way the movement created identity was through circulating images of its founder that were immediately recognisable. From the mid-sixteenth century onwards, Luther's image was printed on a range of material objects—but always as himself, with his lumpy, fleshy face, so that he could hardly be mistaken for a saint. Lutheran churches were beautiful, filled with painted altarpieces, grand organs, stunning mannerist balconies, impressive pulpits, and images of the reformer himself; Lutherans developed their own church aesthetic that was far from austere.[45] Lutherans felt comfortable with their faith taking material forms, and this is partly because Luther himself was so positive about the natural world and about the human body, with its messy and sinful aspects.[46] This was a man who could joke that if you want to make a vow, you should vow not to bite off your own nose, for that was a vow you could keep—an anti-clerical joke with a saucy innuendo, since the nose could stand for the penis.[47]

Attitudes like these meant that Lutherans were not worried about combining the material and the spiritual in the way that Calvinists were. Like Catholics, they believed that Christ was really present in the sacrament—Luther insisted that the bread was both bread and at the same time the body of Christ, the wine both wine and Christ's blood. If reason could not explain how this was possible, then so much the worse for reason—whereas Calvin's instinct was to separate divine and earthly things, and treat the mass as a memorial. Calvinists were iconoclasts; Luther lauded images. Calvinists regulated sexuality and morals; Luther could joke about these issues and stressed the importance of suiting pastoral advice to circumstances, not rules— a stance which got him into trouble more than once. As a result, Lutherans were not allergic to material objects that commemorated their hero, and by producing kitsch, they avoided turning these objects into relics to celebrate a saintly founder.[48]

Why did kitsch feature so prominently in 2017, insinuating itself into all the rituals and even replacing monuments themselves? It is striking that so much of the Luther kitsch was edible—Luther marzipan, Luther chocolates, Luther pasta, Luther cookie-cutters—literally bite-sized. It had to be worn, like the socks; or you had to interact with it, shaking your 'Luther-in-the-snow' to make the plastic flakes whirl around the stout reformer, or putting together your own Playmobil Luther. As we saw in chapter 6, Playmobil Luther was actually based on the nineteenth-century Luther monument on the Wittenberg town square, and it owed perhaps even more to Otto Hörl's plastic Luther replica, part of his art installation of 2010. As Hörl's wonderful artwork demonstrated, if you change the size of a monument, you transform its meaning: once he is barely a meter high, Luther becomes

7.11. Martin Luther
rubber duck.
Photo by John Cairns.

not a hero but something more akin to a garden gnome. Hörl made us reflect on monumentality, German historicism, and national identity. He made us ask what the positioning of a nineteenth-century Luther statue on the main square, under its Schinkel baldacchino, might tell us about the constructed nature of hero worship.[49]

In 2017, however, Hörl's work itself became kitsch: you could buy one in your favorite colour for only €500. Many exhibition organizers did just that, and used plastic Luthers as signposts. One wag managed to present the pope with his own. In a sense, the Playmobil Luther of 2015 marked a logical progression from the nineteenth-century monument and from Hörl's installation, for now Luther was pocket-sized. In place of a single nineteenth-century monument, we had a tiny figurine which, like Luther's works in the sixteenth century, enjoyed a massive print run—over a million were sold.

Above all, however, Luther kitsch was funny. It involved the senses, it was about eating and play, and it punctured any pomposity about the reformer. This, too, reflected a powerful trait of Luther's, his sense of humour and his ability to laugh at himself—unusual for a sixteenth-century reformer. It allowed German nationalism to be treated with irony. When you can put a monument in your pocket, it loses its power to overawe, and it cannot become a focus for a grand ritual event; it has ceded its claim to space.

The secular attempt in 2017 to make Luther a national hero, and to honour him as the founder of the German language, will probably be judged a failure. But this could also be seen as a success. Once Thomas Kaufmann's book on Luther's anti-Semitism became known, Luther could not be a hero, nor could he be lauded as the first modern man. The fact that it was not possible to rekindle a sense of national identity around Luther is itself a major achievement: where Luther has been yoked to national goals, as he was in the late nineteenth and early twentieth centuries, the result has been nationalistic in the worst ways. In 2017 the Luther celebrations did not answer the question of what German culture is or what a German identity might mean in a country welcoming thousands of migrants, and neither did they become the forum for such a discussion. But this is perhaps just as it should be—though these issues certainly shaped the celebrations, 'German-ness' should not have captured them.

Did Luther bridge the gap between Protestant and Catholic? Certainly, many Catholics worked with Lutheran churches and the celebrations often featured cross-confessional events. The Catholic Church now offers laity communion in both kinds and are converging with Protestants on many important issues. Germany's religious map is very different today: where once just about everyone in West Germany paid their church taxes, these days there are also sizeable groups of atheists and agnostics or disillusioned church members who are no longer willing to pay. There are important groups of Muslims and Jews, and it might be argued that the attempts at ecumenical dialogue, encouraging though they were, were less good at reaching out either to Muslims or to those of no faith at all.

Sometimes the best monuments are transient. If the aim was to nurture a new German cultural identity, free of the weight of the history of Nazi Germany, then the Luther celebrations did not succeed. The ritual events did not create a unified collective and those who participated often did so on their own, not as part of a group. The summer sleepover, which was intended to reawaken faith through joining people together in a shared and quite physically demanding experience as well as through participation in liturgy, may have inspired many, and was a profoundly lay event. But it could not appeal to all Germans—indeed, it may even have irritated the many non-religious Wittenberg locals—and it was a denominational event. With the practical demands of tourism dictating the timetable, by the time the public holiday that should have been the anniversary's climax came along, the whole celebration had fizzled out. In the short run, the commemoration could not bring East and West together, and though Saxony and Thuringia did become tourist destinations, it remains to be seen whether this will have a lasting effect. Given the almost complete silence about the Peasants' War, Karlstadt, Müntzer, and those who took different lines on the sacrament from Luther, what the celebrations 'forgot' may be as important as what they 'remembered'. As any historian who works on Luther knows, this is contested terrain, and never more so as Germany has to tactfully negotiate its growing power within Europe. Perhaps, after all, the Playmobil Luther is the best monument to the *Lutherjahr* of 2017, with its whimsy, its refusal to capture public space in a permanent or nationalist monument, its irony, and its limitations.

# ACKNOWLEDGEMENTS

THIS BOOK GREW out of my experiences in 2017, the 500th anniversary of the posting of the 95 Theses. I had just published a biography of Luther, but had never intended to produce one timed for the anniversary: I was simply eight years late delivering the manuscript. So I was totally unprepared for what happened next.

Luther took over my life. I gave over a hundred talks and met extraordinary people: Lutheran bishops, women pastors of the German Lutheran Church, Anglican priests, Lutheran theologians, northern British evangelicals. I met Catholics in Dublin and Lutherans in Kentish Town, and spoke from on top of a box in the eighteenth-century Lutheran Church in Whitechapel. I met people who averred that Luther's anti-papalism had not gone far enough, and I was heckled in Dublin by a woman who insisted she was a Russian princess. I met the pastor of the Ulm Minster, who took me high up into the ceiling and dizzying spires of the cathedral, once the tallest in Europe. I made friends in Wittenberg and attended a conference in Jerusalem in Hebrew on Luther, which finished with sausage and pretzels in a crusader monastery. I met people who idolised Luther, and people who could not abide him. And I met many who were not religious at all, but who were just interested in the man.

As Luther would have understood, this book grew out of the spoken word and it was intended to entertain, to provoke, and to explore ideas. The fact that Lutherans are passionately interested in their subject but equally passionately committed to debate and to questioning authorities of all kinds means that they can welcome someone who is a woman, who is not German, and who is not even a Lutheran. They are a marvellous audience.

The ideas and early versions of these lectures were tried out at the Wiles Lectures which I gave in Belfast in 2015, and I'm grateful to Peter Gray and to the audience and their excellent questions. The Wiles Lectures provide a unique opportunity for scholars to discuss their work with other scholars over the period of a week, and rather like Luther's *Table Talk*, intellectual work is done after dinner, over drinks. Gadi Algazi, Scott Dixon, Renate Dürr, Peter Gray, Joel Harrington, Bridget Heal, Kat Hill, Colin Kidd, Charlotte Methuen, Jenny Spinks, Steve Smith, Ulrike Strasser, and Alex Walsham all gave up time to talk about Luther, and many of their insights, and those of the audience, are in this book. Amongst the murals of Belfast, Catholic and Protestant, we even encountered a Luther mural almost hidden behind a high wire fence, beside a bulldozer. Belfast also taught me how long sectarian hatreds can endure, and forced me to take seriously some of the less pleasant aspects of Luther's legacy.

A revised and different selection of the lectures was delivered at Princeton as the Lawrence Stone Lectures in 2016, and I am grateful to Angela Creager, Nigel Smith, Joan Scott, Tony Grafton, Linda Colley, and David Cannadine, and to the wonderful graduate students I met there. Another version was given as the Miriam Yardeni lectures in Jerusalem, Tel Aviv, and Haifa. This was a life-changing experience, and I am grateful to Gadi Algazi, Yossi Ziegler, Dror Wahrmann, David Katz, and to all those who made it possible.

Several artists in particular made me see Luther differently. My friend Miranda Creswell helped me think about portraiture and visited a Dutch exhibition of Werner Tübke's remarkable work with me. Neel Korteweg showed me her magnificent Luther portraits in Amsterdam and came to London to discuss her work at the National Portrait Gallery. Erwin Wurm's studio has been immensely helpful; and I am indebted to Uwe Pfeifer, who provided a photograph of his wonderful Luther triptych, and explained his intentions in his artwork of 1983–84. And I would never have seen the fantastic *Luther und die Avantgarde* exhibition had it not been for the insistence of Charlotte Methuen; and I might not have discovered Song Dong's *Prison within Prison* if Eva Loeber of the Cranach-Stiftung Wittenberg had not taken me there.

Many people have added to my collection of Luther kitsch. I would especially like to thank Hole Rößler of the Wolfenbüttel Herzog

August Library, whose Luther duck I filched; and Stefan Weszkalnys, Tobias Raubuch, and the Lutheran Church of the Saarland, who sent the History Faculty one of their electric blue gigantic heads of Luther packed in an outsize wooden crate: alas, when it arrived, Luther's head had cracked clean off his neck. I cannot now remember who asked me about Luther's facial hair, and it took many years for me to realize just how helpful a question this was. I am grateful to all those who shared their dreams with me. The Early Modern Workshop provided cake, grapes, and coffee and steered me through conceptual logjams.

The award of the Gerda Henkel Preis made it possible for me to write the book, and I would like to thank the committee and the staff of the Henkel Foundation and the Foundation for its generosity. The Wiles Foundation generously allowed me to publish the book with Princeton University Press, and assisted its publication financially. The Fell Fund of the University of Oxford provided research assistance and publication support. My colleagues at the University of Oxford have assisted me in so many ways, and I am grateful to the then chair of the History Faculty, Martin Conway, who enabled me to travel during 2016–17. In Wittenberg, the staff of the Lutherhalle have been unfailingly helpful, and I would like in particular to thank Jutta Strehle, who has done so much to open up the treasures of the Lutherhalle to the public and to assist scholars. The Herzog-August Bibliothek has been extremely helpful and I would like to thank the Director Peter Burschel, Hole Rößler, and Ulrike Gleixner for their advice and inspiration, and for the marvellous exhibition *Luthermania*.

So many individuals have contributed to this book that I cannot remember who they all are, so I apologize if I have forgotten anyone. I owe a particular debt to my students who took the Luther Special Subject at the University of Oxford. I would like to thank Mette Ahlefeldt-Laurvig, Charlotte Appel, Nick Baines, Giulia Bartrum, Wolfgang Behringer, Paul Betts, Johannes Block, Sue Bottigheimer, Susanna Burghartz, Mark Byford, Patrick Cane, Charles Colville, Natalie Zemon Davis, Irene Dingel, Martin Dinges, Michael Drolet, Renate Duerr, Dagmar Engels, Liz Fidlon, Etienne François, Robert Gildea, Daniel Görres, Laura Gowing, Bruce Gordon, Stephen Green, Robin Griffith-Jones, Rebekka Habermas, Christa Haemmerle, Amalie Häntsch, Tim Harris, Pastor Maring Helmer-Phan Xuan, Daniel

Hess, Olenka Horbatsch, Jan Hennings, Adalbert Hepp, Tamar Hertzig, Michael Hunter, Geert Jansen, Daniel Jütte, Robert Jütte, Susan Karant-Nunn, David Katz, Annette Kehnel, Chris Kissane, Valerie Kivelson, Sarah Knott, Manfred Krebs, Simone Laqua, Hermione Lee, Volker Leppin, Alison Light, Andreas Loewe, Machteld Löwensteijn, Peter Macardle, Jan Machielsen, Julian Masters, Hans Medick, Erik Midelfort, Birgit Münch, Hannah Murphy, Johannes Paulmann, Helmut Puff, Glynn Redworth, Mathias Riedl, Tom Robisheaux, Ailsa Roper, Cath Roper, Carla Roth, Miri Rubin, Renate Schmidtkunz, Luisa Schorn-Schütte, Anselm Schubert, Alex Shepard, Nina Sillem, Peter Sillem, Pat Simons, Ruth Slenczka, Jeffrey C. Smith, Philip Soergel, Andreas Stahl, Nick Stargardt, Willibald Steinmetz, Barbara Taylor, Sarah Toulalan, Amanda Vickery, Ed Wareham, Bernd Weisbrod, Ulrike Weckel, Gisa Weszkalnys, Stefan Weszkalnys, Chris Wickham, Merry Wiesner, Karin Woerdemann, Anthony Wright, Heide Wunder, Sylvie Zannier-Betts, and Yossi Ziegler. They are not, of course, responsible for its errors.

The late Marianne Adams taught me German at school and then at university, and her fierce hatred of Luther for his views on women was a deeper influence on me than I realized. Charles Zika inspired me to become a historian of sixteenth-century Germany. Jenny Spinks has helped me work with visual materials; she also read and commented on most of the chapters. I have learnt much from Christiane Andersson and Pat Simons; and I am grateful to the History Faculty at Michigan for advice and discussion. Gunnar Heydenreich shared his immense knowledge of the Cranach corpus with me; the members of the Luther portraits project at the Germanisches Nationalmuseum Nuremberg were generous with advice. Tim Wilson, Matthew Winterbottom, and Jim Harris introduced me to the Ashmolean's holdings and I profited from their course on material culture. Long ago, Hartmut Lehmann made me think about Luther's legacy in the USA and in Australia. Kat Hill's work on the cultures of Lutheranism has paralleled my own, and I have learnt hugely from her creative intelligence. Thomas Kaufmann has been an indulgent critic, and a true friend: I owe a great deal to his open-mindedness. Henrike Lähnemann and I worked together on Luther celebrations in Oxford, and we are all indebted to her linguistic, book historical, and musical skills.

Clare Alexander, my agent, has been a rock of support. Peter and Nina Sillem, my friends and publishers in Germany, were behind the project from the outset; Tanja Hommen helped make it happen, and Karin Woerdemann's eagle eyes spotted mistakes and improved interpretations. At Princeton University Press, Brigitta van Rheinberg sat down with me and showed me what the book was about; Eric Crahan and Priya Nelson have been its supportive editors; and Thalia Leaf and Sara Lerner energetically moved it along; Bethan Winter did a superb proofread. Wendy Washburn's copy-editing was always right; David Luljak compiled a superb index; and Kourtnay King was a fantastic picture sourcer. Rosi Bartlett inspired me to think about how to communicate with an audience; Simon Ponsonby read and commented on the chapter on the Jews and shared his insights on Luther over cups of coffee, as did Pastor Block of the Wittenberg Stadtkirche. Daniel Pick suggested how to think about Luther psychoanalytically, and Mike Roper's insights are everywhere in this book. Ulinka Rublack, whose work I so admire, showed how to think about Luther and material culture. Clare Copeland read the book, edited it, found the images, spotted many mistakes, compiled the bibliography, and also told me that I needed to write one more chapter. As ever, she was right. My warmest thanks to her.

Ruth Harris read every chapter not once but many times. Most of the ideas in this book arose from conversations with her, as she made me see how to do the history of religion differently and showed me why Luther is not a hero. She is a wonderful friend and her contribution to this book is immense. My son Sam Stargardt asked great questions and helped me finish. When it comes to religion, my stepson Anand Narsey never lets me get away with answers that are less than honest. Eugene and Mary Donnelly helped me understand Catholicism, and their family welcomed me warmly. Finally, another Martin, Martin Donnelly, supported me, went with me to many of these places, spotted images of Luther in the strangest settings, and asked questions I usually could not answer.

# NOTES

## ABBREVIATIONS

LW      *Luther's Works,* Philadelphia, 1957–.

VD 16   Verzeichnis der im deutschen Sprachbereich erschienenen Drucke des
        16. und 17. Jahrhunderts.

WB      *D. Martin Luthers Werke: Kritische Gesamtausgabe,* Briefe, 18 vols.

WDB     *D. Martin Luthers Werke: Kritische Gesamtausgabe,* Deutsche Bibel, 15 vols.

WS      *D. Martin Luthers Werke: Kritische Gesamtausgabe,* Schriften, 72 vols.,
        Weimar, 1903

WT      *D. Martin Luthers Werke: Kritische Gesamtausgabe,* Tischreden, 6 vols.

## PREFACE

1. The pulpit is figuratively Luther's. The pulpit in the church today is neo-Gothic;
   Luther's first pulpit was a simple wooden affair dating from the late fifteenth
   century, a small 'wine glass pulpit' and not apparently very high. It was later
   replaced by the Town Council with the 'great pulpit'. See Gutjahr et al., *Martin
   Luther. 95 Treasures. 95 People,* 264–65: it was destroyed during the French occupa-
   tion in 1806 and the fragments rediscovered and reassembled in 1883; Bellmann,
   Harksen, and Werner, *Die Denkmale der Lutherstadt Wittenberg,* 177, 273.
2. Kaufmann, *Luther's Jews,* 26.

## INTRODUCTION

1. It was also in part financed by the state. Funds from the German Federal Foreign
   Office supported the Google online version of the massive exhibitions that were
   held in the USA; committees for celebrating the quincentenary were formed
   at the behest of the embassy in many countries and there were funds for which
   one could apply; Goethe Institutes internationally were actively engaged in celebrating Luther.
2. Kaufmann, *Luther's Jews.*
3. Roper, *Oedipus and the Devil,* 146–69.

4. Roper, *Martin Luther*, 321–42.
5. WT 2, no. 1555, 130; 1975, 285; 'Rhetorica ist, wenn einer wol waschen kan; dialectica, wenn einer dasselbig wol verstet'. WA TR 5, no. 5987, 417.
6. On Bugenhagen, see Baumann, Krüger, and Kuhl, eds., *Luthers Norden*; on Cochlaeus and his relationship with Luther, see Roper, 'The Seven-Headed Monster'.
7. Thomas Müntzer, *Hoch verursachte Schutzrede*, in *Kritische Gesamtausgabe*, vol. 1, 388; Matheson, *Thomas Müntzer*, 338.
8. Mundt, *Lemnius und Luther*, II, 143.
9. Luther's Bible has, in its 1534 edition, 'Wenn ich meine seele nicht setzet vnd stillet, So ward meine seele entwenet, wie einer von seiner mutter entwenet wird'. This is a somewhat contorted sentence, grammatically hard to disentangle, and in the first printing of the Psalter the 'und' was mistakenly repeated by the printer. The sentence means, loosely translated, 'if I, my soul, does not still and quieten itself, then it would be weaned like a child from its mother'; that is to say, the weaning is a threat and is not a positive experience. Most translations of the passage, including the Vulgate, do not interpret the passage along these lines, but see the child as at peace with the mother from whom it has weaned itself. Since Luther often refers to the child as a 'baby', this was an important passage for him. I am grateful to Henrike Lähnemann for help in interpreting this passage. See chapter 2.
10. Erwin Wurm, 'Boxhandschuh', 2016, photograph in Smerling, ed., *Luther und die Avantgarde*, 308–11; it is described as 'signal red' but seemed to me to be orange.
11. Song Dong, 'Prison in Prison', 2017, photograph in Smerling, *Luther und die Avantgarde*, 276; when I was there in summer 2017, the transparent boiled sweets could be removed and shared.
12. Around sixty-five artists took over the cells of the prison. There were also associated shows in Kassel and Berlin. Artists involved included Gilbert & George, Ai Weiwei, Alexander Kluger, Csilla Kudor, and Zhang Huan—and many others. Smerling himself, whose idea it was, held lectures and guided tours.
13. For the catalogue that finally begins to make the extent of the Lutheran contribution to church art evident, at least in the North, see Steiger, *Gedächtnisorte der Reformation*; and on the rich material culture of Prussia and Brandenburg, see the exhibition and catalogue by Slenczka, ed., *Reformation und Freiheit*.

## Chapter 1. The Luther Cranach Made

1. Erasmus is the other obvious comparison, and portraits by Massys, Holbein, and Dürer made his face known around the same time. But many of these portraits were commissions, not mass-produced woodcuts, and did not have as wide a circulation as Luther's portraits began to have.
2. Many of Cranach's invoices survive, so we know what paint products he used; he imported materials from Frankfurt as well as Leipzig fairs, which were themselves imported from further away. See Heydenreich, *Lucas Cranach the Elder*,

NOTES TO CHAPTER I

130–31. Luther's interest in cloth in Cranach's workshop is noted in WB 2, 287, 13 May 1520. For the complex history of the workshop buildings, see the definitive Hennen, '"Cranach 3D"; see also Cranach-Stiftung, *Lucas Cranach d. Ä.* On Cranach, see Ozment, *The Serpent and the Lamb.* For a brilliant exploration of their relationship, see Körner, *The Moment of Self-Portraiture in German Renaissance Art.*

3. Luther, letter to Cranach after the Diet of Worms: WB 2, 400, 28 April 1521, p. 305. Katharina von Bora lodged in Cranach's house before she married Luther.

4. For marriage jokes, WT 1, 814; WT 4, 4847; WT 5, 5524. Apple pips: WT 3, 3210.

5. WT 4, 4787.

6. Dürer was a presence in Wittenberg too: his *Martyrdom of the Ten Thousand* had been painted for the Wittenberg Schlosskirche in 1508, where it sat alongside Cranach's work: Heydenreich, *Lucas Cranach the Elder*, 298.

7. Heydenreich, *Lucas Cranach the Elder*, 22: the idea that he was fast seems to have stemmed from the Nuremberger Christoph Scheurl who eulogises it in a letter of 1508. Speed was taken to be an indication of skill and Cranach's grave reads 'pictor cellerimus'.

8. Georg Mylius refers to a whole series of techniques for multiplying images in his funeral speech for Cranach the Younger: Heydenreich, *Lucas Cranach the Elder*, 23.

9. There are indications of other artists, such as the mysterious Stefan Schmelzer, who seems to have been independent but also worked occasionally for Cranach: no existing work of art has been ascribed to him (Hennen, '"Cranach 3D"'), but he did receive a stipend from the elector; another independent artist and craftsman in Cranach's circle was Simprecht Reinhart. Thomas Lang, 'Simprecht Reinhart: Formscheider, Maler, Drucker Bettmeister—Spuren eines Leben sim Schatten von Lucas Cranach d. Ä'. In Lück et al., eds., *Das ernestische Wittenberg.*

10. Even the picture formats became standardized: between 1520 and 1535, 70 per cent of the workshop's single panels fell into one of six standard sizes; see Heydenreich, '". . . That You Paint with Wonderful Speed",' in Brinkmann, *Cranach*, 29–30. See also Heydenreich, *Lucas Cranach the Elder*, 297–301. The workshop often worked from sketches which were then transferred, sometimes by means of pierced holes on the original design with the lines then drawn by brush; see for example, an investigation of a Luther portrait from c. 1540 examined with infrared light in Sandner, *Unsichtbare Meisterzeichnungen*, 132–3. The original workshop designs with holes pricked through survive for portraits of both Luther and Katharina von Bora. On Luther as designer, working with the workshop, see Grimm, 'Die Anteile', in Sandner, ibid.

11. See Enke, Schneider, and Strehle, *Lucas Cranach der Jüngere.*

12. For a brilliant discussion of the images of Luther between 1519 and 1525, see Scribner, *For the Sake of Simple Folk*, 14–36.

13. It is, however, missing the cross and heart which were part of the full design.

14. See Warnke, *Cranachs Luther*, 32.

15. *(Ein) Sermon kürzlich gepredigt und dabei den Verstand, wieviel Kraft die heiligen Evangelien über die Concilia haben* (Erfurt, 1522) and VD 16 L 6200, final page. For a catalogue of images of Luther in printed books held by the HAB Wolfenbüttel, see Maria von Katte, *Katalog der Wolfenbütteler Luther-Drucke 1513 bis 1546*, in the online resources of the Herzog August Bibliothek, Wolfenbüttel (http://lutherkat.hab.de).

16. Warnke, *Cranachs Luther*, and see Eser, 'Martin Luther im Habit eines Augustinermönchs', Catalogue entry, in Eser and Armer, eds., *Luther, Kolumbus und die Folgen*, 76. There are only two copies from the original plate, possibly test printings, one in Washington and one in the Albertina, Vienna; a third, in Coburg, is from the second state of the original, which includes a doodle of a man with a beard, and which can be dated by the watermark on the paper to between 1540 and 1550. All the other surviving ones date from after Luther's death and show the doodle in fainter form: Messling, *Die Welt des Lucas Cranach*, 219.

17. Messling, *Die Welt des Lucas Cranach*, 219–20.

18. See Maria von Katte, *Katalog der Wolfenbütteler Luther-Drucke 1513 bis 1546*, in the online resources of the Herzog August Bibliothek, Wolfenbüttel (http://lutherkat.hab.de), for portraits of Luther.

19. The University had only been founded in 1502; see Roper, *Martin Luther*, 77–103.

20. Originally published in Latin, *On the Babylonian Captivity* was soon translated into German—ironically by his opponent Thomas Murner, who thus secured it an even larger audience.

21. Hans Baldung Grien, *Martin Luther als Augustinermönch*, in Martin Luther, 'Acta et res gestae D. Martini Lutheri', in *Comitiis Principum Vuormaciae* [VD 16 ZV 61], Strasbourg 1521, f. 3 v. For a discussion, see Toussaint, 'Luther wird heilig', 150–53.

22. The papal legate Aleander complained that portraits of Luther with a halo were being sold in Augsburg, and images without the halo were selling like hotcakes in Worms; Toussaint, 'Luther wird heilig', 151.

23. Hans Schwarz attended the Diet and made many medals of the participants. The Victoria and Albert Museum collections include a medal of Franz von Sickingen after Hans Schwarz, dated 1521: Museum Number 274–1864; there is a gilded bronze medal of Charles V from 1521 by Hans Schwarz at the Walters Art Museum, Accession Number 54, 1011.

24. See Warnke, *Cranachs Luther*, 40–49. The medal of Luther, closely based on the Cranach profile portrait and dated 1521, exists only in a one-sided copy, in lead (now held at Gotha, Schloss Friedenstein) and silver (Berlin Coin Collection), and was probably made at the time of the Diet; Kluttig-Altman, *Martin Luther. Treasures of the Reformation*, 163.

25. Daniel Hopfer, 'Portrait of Martin Luther', British Museum, 1845,0809.1371. Albrecht Altdorfer, 'Martin Luther with Doctoral Cap'; see, for example, the copy at the Metropolitan Museum of Art, 20.64.18: only 'D.M.L.' in a frame above the reformer's head indicates that it is Luther. The profile is framed by a round

classicizing wreath and the rest of the surrounding picture space is decorated with fashionable mannerist vegetative forms. There is also a medal from 1521 based on this profile portrait; Kluttig-Altmann, *Martin Luther*, 163.

26. I am grateful to Christiane Andersson for pointing this out. H. S. Beham, 'Luther as Evangelist, after Cranach's engraving': see Max Geisberg, *Die deutsche Buch-illustration* VI, No. 605, and used in *Apostolorum Romanum non venisse*, Nuremberg 1520, and *Das new Testament Deutsch* (Nuremberg, Hans Herrgott, 1524).

27. Kalkoff, *Depeschen des Nuntius Aleander*, 133.

28. Lucas Cranach d A., Luther as Junker Jörg, British Museum O,3.190: 'Though so often sought and persecuted by Rome, I, Luther, still live by Jesus Christ in undeniable hope. As long as I have this, farewell perfidious Rome!' The woodcut has three parallel paragraphs below the image which explain the significance of three historical dates: 1521 and Worms, 1522 Luther in his Patmos, and 1522, Luther's return, an organization that suggests this woodcut is itself part of the creation of the history of Luther. For a description of the image and a reproduction including the bottom section, see Kluttig-Altmann, *Martin Luther*, 204.

29. For some time it remained important to distance the elector from Luther's actions; see Roper, *Martin Luther*, 230–33.

30. WS 10 part 3, 1:13; one printed version of the *Invocavit* sermons mentions that they were preached as Luther returned from his 'Pathmos'; the other does not.

31. See, on this image, Warnke, *Cranachs Luther*, 49–51; and Kluttig-Altmann, *Martin Luther*, 204, for Wolfgang Holler's translation of the Latin verses. The image is commonly taken to have been printed in 1522 or 1521/2; but the date on the image refers to the point in Luther's life; some have argued that it is a reverse copy of Cranach's painting of Luther as Junker Jörg and so must have been produced later than the paintings. There are several versions of the woodcut including one which is reversed and attributed to Hans Sebald Beham. The Latin inscriptions, when German might have been more usual at this point, together with the imprecations against the Pope and the historicising strategies of the image, suggest that the woodcut may date from a later period than 1522, inspired by an interest in Luther's biography. It certainly forms part of the narrative of Luther, the great reformer, returning in support of Saxony (Luther's luxuriously tended beard is very similar to the Cranach studio's representations of Frederick the Wise's beard) and quashing Karlstadt and the radical Reformation in Wittenberg. Hans Brosamer's 'Seven-headed Luther' of 1529 includes a 'Martinus' head with beard and moustache which could perhaps be said to resemble Cranach's image, but the head hides under a capacious hood which is absent from the Cranach original: does this mean that the Brosamer image is indebted to the Cranach Junker Jörg and must therefore have been current by 1529, or does the addition of the hood suggest that it owes nothing to Cranach's Junker Jörg? On the myth-making around Luther's return, see Krentz, *Ritualwandel und Deutungshoheit*, and, now, Thomas Kaufmann, *Neues von 'Junker Jörg'*.

32. WS 10, 3, p. 7.

33. The Muskegon Museum of Art, Michigan, US_MMA_39–5. The Museum links this picture to another of Katharina von Bora with a green background also by the Cranach workshop, and since the bearded Luther picture is dated 1537, it concludes the other must be the matching half, dating it as 1537 too. The painting was restored in 2013–14 (see http://www.baumanconservation.com/SolvingTheCranachMystery.html), and in the course of the restoration it became clear that there were two inscriptions on the Luther portrait, now faded, one reading 'Propheta Germanvs anno 1521' and a lower inscription, 'Pestis eram vivens moriens ero mors tva papa', a slogan which became widely attached to images of the reformer after his death (see chapter 5). The Muskegon painting restoration also turned up a similar painting pair in a church in the Saxon town of Penig, dated 1537, which is not currently included in the Cranach Digital Archive (www.lucascranach.org), and to which the portrait in Muskegon seems to be closely related; it also includes the imprecation 'Living I was your plague'—though the Penig version looks less obviously like an original Cranach. (See, for a reproduction, Wartburg-Stiftung, *Luther und die Deutschen*, 216.) There may also be another version of this '1537' pair in private possession in Switzerland.

   However, there remain problems with these works. It is probable that the two other paintings of Luther as Junker Jörg which *are* included in the Cranach Digital Archives at the time of writing are also of a later date, long after his return from the Wartburg, and are part of the historicising of Luther and his life story; the one at the Museum der bildenden Kuenste in Leipzig is presumed to be from 1521, and that in Weimar, Klassik Stiftung Weimar, from 1521–22, but there is no dating or signature on either painting. A version in the Royal Collection UK, RCIN 402656, is now thought to be a copy of a Cranach. Thomas Kaufmann has argued persuasively that these portraits of the bearded Luther relate to Luther's near death at Schmalkalden in 1537 (Kaufmann, *Neues von Junker Jörg*), and this would explain the 'Living I was your plague' caption, since Luther supposedly made this remark at that point; but this might not prove that the other two portraits at Leipzig and Weimar were not taken to be portraits of 'Junker Jörg' whenever they were painted; they also lack a matching portrait of Katharina. The 1537 date on the Muskegon painting would not definitively prove that the portraits date from that year. I am very grateful to Thomas Kaufmann for sharing his work with me.

34. I am grateful to Daniel Görres, Daniel Hess, Anselm Schubert, and Amalie Häntsch of the Critical Catalogue of Luther Portraits (1519–1530), Germanisches National Museum, for their advice.

35. See for example the copy in the British Museum London, Museum Number, O,3.190. There may be an original drawing on which it was based.

36. Heinrich Göding, 'Luther as Junker Jörg', dated 1598. He stands in front of Worms, not Eisenach, so he is not actually in his 'Pathmos' here; the image refers to the Diet of Worms which has preceded his move to the Wartburg.

37. The exception is the image of Katharina in the Muskegon Gallery, US_MMA_39–6. The painting is said to date from 1537, although only the Luther

portrait includes a date and his portrayal as a monk is problematic: see n. 31 above. Three other post-1530 double portraits are included in the Cranach Digital Archive, but they are copies based on Cranach the Elder's originals, not workshop productions. So far as I know, there is no image of Luther and Katharina von Bora produced by Cranach the Younger, although he did produce double portraits of Melanchthon and Luther.

38. National Gallery of Art, Washington, D.C., US_NGA_1959-9-1; see http://www.lucascranach.org/US_NGA_1959-9-1.

39. Heydenreich, *Lucas Cranach the Elder*, 78–81. The pair originally owned by the Landgraves of Hesse and now in the Hessisches Landesmuseum Darmstadt, Inv.-Nr. GK 73, still has the original hinges; see Ermischer and Tacke, *Cranach im Exil*, 286–7. The circular forms resemble the carved double portraits of princes and their wives or concubines that can also be hidden in their round capsules.

40. See Roper, 'Venus in Wittenberg', 81–98. On the double portraits, Kluttig–Altmann, *Martin Luther*, 234–41; Baumann, Krüger, and Kuhl, eds., *Luthers Norden*, 72–6.

41. See Meller, *Fundsache Luther*, 322–23.

42. Hans Brosamer, *Martin Luther*, 1530, printed by Wolfgang Resch, measuring 364 × 284 mm. There is a matching woodcut of Katharina von Bora. See Geisberg and Strauss, *The German Single-Leaf Woodcut*, 1: 391. This image of the reformer influenced the medallion-like green 'Luther tiles' which were produced after Luther's death for decorating the ceramic heating stoves that were used in Germany at this time: Kluttig-Altmann, *Martin Luther. Treasures of the Reformation*, 379, object 392. Interestingly, Brosamer is also credited with the anti-Lutheran 'Seven-Headed Luther' image which fronted Johannes Cochlaeus's *Sieben kopffe Martin Lutthers*, Dresden 1529 [VD 16 C 4389, 4390, 4391]; the 'Doctor' and the 'Ecclesiastes' heads caricature Cranach's versions of about the same period. See also Warnke, *Cranachs Luther*, 51–54.

43. Syndram, Wirth, and Wagner, *Luther und die Fürsten*, Katalog, 96–98.

44. De Luca and Fara, *I volti della Riforma*, especially de Luca, 'I volti della Riforma nelle collezioni granducali', 43–47, and Catalogue, 64–68. In addition to the double portrait of Katharina and Luther of 1529 from the Cranach workshop, they had a double portrait of Luther and Melanchthon from 1543. I am most grateful to Francesca de Luca who took me through the exhibition, and to Giovanni Maria Fara for his help.

45. *Martin Luther after Lucas Cranach the Elder*, etching (1525), National Portrait Gallery London, NPG D47378. See NPG D47387 for a rather poor engraving copy of the Katharina image by Engelhardt Nunzer, c. 1692–1733, who also produced a copy of Martin Luther; this one appears to be a copy of the pair from 1526.

46. I am indebted to Jutta Strehle, who curated the exhibition at Wittenberg in 2017 in which this was included and who sent me a copy. Unfortunately there was no catalogue for this excellent exhibition. See, however, Jöstel and Strehle, *Luthers Bild und Lutherbilder*, 23–25.

47. See, for example, the pair from 1532, now in the Dresden Gemäldegalerie Alte Meister, Nrs. 1918, 1919. On this pairing, produced particularly in 1532–33, see Marx and Mössinger, *Cranach*, 473–79: there is evidence that techniques of reproduction were used on the image.

48. There are also triple versions, which include Bugenhagen, Luther's confessor and the parish priest of Wittenberg: see, for example, that from the National Trust Collection, NT 129808, held at Knole, Kent, produced by a follower of Cranach at some time between 1560 and 1599.

49. Medals were an early favoured medium for representing Luther's face. Produced throughout his lifetime, they proved an enduring form for commemoration; the three-quarter format commonly used owes a great deal to Cranach, and the 'head' portrait was perfectly designed for transfer to the medal form. Wolf Milicz of St Joachimstal produced medals based on the Brosamer version of Cranach's original in the 1530s; see Kluttig-Altmann, *Martin Luther. Treasures of the Reformation*, 166, no. 162, for one from 1537, fire-gilded in silver; see also Dresden Kunstsammlungen, Münzkabinett, 1914/198b, silver-gilded, and BID2545 for the same design in lead. Medals could be worn on the hat or passed from hand to hand. For book-bindings, drinking vessels, tiles, and a host of other objects with Luther portraits, see chapter 7.

50. The portraits of Müntzer and Karlstadt that we have date from after their deaths.

51. See Ottomeyer, Götzmann, and Reiß, *Heiliges Römisches Reich*, 60–61: the Bible is held in Bad Windsheim, Stadtbibliothek, Sign. I a 20, and was presented to Georg Vogler in 1536 when he visited Wittenberg. The picture is tempura on linen and has been pasted into the flyleaf; opposite it is a dedication in Luther's hand. Cranach the Younger produced a similar image for the Bible of Nikolaus of Ebeleben in 1562, Staatsbibliothek zu Berlin—Preußischer Kulturbesitz, Abt. Historische Drucke, DE_SBB_fol-12-Iv; this image owes a great deal to the Vogler Bible. It too, unlike many of the images of the reformer, shows the mighty stubble in detail. I am grateful to Patricia Simons, who drew my attention to the significance of the stubble.

52. Bellmann, Harksen, and Werner, *Die Denkmale der Lutherstadt Wittenberg*, 63. For a relief medallion portrait of Luther in sandstone carved on a pillar at the entrance of the Festsaal in Torgau, Schloss Hartenfels, see Slenczka, 'Die Reformation als Gegenstand der Herrschaftsrepresentation', 161–3; roundel portraits of Johann Friedrich and his wife Sibylle von Cleves were on either side of the doorway itself, while there was a bronze memorial tablet in the chapel commemorating not only Johann Friedrich and his sons, but also Luther, whose head appears in a roundel at the bottom (Torgauer Schlosskapelle, after 1544). Both these images of Luther were also indebted to Cranach's version of his face, as was the Croy tapestry from 1554, where the workshop supplied designs and the relationship to a large Cranach woodcut of Luther preaching is evident; Slenczka, 'Die Reformation', 167.

53. Kluttig-Altmann, 'Archäologische Funde', 384, shows one such black oven tile from Rothenburg ob der Taube, while the Tyrolean Folk Art Museum Innsbruck contains a superb green oven tile portrait of Luther; both are loosely based on Cranach designs. The position of such portraits—on the oven which was the source of heating and the centre of a household—suggests how important they were to a sense of family identity, though they might have been hidden on the back side of the oven. Luther regularly uses sayings in his writings that refer to the oven.

54. See Toussaint, 'Luther und der Teufel', 213–15, and Hecht, 'Luther bekommt Hörner', 223–27.

55. There is a marvelous depiction of Pelagius, Luther, and Mohammed, all in the flames of Hell, in the bottom half of a painting of the Assumption of Mary painted in about 1551 by Francesco da Citta di Castello and now in S. Maria in Monserrato degli Spagnoli, the Spanish church in Rome. The image owes rather less to Cranach and shows Luther as a tonsured monk in Augustinian habit in Hell; I am grateful to Martin Donnelly for spotting Luther in Hell. In a room commemorating the Farnese family in the Palazzo Farnese nearby, there is another fresco depiction, almost certainly of Luther, by Francesco Salviati, showing him with Paul III: he is depicted with the famous deep-set 'demonic' eyes, heavy jowls, broad forehead, and without a tonsure; he wears a rich fur-lined gown. This depiction from c. 1560 is not a copy of a Cranach, and the clothes he wears are not the clerical garb Cranach made famous; but Salviati may well have seen a Cranach because the face is strikingly similar even though it is painted in a very different style. On Palazzo Farnese, see Gruau, *Palazzo Farnese*, 50. There were also many hostile images of Luther in New Spain: Mayer, '"The Heresiarch that Burns in Hell".'

56. See Christensen, *Princes and Propaganda*, 48–50. On Luther's body, see Roper, 'Martin Luther's Body', 351–84.

57. Neugebauer and Lang argue that this constituted a new iconography, the memorial full-size image of the cleric. A life-size double image of Luther and Melanchthon was painted for the castle in 1562; it was destroyed in 1760 in the bombardment of Wittenberg during the Seven Years' War; Neugebauer and Lang, 'Cranach im Schloss,' 68–69.

58. On this image, see Eser, 'Riesenholzschnitte auf Martin Luther', 77. Many of them were hung in churches and the one on display in the Nuremberg exhibition had been kept in a church which originally had versions with Hus and Melanchthon in the same format. See also Jöstel and Strehler, *Luthers Bild*, 8. There was a full-body Luther on the wall of the church of Rychnowo in former Ducal Prussia from 1714 to 1718; Bahlcke, Störtkuhl, and Weber, *The Luther Effect*, 187. And a life-size Luther was discovered in Krupka, Bohemia, in 1927, painted on the wall opposite the pulpit (ibid., 272). Both images betray the influence of the Cranach full-body Luthers complete with their gigantic boots.

59. See, for example, the portrait of the preacher Caspar Eberhard by Lucas Cranach the Younger, of 1576, which is in the style of his Luthers, and is now in the church of Our Lady, the parish church, in Wittenberg; Neugebauer and Lang, 'Cranach im Schloss', 69. Lucas Cranach the Younger, *Georg III, der Gottselige, Fürst von Anhalt* (1575), Kunstsammlungen der Veste Coburg, Inv. Nr. M 360; Georg became Bishop of Merseburg and his painting is in exactly the same format as Luther's, Inv. Nr. M 304. See Braunfels, *Mit Luther durch die Kunstsammlungen*, 8–11. One remarkable altar by Cranach the Younger shows full-length depictions of Luther and Melanchthon when the two outside wings are closed; they are not shown as saints but as theological authorities—but the position they occupy in the altar's architecture is where you would expect to see a saint. Lucas Cranach the Younger, *The Vineyard Retable*, 1582, Salzwedel, Johann-Friedrich-Danneil-Museum, image in Dettmann, 'Martin Luther as a Saint?', 274.
60. For the original sketch of the dead Martin Luther, and the Cranach version with the trademark winged serpent, see Catalogue, Brinkman and Gabriel Dette, 'Portrait of Martin Luther on his Deathbed', in Brinkman, *Cranach*, 196–97; at least twenty of these paintings survive. An unnamed painter from Eisleben also sketched the reformer on his deathbed; Furtenagel had to travel from Halle.
61. Cranach Digital Archive, DE_NLMH_KM107 (Niedersächsisches Landesmuseum Hannover); DE_SKD_GG1955 (Staatliche Kunstsammlungen Dresden); one from the 'circle' of Cranach the Elder, DE_KSUL_0633–90 (Kunstsammlung der Universität Leipzig). There are three by Cranach the Younger: DE_KSUL_1951–180 (Kunstsammlung der Universität Leipzig), 1574; DE_SKD_GG1955 (Staatliche Kunstsammlungen Dresden), c. 1574?; and DE_SKK_0121, (Staatliche Kunsthalle Karlsruhe), dated c. 1600. There are other copies, for example, Deutsches Historisches Museum Berlin, DE_DHM_Gm2010–1, from after 1672.
62. See, on this image, Körner, *The Moment of Self-Portraiture*, 67–68.
63. Wolfgang Stuber, *Bildnis des Martin Luther als Hieronyumus im Gehäus*, 1587–97, Germanisches Nationalmuseum Graphische Sammlung Nuremberg St.N. 4493 Kapsel 141, obj/33700704; this version has 'FIFVS' corrected to 'VIVVS'. I am grateful to Christiane Andersson for discussion of this image. There are also some hand-coloured versions.
64. On the history of the publication of the *Table Talk*, see Junghans, 'Die Tischreden Martin Luthers', 26, and Schilling, 'Bibliographie der Tischredenausgaben', 747–60. See also Roper, 'Martin Luther's Body', and Tudor-Craig, 'Group Portraits', 87–102.
65. See, for example, 'The candle is lighted, we can not blow out', London, ca. 1620–40, published by Thomas Jenner: The British Museum, London, no. 1907,0326.31. Amongst other versions, see, published by John Garrett, a line engraving after 1673, The National Portrait Gallery, London, NPG D24005; a version from 1683, NPG D23051 and D43263; and another from 1769, 'The Primitive Reformers', NPG D 42454. Hertford College, Oxford has a painted version of this image

and I am grateful to Mia Smith for showing it to me. The iconography was also used as a design for plates, see Walsham, 'Domesticating the Reformation', 566–616. For continental versions, see, for example, *Luther in the Circle of Reformers, 1625–1660*, Deutsches Historisches Museum, GM 97/24.

66. Johannes Nas, *Sihe wie das ellend Lutherthumb, durch seine aigne verfechter, gemartert, Anatomiert, gemetzget, zerhackt, zerschnitten, gesotten, gebraten, und letzlich gantz auffgefressen wirdt* [Ingolstadt, 1568], The British Museum, London, no. 1880,0710.336. See also, on a related image, Spinks, 'Monstrous Births and Counter-Reformation Visual Polemics', 335–63.

67. Körner, *The Reformation of the Image*, 379–86, 260, 396.

68. Pfeifer himself explains that Cranach was not the inspiration, but Dürer's Adam and Eve, now in the Prado. However, Cranach was himself inspired by Dürer's image as his many versions of the subject show.

69. In an email to the author, Pfeifer explained that the picture was a reaction to the arms race between East and West, a topical issue in 1983–84, when the picture was painted. It represents a peace discussion: will force or diplomacy win out? Luther, Pfeifer argues, was opposed to the Peasants' War.

70. McLellan, 'Visual Dangers and Delights'.

71. Smerling, ed., *Luther und die Avantgarde*, 308–11. Wurm responded to the invitation by writing, 'Ich werde meine Teilnahme nutzen, um gegen die Verlogenheit anzukämpfen' (I will use my participation to fight against hypocrisy).

72. Fabian von Auerswald, *Ringer kunst*, Wittenberg 1539 [VD 16 A 4051].

73. WB 10, 3807 (6 Nov. 1542), 174–5:3–8, to Jonas: 'Solchs wissen die Drucker, die Vniuersitet, die Stadt, das es gantz vnuerborgen vnd nicht heymlich ist. So wirdt es die Brauth zu Meyntz selbst wol wissen, Dan ich habs also gemacht, Das ich hab wollen vormerckt seyn, vnd wehr es lieset, so Jhmands meyne fheder vnd gedancken gesehen, muss sagen: Das ist der Luther'.

## CHAPTER 2. LUTHER AND DREAMS

1. Hsia, 'Dreams and Conversions'. Ricci's dream was modeled on Ignatius Loyola's vision that founded the Jesuits. See Hsia, *A Jesuit in the Forbidden City*; Laven, *Mission to China*; Kagan, *Lucrecia's Dreams*. See also Rublack, *The Astronomer and the Witch*, on Kepler's extraordinary Somnium manuscript.

2. Price, 'The Future of Dreams'; Burke, 'L'histoire sociale des rêves'; Pick and Roper, *Dreams and History*; Plane and Tuttle, *Dreams, Dreamers and Visions*.

3. See Gantet, *Der Traum*, esp. 111–20, and Gantet, 'Dreams'.

4. WT 4, 4444 a, 4444 b, pp. 315–16; and Luther refers to Melanchthon's dream at Schmalkalden, WB 8, 3310, 14 March 1539, 391, and see n. 10; the Wittenbergers attempted to paint the picture in Melanchthon's dream. Friedrich Myconius was also writing about this dream (WB 8, 3308, 3 March 1539, 386). It or another dream or vision is mentioned again in WB 8, 3314, 26 March 1539, 397–8, n. 3, and it may be this which was collected by Johannes Manlius; it involved peasants

and may well be the one referred to here since Luther immediately goes on to talk about peasants, students, and poverty. The dream discussed in WT 4444 b featured Luther, the Wittenbergers, the pope, Campeggio, and Lutherans; it is about peace in the church, and the Pope calls on Melanchthon to recant, which he refuses to do.

5. Gantet, 'Dreams'; see, for example, WT 1, 617, p. 292: here Melanchthon describes a dream which signified commotion in the church and either he or Luther adds an account of a dream in which he tries to put the body of Christ into a cradle which looked 'gresslich vnd erschreklich', but he could not get it in.

6. 'Oravi Deum, ut non det mihi somnia' (WT 1, 382:10); see also WA 3, 3049, p. 157.

7. WT 3, 2952 b, p. 114.

8. For example, he told stories of people who had come to him insisting on the veracity of their dreams in place of God's Word; WT 6, 6211, 541–42. He calls these people 'Schwärmer'. He also used the expression 'lauter Somnia' to refer to legends about water sprites, WT 6, 6831, 218:19; 24. He spoke of the dreams and lies of false human doctrine, and condemned the Anabaptists for trusting their dreams, e.g., WS 34, I, 508:29.

9. 'Wie ihn die nächste Nacht geträumet hätte, wie ihm ein großer Zahn wäre ausgefallen, so groß, daß er sich nicht genug hätte können verwundern'; WB 5, 1595 b, 19 June 1530, 379:21–3. This dream is problematic. We know about it only second-hand through Luther's secretary Veit Dietrich's report in a letter to Katharina von Bora. He appears to be telling her the dream in order to reassure her that Luther has overcome his grief, and convey to her how he is reacting, since she is not there. Luther was not apparently writing to her about his father's death, though there may be letters which have not survived. Dietrich's letter is printed in Mayer, *De Catharina Lutheri coniuge dissertatio*, Section 28, pp. 61–62, but the manuscript to which Mayer refers as his source is not referenced. The letter was included in the Walch, Enders, and Weimar editions of the letters, although Mayer is apparently the only source.

10. WB 10, 3905, 26 Aug. 1543, 373; and see Rankin, *Panaceia's Daughters*, 99–100. Luther's headaches seem to have become particularly severe around 1530.

11. 'Nimis me derelinquis. Ego super te, sicut ablactatus super matre sua, tristissimus hac die fui'. WB 1, 202, 3 Oct. 1519, 514:49–50.

12. 'Jch hab all mein ding von Doctor Staupiz; der hatt mir occasionem geben', WT 1, 173, pp. 80:6–7 (1532): here, Luther explicitly denied having any debt to Erasmus. On Staupitz, see Posset, *The Front-Runner of the Catholic Reformation*.

13. WB 2, 512, 27 June 1522, 566, reference to letter of Staupitz to Linck.

14. See Brecht, *Luther*, vol. 1, 286–89 on this work which was a revision of his lectures from 1516–17 and was published in September 1519, the first full statement of his theology following the Leipzig debate. The additions Luther made to the original lectures strengthen the importance of the sinfulness of man, grace, and the role of the church as preacher of the gospel, not steward of papal power. It was therefore a work of which he was proud, and which encapsulates the ideas

that were then most important to him; Galatians remained a key text for him and he later described it as his 'Katharina von Bora'. WS 2, 436–618.

15. WB 1, 202, 3 Oct. 1519, 514:44–48.

16. 'Vitam odi pessimam, mortem horreo, et fide vacuus sum, aliis donis plenus, quae scit Christus quam non desiderem, nisi ei serviam'. WB 1, 202, 3 Oct. 1519, 514:51–53.

17. 'Hac nocte somnium de te habui, tanquam recessuro a me, amarissime me flente et dolente, verum te manu mota mihi dicente, quiescerem, te reversurum esse ad me; hoc certe verum factum est hoc ipso die'. WB 1, 202, 3 Oct. 1519, 514:75–77.

18. 'Deus rapit, pellit, nedum ducit me; non sum compos mei, volo esse quietus, et rapior in medios tumultus'. WB 1, 52, 20 Feb. 1519, 344:8–9.

19. WB 1, 202, 3 Oct. 1519, 513:4 (and see footnote 1) and 623, note to p. 515.

20. See Roper, *Martin Luther*, 69–73; 101–3.

21. Indeed, the psalm can be read not as expressing the sorrow and abandonment of weaning, but as celebrating the peace of the weaned child and its altered relationship with its mother. In the Bible of 1534 Luther translated this as 'Wenn ich meine seele nicht setzet vnd stillet, So ward meine seele entwenet, wie einer von seiner mutter entwenet wird' (*Biblia*, Wittenberg 1534 (Taschen facsimile), Der Psalter, fo. LVII (v)). The King James version by comparison has 'Surely I have behaved and quieted myself, as a child that is weaned of his mother: my soul is even as a weaned child'. See WBibel 10, I Band, 1524–45, 542, 543a, 543b; the translation was consistent through editions of the Psalter 1524, 1531, and 1545. I am grateful to Henrike Lähnemann for help with this passage.

22. Müntzer, *Auszlegung des andern vnter‖schyds Danielis*; Matheson, *Thomas Müntzer*, 226–52.

23. 'Das er toethen wil alle wollust des fleisches', 'Muss sich der mensch von allen Kurtzweil absondern/ vnd eynen ernsten mut zur warheit tragen', drumb ists nicht wunder das sie bruder mastschwein vnde bruder sanffte leben sie vor wirffet.' Thomas Müntzer, *Auszlegung des andern vnter‖schyds Danielis*, Allstedt, 1524 [VD 16 M 6746], fo. B iii (v); fo. C (r); Matheson, *Thomas Münzter*, 240, 242. On Müntzer's dreams, see Dieter Fauth, 'Träume bei religiösen Dissidenten in der frühen Reformation', 71–106.

24. Luther had also had to deal with the possibility of martyrdom as he prepared for the Diet of Worms in 1521. He remained deeply concerned about martyrdom and wrote descriptions of the martyrdoms of some of the early evangelicals, such as Heinrich von Zütphen and Leonhart Keyser; he was also aware of his own attraction to martyrdom, and of the irony that he later could seem to be making martyrs of others. See Roper, *Martin Luther*, 315–17.

25. 'Hic plus de visionibus et somnii dixi quam aliquis professorum', Müntzer, *Kritische Gesamtausgabe*, vol. 2 (Briefe) 153:6–7; Matheson, *Müntzer*, 54, letter from Karlstadt to Müntzer, 21 Dec. 1522.

26. 'Das Paulum keynmal getreumet hat, mus yhr allegat seyn. Aus zum teuffel mit solchen predigern! . . . Do kommen den vnser lose freche bachanten . . .' Müntzer, *Kritische Gesamtausgabe*, vol. 2, 240–52, 249; Matheson, *Müntzer*, 92.

27. 'Disse rotten geyster nichts ynn der schrifft verstehen, widder Mosen noch Christum, und nicht drynnen suchen noch finden denn yhr eygen trewme', WS 18, 76:10–12; LW 40, 92, *Against the Heavenly Prophets*. See also WT 1, 153, p. 73:6. He claimed that they took all their own dreams for God's word: 'Ja alle yhre trewme sind eyttel Gottes wort' (WS 18, 138:8), and that they rejected all externals. The word 'dream' recurs throughout the tract. In fact, Karlstadt did not place such emphasis on the prophetic importance of dreams, nor did he follow Müntzer's revolutionary path. But Gelassenheit was extremely important for him, featuring prominently in his theology as early as 1519; and it would be through his understanding of Gelassenheit that he would reach an acceptance of the possibility of martyrdom. For Luther, Karlstadt's mystical adoption of Gelassenheit was just a new kind of 'works righteousness'. On Karlstadt's theology of the Eucharist, see Burnett, *Karlstadt and the Origins of the Eucharistic Controversy*.

28. 'Wie were es sonst muglich das solche gelerte menner, on wirckunge des Satans, so blind solten sein, vnd solche lose trewme so hoch rhümen vnd ynn die welt treiben fur die aller sterckesten grunde des glaubens?'; 'Drumb meinen sie, wenn yhn ettwas trewmet, so sey es bald der heilige geist', WS 23, 100:26–29; 112:27–28; LW 37, 45, *That These Words of Christ 'This is my Body, Etc' Still Stand Firm Against the Fanatics* (1527). For a brilliant interpretation of Müntzer's and Luther's different understandings of Daniel, see Gantet, *Der Traum*, 60–64.

29. Zwingli, *Opera*, vol. 3, 341; Gordon, 'Huldrych Zwingli's Dream'. Luther was also able to make this allegation against Karlstadt, who according to Luther 'tobet da her: Myr hat getrewmet, das Missa auff Ebreisch eyn opffer heysse' (WS 18, 104:4–5); that is, 'raves: "I have dreamt that mass in Hebrew means sacrifice"' and so the doctrine of the Real Presence was false. He has just accused Karlstadt of having little knowledge of Hebrew: 'er muess es yrgent ym rauchloch geschrieben funden odder eyne eygen Ebreische sprache newlich ertichtet haben, wie er sunde und gesetze und boese gewissen ertichten kan odder die hymlische stym redet villeicht so' (WS 18, 103:28–31); that is, 'I think he must have found it [the idea that Mass means sacrifice] written in the vent of a chimney, or recently invented his own Hebrew language, as he can invent sins and laws and a bad conscience, or probably the heavenly voice speaks in this way' (LW 40, 120); however, *rauchloch* (vent of a chimney) means privy or anus.

30. 'Der den heyligen geyst mit feddern und mit all gefressen habe'. WS 18, 66:19–20; LW 40, 83, *Against the Heavenly Prophets* (1524–25). Dreams and visions continued to be important to many in the Reformation movement, particularly Anabaptists and spiritualists. They offered women in particular a source of authority and legitimation. See Barrett, *Wreath of Glory*; Hill, *Baptism, Brotherhood, and Belief*; and Goertz, 'Träume, Offenbarungen und Visionen'.

31. WS 18, 281.

32. Martin Luther, *Eyn Schrecklich geschicht vnd gericht Gotes vber Thomas Müntzer....* [Josef Klug: Wittenberg 1525], [VD 16 L 5852].

33. 'Steche, schlahe, würge hie, wer da kan, bleybstu drüber tod, wol dyr, seliglichern tod kanstu nymer mehr uberkomen, Denn du stirbst ynn gehorsam goettlichs worts und befelhs Ro. am 13. und ym dienst der liebe, deynen nehisten zurretten aus der hellen und teuffels banden' (WS 18, 361:25–28); *Luther's Works*, vol. 46, 54–55.

34. An interesting example of a dream by one of Luther's inner circle which entered Reformation tradition is that of Friedrich Myconius in 1517. The carefully stylized account of his dream and conversion is to be found in Lehmann, *Historischer Schauplatz*, 799–809, in a long section which includes accounts of different kinds of dream. Myconius said he dreamt it just after he had entered a monastery. The dream is crafted into Myconius's account of his own Anfechtungen—he describes himself as like a 'blutflussigem Weibe mit dem es immer aerger wurde, ob sie gleich alles verdoctert' (808), from which he was freed only by Luther in 1517. He spent seven years as a monk. In the dream Myconius found himself in a stony desert devoid of plants or comfort, with only rocks and crags, rather like the landscape near Schloss Stolpen in Meissen, he explains. A man with chestnut hair and long beard, dressed in a green short *Rock* and red coat appeared to him: St Paul. Interestingly two of Cranach's paintings of St Paul do indeed show him with a chestnut brown long beard, slightly greying chestnut hair, red coat, and green robe; only the green robe is long and not short. CDA PRIVATE-NONE-P102c, Fellitzsch Altarpiece, right wing, verso; and CDA F-MdLP-MNR939, Louvre, Paris. The landscape around Burg Stolpen was craggy; and castles with landscapes with surreal rock formations often appear in the backgrounds of Cranach's paintings. In this case it is impossible of course to know whether the dream actually drew on Cranach's imagery or whether this was added much later. But the coincidence between the visual world of the dream and Cranach's art is significant.

35. Freud, *Die Traumdeutung*.

36. Pick and Roper, eds., *Dreams and History*.

37. WB 5, 1559, 4 May 1530, 299–300.

38. Dreams were apparently often shared amongst the Wittenbergers. One moving example is the dream of Luther's wife, Katharina von Bora, the night before their daughter died. She dreamt that two well-dressed young lads had come to take Magdalena to her wedding. She told Melanchthon the dream and he reacted with shock because he immediately knew that the dream was about her heavenly bridegroom and portended Magdalena's death, as he told others. WT 5, 5494, p. 191.

39. 'Dominam meam'; 'Jhr seid sehr bose Buben, den guten Mann zu vexiren' (WB 5, 1569, 15 May 1530, 320:4–5).

40. 'Quare non est, ut de his multa scribam. . . . veniet, ne dubita, veniet Lutherus hanc aquilam liberaturus magnifice' (WB 5, 1704, 28 Aug. 1530, 582:4; 583:14–15). Luther concludes by suggesting that Spalatin take a leaf out of the ever forthright Amsdorf's book and say 'Dass uns der Papst und Legat wollten im Ars lecken!'

41. There were other examples of dreams during the Diet. The elector had dreamt that a large, high mountain lay on top of him, and that Duke George stood on top of the mountain, but the mountain had collapsed and Duke George had rolled down to him. Luther, who purported to make light of dreams, described it and interpreted it in 1533, three years after the dream, as having come true. The mountain was the emperor, upon whom Duke George had set all his trust, but the mountain had collapsed because the emperor was no longer so well inclined towards him. Duke George should therefore humble himself towards the elector. WT 3, 2941, pp. 102:12–25. This example is fascinating because it shows that dreams were discussed amongst the Wittenbergers, even including Saxon political circles. Here too, though Luther mocked dreams, he did not forget them either and clearly thought they could be prognostications. This dream image, which Luther conveys very powerfully in the condensed language he employs here, also allowed him to imagine the collapse of ducal Saxon power, and to visualize the struggle between the two Saxon rulers which was such a driver of the masculine rhetoric discussed in the next chapter. It also presented the political relations between them and the emperor in visual terms, with the huge mountain buoying up the Duke's power; and it expressed Luther's hope that this could change. A dream enabled a conversation about the unthinkable, a discussion which could not easily be had in other terms, long before the formation of the Schmalkaldic League.

42. WT 2, 2756 c, 637; 638: 'denn er hätte dies halbe Jahr viel gräuliche, schreckliche Träume vom jüngsten Gericht gehabt'. In one version of the ensuing conversation, Luther first gloomily ponders time and the impending Last Days, but then undercuts this, joking that everyone who becomes a pastor at Lochau seems to go crazy and become a Schwärmer. He tells the story of Michel Stiefel who became convinced that he was the Seventh Angel and the Last Days were about to arrive, and gave away all his books and household goods.

43. 'Mein Traum wird wahr werden, denn mich dunkte, ich wäre gestorben und stunde bey dem Grabe als nackend, mit geringen Haderlumpen bedeckt. Also bin ich lang verdammt zum Tode, und lebe gleichwol noch'. WT 1, 1109, 554:17. See also 'wirt mir war werden. Videbar mortuus, et circa sepulcrum steti quasi nudus mit geringen hülsen bedeckt. Ita ego diu damnatus attamen adhuc vivo' etc. in WT 3, 3510 a, p. 369.

44. 'Nam hac nocte (quod non memini factum antea a me) dormivi in latere dextro sex horas, cum soleam dormire in sinistro semper: ita fessus eram. Nam praecedente nocte usque ad multam diem portavi lapides et ligna in inferno, non in Aegypto. Erat fornax non illa ferrea Aegypti, sed talis, quam non licet dicere, ut esse funus mihi viderer. Sed scribo haec, ut videas verum esse, Christum esse regem virtutis in infirmitate, qui calida cum frigidis, dura cum mollibus, mortem cum vita, peccatum cum iustitia, denique omnia contraria cum contrariis regere, temperare et componere potest, pro magnitudine potentiae suae gloriosae, cui laus et gloria'. WB 6, 1791, 7 March 1531 to Justus Jonas, 49–50:8–18. He may be

referring to the harsh labour of the Israelites in Egypt carrying bricks and mortar, or to Erasmus's *Adages*.

45. 'Traurige Träume kommen vom Teufel'; WT 1, 1109, 554:9–10; 'Der Schlaf ist des Todes Bruder'; WT 1, 1109, p. 554:7.

46. WT 6, 6893, 253:6–8. The passage comes in a section on eclipses, which is very gloomy, and which probably dates from some point before 24 September 1545, as it mentions Albrecht of Mainz as still alive. This dream fragment, about which we know very little, is interesting because Luther identified closely with St Paul. About this time, in the introduction to his Latin works, Luther wrote an account of his recognition of the grace of God in terms of a single moment of salvation; that moment in a sense parallels Paul's conversion experience, just as it is also based on St Augustine's. The words Luther uttered in the dream were apparently from the Vulgate version of Psalm 4, not from his own German translation, and the psalmist, generally thought to be King David, asks for God's protection whether in rest or asleep, so they are closely connected to thoughts of his own impending death.

47. 'Der Teuffel kan mich so engsten, das mir der schweys im schlaff ausgeht'; WT 1, 508, pp. 232:32–3.

48. Here it is interesting to note that 'Anfechtung' is sometimes replaced by 'dream' in German notes of the *Table Talk*.

49. 'Traurige Träume kommen vom Teufel; denn Alles, was zum Tode, Schrecken, Mord und Lügen dienet, das ist des Teufels Handwerk. Er hat mich oft vom Gebet abgetrieben und Gedanken eingegossen, daß ich bin davon gelaufen'. WT 1, 1109, 554:9–12.

50. 'Jch hab kein grossere gehabt vnd schwerere denn de praedicatione, das ich dacht hab: Das wesen richstu allein zu; ist es nun vnrecht, so bistu schuldig an so uill seelen, die in infernum faren. Jn der tentatio bin ich oft dahin gangen in infernum hinein, donec me Deus revocavit et confirmavit me, quod esset verbum Dei et vera doctrina'; WT 2, 1263, pp. 15:12–16. Luther also often dreamt that he had to preach but had no notes: WT 3, 3494, p. 358. One of the ways Satan attacked people was to send them bad dreams, another was to 'hang evil mouths on them' (henget yhm bose mauler an), that is, to subject them to gossip, one of the things that deeply offended Luther: he mentioned this in the same sentence as the evil dreams. WS 36, 336:21, Sermon, 29 Sept. 1532.

51. WT 2, 1263, pp. 15:28–35.

52. 'Non, respondet illa, bene dormivi absque ullis somniis' (the German version of this story has 'Anfechtung' in place of dreams); WT 1, 122, pp. 50:1–12; 52:5–18. Luther added, in one of his usual twists, that the advice about drinking before bed to drive away Anfechtung and sleep well did not apply to young people, but only to him, as an 'old man' (52:15–17).

53. 'Denn es ist mir so: wenn ich auf wache, so kompt der Teufl baldt vnd disputirt mit mir, so lang bis ich sage: Leck mich in dem a.'; WT 2, 1263, pp. 15:35–37.

54. Duke George traduced Luther as a 'wechselbalck, einer badmagdt sonn' in a letter, a fact which Luther mentioned on 16 April 1538 (WT 3, 3838, 649–50, 650:3–4), an accusation taken up by later Catholic polemicists. Luther's immediate response as captured in the *Table Talk* was to insist that he was born of peasant stock in 'Moer bey Eisennach', yet was a Doctor of Holy Scripture and 'adversarius papae' (650:5–7). It is revealing that this brief summation of his identity, prompted by Duke George's insult, should place his role as 'adversarius papae' so prominently, a theme explored in chapter 5.

55. For example, he spoke of the Devil making people dream and sleepwalk, and leading them to high places where, if angels did not protect them, they would fall to their deaths, an elaboration of Jesus's temptations in the wilderness, WT 1, 802, p. 382.

56. On dreams and witchcraft, see Amelang, 'Sleeping with the Enemy'.

57. See British Museum, 1880,0710.299; and for other versions, see Paas, *The German Political Broadsheet*, vol. 1, 234–38; 373–78; vol. 2, 94–103; there was also a version printed in Strasbourg in 1668 with different verses.

58. See Volz, 'Der Traum Kurfürst Friedrichs'; and see also Pettegree, *Brand Luther*, 308–12.

59. Iserloh, *Luthers Thesenanschlag*; Iserloh, *Luther zwischen Reform und Reformation*.

60. Volz, 'Der Traum'.

61. Luther himself had been interested in prophetic intimations of his own role. So he collected information about the monk Johannes Hilten, who had prophesied that another would come and preach against the monks. He also believed that the dream of the Franciscan which Staupitz had reportedly heard in Rome in 1511—that an 'Eremit' would attack Pope Leo X—referred to himself. Commenting on this dream in 1536 he remarked that back then he never thought that the dream was about him; but 'Eremit' (hermit) could mean 'Augustinian' (he was an Augustinian 'Eremit'). He went on to remark that at that time (i.e., in Rome), we saw the Pope's face, but now we see him in the arse, without his majesty: 'Wir sahen dem Papst ins Angesicht, jtzund sehen wir ihm in Ars, außer der Majestät'; WT 3, 3478, p. 347:11.

## Chapter 3. Manhood and Pugilism

1. On Luther's manhood, see in particular Karant-Nunn, 'The Masculinity of Martin Luther'. See also, Karant-Nunn, 'The Tenderness of Daughters', and Rublack, *Dressing Up*, chapter 3.

2. See Purvis, 'Martin Luther in German Historiography': Fritz Fischer and Hajo Holborn both argued that Luther predisposed Germans to accept authoritarianism, and linked Luther's legacy to the idea of a German *Sonderweg*; William L Shirer's influential *The Rise and Fall of the Third Reich* (1960) had earlier linked Luther to Hitler, connecting Luther with anti-Semitism and fascism. I am grateful to Tom Brodie for his help here.

3. 'Ja, wenn sie in der Wiegen sterben, denn da sie auffs Pferd kemen, rennten sie gemeiniglich gestracks zur Höllen zu' (Mathesius, *Historien*, Sermon 8, 196). Luther did, however, certainly approve proverbs such as 'Princes are rare birds in Heaven' (WS, 27, 419:3).

4. Or to frighten them into joining monasteries in their old age: princes, Mathesius averred, could be saved if they remained faithful to their baptism and believed in Christ. Mathesius, *Historien*, 196–97.

5. On the debate over whether the Theses were posted or not, see Roper, *Martin Luther*, 1–2, 430.

6. Luther threatened that if Albrecht did not withdraw his manual of instructions to the preachers, then 'someone may rise and, by means of publications, silence those preachers and refute the little book'. Luther claimed to 'shudder at this possibility', but the implicit threat is clear. LW, 48, 48–9?; WB, 1, 48, 31 Oct. 1517, 108–113, 112:57–8; 59.

7. WB, 10, 3807, 6 Nov. 1542: 'Brauth zu Meyntz'. Luther repeatedly refers to him in this letter as the 'Brauth', and had also earlier dubbed him the 'Abgott' of Halle. Both insults had form, for in 1521 Luther had written 'Wider den Abgott zu Halle' which had been suppressed by Spalatin; and then in December 1521, Luther had written privately arraigning him for his sexual relationships and threatening to publish, to which Albrecht had written an emollient reply; WB, 2, 442, 1 Dec. 1521, 406–8; 448, 21 Dec. 1521, 421. See also WS, 30, II, 'Brief an den Kardinal Erzbishof zu Mainz', 1531; WS 30, III, 'Notizen zu einem offenen Brief an die Christen in Halle gegen Erzbischof Albrecht von Mainz'.

8. See Tacke, 'Agnes Pless und Kardinal Albrecht von Brandenburg', 347–65; Tacke, 'Luther und der "Scheissbischof"', 114–25.

9. WB, 3, 882, 2(?) June 1525, 521; 883, 3 June 1525, 522; VD 16, L 3772, An den Durchleuchtigsten hochgebornen Fürsten . . . Albrechten Ertzbischoffen zu Meintz vnd Magdenburg, Churfürsten vnd Marggraffen zu Brandenburg. Eyn sendbrieff vnd Christliche ermanung (etc.) D. Martini Luthers, Nürnberg, 1526, 'ich sei nicht tüchtig gnug dazu' (522:18–9). On the type of marriage, Luther refers to 'eine verlobte Josephsehe' (WB, 3, 883, 522:18). He may be playing with the idea that he is not long for this life but he is also evidently wondering whether he will manage consummation.

10. 'Vorherzutraben', 522:15. Luther imagines that his own marriage might be an example and a 'Stärkung' for Albrecht. (There were rumours circulating even in Rome that Albrecht was thinking of marrying, secularizing his lands, and joining the Reformation. WS, 18:403. Wolfgang Capito, who had earlier worked for Albrecht, had informed Luther of similar hopes.) Luther may have intended the letter as part of a public campaign to present Albrecht's impending marriage, and this was clearly behind his uncharacteristic tact. However, the marriage came to nothing. The open letter was not published until 1526 (WB, 3, 522 n.1; WS, 18, 405), and then it was not published at Wittenberg, though there were several editions, including from Nuremberg, Leipzig, and Magdeburg, often in

collections with other pamphlets. See WS, 18, 408–11 for the text 'Dem durch-leuchtigisten hochgebornen Fuersten unnd Herren. . . .' For an edition from Magdeburg from 1527, see VD 16 ZV 9967. Luther insists that he is making this appeal so as (amongst other concerns) 'dise leydige/ vnd grewliche empoerung zu stillen' (408:12–3; see also 409:1–6); that is, he links Albrecht's behavior to God's punishment, and his reform would therefore help stop the Peasants' War. As Luther mentioned the work on 21 May 1525, it must have been writ-ten before or around that date (the Battle of Frankenhausen took place on 15 May, and Frederick the Wise had died on 5 May; but the decisive battle in Albrecht's lands, that of Königshofen, did not take place until 2 June). Luther admonishes the archbishop that he is a 'menliche person von Got gemacht' (410:23), and if God does not perform a miracle and turn a man into an angel, 'kan ich nicht sehen, wie er on Gottes zorn und ungnad alleyn und on weyb bleiben mueg' (410:29–30); waiting until he is on his deathbed to marry would be risky. Albrecht gave Luther a gold gulden as a wedding present, perhaps in recognition of the fact that Luther had not published this tract; perhaps because he was still keeping his options open.

11. 'Das er sie aus ehlichem eyver mit eym stumpffen messer ein wenig gestochen hette' (WB, 5, 1523, 1 Feb. 1530, 226–27, 226:24–25); 'mit einer bratworst versiegelt ist' (WB, 5, 1523, 1 Feb. 1530, 226:30–31).

12. WB, 4, 1309, 21 Aug. 1528, 540:17–18: Joachim had been warned already by Luther 'ob ich dem kurfürstlichen hut wurde ins futter greiffen, das die har vmbher stieben'. On 5 October 1528 he published an open letter to Joachim; he published another on 1 Feb. 1530, WB, 5, 1523, 225, following this with a letter to the Bishops of Brandenburg, Havelberg, and Lebus, and again to the estate of the nobility of Brandenburg asking them to take action in the case. For his part, Luther maintained that his open letters were not a 'Schmachschrift', but the campaign of challenging letters drew on the logic of the feud.

13. It was compounded by the fact that Elector Joachim's wife was a Lutheran who had fled to Wittenberg in 1528.

14. Some were moved to Mainz and Aschaffenburg, and Albrecht cancelled the usual exhibition of relics in Halle. See also Nickel, *Das Hallesche Heiltumbuch von 1520*; and on relics, see Laube, *Von der Reliquie zum Ding*.

15. WS, 53, 402–5, 'Zwo Feddern und ein Ey, vom heiligen Geist' (404:21); 'Ein halber Fluegel von Sanct Gabriel dem ErtzEngel' (404:25); 'Ein gros schwer stück vom geschrey der kinder Jsrael, da mit sie die Mauren Jericho nidder worffen' (405:1–2); 'Ein gantz Quentin von seinem trewen fromen hertzen. Und ein gantz lot von seiner warhafftigen zungen' (405:10–12).

16. WB, 10, 3807, 6 Nov. 1542, 174–5:3–8, to Jonas: 'Solchs wissen die Drucker, die Vniuersitet, die Stadt, das es gantz vnuerborgen vnd nicht heymlich ist. So wirdt es die Brauth zu Meyntz selbst wol wissen, Dan ich habs also gemacht, Das ich hab wollen vormerckt seyn, vnd wehr es lieset, so Jhmands meyne fheder vnd gedancken gesehen, muss sagen: Das ist der Luther'. The printer

had been imprisoned. Luther had sent the letter to Jonas in Halle and it was intended for publication, but was not in fact published, WS 53, 402–3 (Introduction).

17. WS, 51, 463: 'es sei zu vil schmach von ainem hauptlerer unsers heiligen evangelions'; 464: 'satanisches Wüten' (Georg Witzel); 'acerrime' (Sleidan).

18. LW, 41,187; WA, 51, 471:10–13, 'das er von Gottes (dem jr feind seid) gaben starck, fett und volligs leibes ist. Aber meinet, was jr wollet, so thut in die Bruch und henget sie an den Hals, und machet davon euch ein galreden und fresset, jr groben Esel und Sewe'.

19. On the codpiece, see Wolter: *Die Verpackung des männlichen Geschlechts*.

20. See Roper, *Martin Luther*, 20–31.

21. LW, 48, 201; WB, 2, 400, 28 April 1521, 305:6–7, 'wiewohl ich lieber hätte von den Tyrannen, sonderlich von des wütenden Herzog Georgen zu Sachsen Händen den Tod erlitten . . .'

22. RTA 2, 534–37. This version entered Lutheran tradition through the work of Ratzeberger, an otherwise not very reliable source: Ratzeberger, *Luther und seine Zeit*, 51.

23. WB, 3, 928, 29 Sept. 1525, 584:5–6 (Michael Stifel); 929, 8 Oct. 1525, 585 (Leonhard Beyer); WB 4, 969, 9 Jan. 1526, 14–15 (Beyer). Some of their travel may well have been done by cart.

24. 'Eyn seliger reuber' (WS 11, 394:30–395:4), where Luther also explicitly points out that the time was fitting: Easter, thus underlining the comparison with Christ. See also Brecht, *Martin Luther*, 2:100; WB 3, 600, 10 April 1523, 54–58: amongst the nuns was Staupitz's sister. Luther's pamphlet defending his actions (in the form of a public letter to Koppe) named the nine women, putting Staupitz in first place; WS, 11, 400:19–22; 'rapui tyranno furenti hoc spolium Christi'. WB, 3, 928, 29 Sept. 1525, 584:9.

25. WS, 30, II, 4.

26. WB, 4, 1065, 1 Jan. 1527, 148.

27. Their exchanges had become even more bitter in the wake of the Pack affair when falsified letters made it appear that George had been in league with other Catholic princes to suppress the Lutherans. Luther had written an unguarded letter to Wenzeslas Link, a copy of which fell into George's hands and had given rise to a bitter polemical battle in 1528. WS, 30, II, 1–24.

28. See, for example, *Ein Sendbrief D. M. Luthers an Herzog Georg*, published together with George's reply. Here, interestingly, George states that he won't get drawn into a theological dispute with Luther, comparing himself to David who refused to take Saul's armour when he fought Goliath: WB 3, 954, 21 Dec. 1525, 637–643, 646–651. George sent copies of Luther's letter and his reply to Philip of Hesse. See *Wider den Meuchler zu Dresden*, 1531, WS, 30, III, 413–445, editorial introduction; text 446–71.

29. *Warnung an seine lieben Deutschen*, 1531, WS, 30, III, 252—320; *Glosse auf das vermeinte kaiserliche Edikt*, 1531, WS, 30, III, 321–88.

30. So, for example, in 1529, in his *Von heimlichen und gestohlenen Briefen* (WS, 30, II, 25–48), Luther castigates George for complaining to Elector John, his ruler.

31. The text of George's *Wider des Luthers Warnung an die Deutschen ein ander Warnung durch einen gehorsamen Unparteiischen* is given in WS 30, III, 416–423, along with Arnoldi's own reply; see WS 30, III, 438–9.

32. WT, 5, 5367, 96:7: 'Jm selben titel war ich ein schalck'. In his writings, Luther uses the term 'schalck' (rascal) to refer to the pope, the Archbishop of Mainz and the devil, amongst others, so this is quite an admission—with tongue in cheek of couse.

33. WS, 30, III, 469:6; 469:7, 'So wil jch dich fur einen man halten'.

34. WS, 30, III, 469:8–16: 'leuffest uberhin, treibest die weil viel speyens und beklickest das papir mit unnoetigen worten, wie man die auffruerisschen straffen sole, als kemestu mit solcher newer kunst erst vom himel herab. Schilltestu uns gleich wol auffruerer und kanst es nicht war machen noch beweisen. Weistu, wie man solche gesellen nennet jnn Deudschen landen? Man heist sie verzweivelt buben, verrether und ehrlose boesewichter, die frumen unschueldigen leuten mit jrem gifftigen maul jr ehre nemen und umb leib und leben bringen wollen. Das ist dein rechter name, Du seiest, wer du wollest'. This allergic reaction to slander and to the harm it causes is something that runs deep in Luther, and was the topic of his famous sermon in Gotha in 1515: WS, 1, 44–52.

35. WS, 30, III, 469. Names play quite a role in this tract. Luther accords himself the doctoral title George omitted, and addresses George as Juncker Meuchler (456:12; 461:14). The power of cursing is also freely used. In his tract on stolen letters, Luther concludes by appealing to the reader to pray *against* Duke George, a remarkable and deliberate breach of the duty to pray for the authorities. He then supplies a gloss on Psalm 7, turning its imprecations on the enemy against George, and calling on the reader to pray the psalm against him and his helpers if they will not desist: 'Diesen Psalm wil ich widder Hertzog Georgen gebetet und gesetzt haben sampt allen seinen Brieffs dieben und anhengern, wo sie sich nicht bessern' (WS, 30, II, 48:1–2). And in his 1533 tract he goes one better, concluding with a bizarre inverted Lord's Prayer which curses the papists. Instead of 'Geheilig werde dein name', the pious reader must say 'Verflucht, verdampt, geschendet muesse werden der Papisten namen und aller, die deinen namen lestern', and so on. WS, 30, III, 470:20–2. In response to *Der Meuchler*, Franciscus Arnoldi published *Auff das Schmaebuchlein, welches Martin Luther widder den Meuchler zu Dreßden . . . hat lassen außgehen*, Dresden, 1531.

36. WB, 6, 1814, 8 May 1531, 91; indeed, he even went so far as to ask for his help in continuing *Von dem Meuchler*.

37. 'So fern es je müglich sein wollt meines Gewissens und der Lehre halben' (WB, 6, 1848, 29 July 1531, 154:5–6; 154–55). Luther was willing to accept this but only on condition that other papists and George did not insult him either.

38. 'Verlauffenem Münch' and 'trewlos vnd meyneydig'; Johannes Cochlaeus, *Hertzog Georgens zu Sachssen Ehrlich vnd grundtliche entschuldigung*, M.D.XXXiiij, Leyptzigk, fo. C iv (r). In his personal introduction to the tract, George called

Luther a 'bosshafftiger luegner, ketzer vnd auffruerer', going on to say that if he persisted in his views, then George would regard him as worse than a 'grober Bacchant' [fo. A I (v)], an insult that insinuated he was a drunkard. In the tract itself, written by Cochlaeus, he calls him 'Babst Luther' [fol. A ii v] and insults him as 'ein lausiger ausgeloffner Muench vnd Buebischer Nonnenfetzer / der weder land noch leut hat. Als ein vnedler wechselbalck / von einer Badmeyd geborn [fo. A iii v]. In 1534 an anonymous pamphlet went even further: *Martin Luthers Clagred daß er so gar nit hippen oder schenden kann*, Worms 1534 [VD 16 M 1187]. This is a drama featuring the Meuchler, a soldier, Holhipper, and Luther. Luther, shown on the title page dressed as a monk, soon learns the art of insulting better than his instructor, but the Holhipper gets his own back and the drama culminates in a long passage of insult against Luther (fo. D ii (v) ff). Luther is the son of Satan, responsible for the deaths of 200,000; he is 'trelowß, meyneydig', a 'Venus kind', and devotee of Priapus, a drinker and gormandizer bound for Hell (fo. D iii (r)); and a monk who has married a nun and lives in the monastery itself. It culminates with the accusation that Luther is an insulter of princes and hence foments rebellion: 'Pfey dich an / du fürsten schender / Aller auffrur bist ein anfenger' (fo. D iii (v)).

39. George's coyness about authorship offered Luther an open target which he could not resist: when the mayor of Leipzig wrote to Luther in 1533 inquiring whether he was the author of a letter in his name addressed to the evangelicals in Leipzig—he was, of course—which compared George to a 'murderer or robber' (WB, 6, 2009, 450:19–20: 'morder vnd reuber'), Luther teasingly asked the mayor who had told him to inquire. Playing with George's many cover names, he asked was it 'der pfarer von Collen' (pastor Arnoldi)? Or perhaps the Meuchler zu Dresden? Or Duke George? WB, 6, 2009, 2011, 2012, and Nachgeschichte. The terms 'murderer and robber' were insults, and in the same letter Luther had also called him an enemy of the gospel and an apostle of the devil. George complained to the elector, and a waspish correspondence between the two ensued: WB, 6, 2009:452; 2012, 458.

40. WS, 38, 141:7–9; 142:2 and throughout. On his complex relationship with Cochlaeus, see Roper, 'The Seven-Headed Monster'.

41. WS, 38, 143: Here Luther avers that he was such a strict monk that if anyone had got to heaven through monkishness, he would have; he would have martyred himself to death with 'wachen, beten, lessen und ander erbeit' (143:29); and see passages on monkishness and the 'baptism of the monks' (146–49); and a passionate defence of marriage (162).

42. WB, 7, 2160, 21 Dec. 1534, 136; and WB, 7, 2161, 21 Dec. 1534, 137–39 for Brück's letter advising Luther to get his side to check for insults in Cochlaeus's publications that might infringe the agreement made at Grimma, in case the other side did the same. In a postscript he told Luther to report on what he said separately for the archbishop and the duke, suggesting he go 'ein wenig leis' in the case of the duke, 139:54–55.

43. The son of Elector Johann, who was Friedrich's brother, his assumption of power marked a transition to the next generation.
44. WB, 7, 2163 a, 23 Dec. 1534, 141; WB, 7, 2163 b, 141–2, 142:12–3: 'Jch sehe E. k. f. g. nicht gern ynn solchen sachen dienen'. WB, 7, 2164, 24 Dec. 1534, 143–4; 143:6–9: 'War ists, Jch were wol gern an H. Georgen vnd den Bisschoff. Vnd dieser brieff Herzog Hans were mir wunder gut. . . . Jch wolt dem Esel die ohren krawen'; 144:23–4: 'So sag ichs noch itzt vnd wills nü mehr thun vnd sagen denn zuuor. Las doch sehen, ob ichs verteidige mit meinem halse!'; 144:27: 'Aber, lieber, last sie komen vmb Gotts willen!'
45. WS, 38, 143:15–17: 'Ach, lieber herr, lasst uns doch ein kennlin biers mit einander trincken, wie wol jr stercker moecht sein, mehr kennlin zu trincken denn ich jnn solchem fall'; 143:7: 'Jch schreibe itzt mit der pflaum feddern'.
46. 'Herzog Georg wolt weder Bepstisch noch Lutherisch sein, sondern nach vnterdruckung der Lutherischen selbs der Man sein, der die kirchen reformirte'. WB, 9, 3454 (c. 16 March 1540), 74:2–5.
47. 'Lieber Erasme, wasche mir den Beltz, vnd mach mirn nit naß, Jch lobe noch die von Wittenberg, die behalten doch kein Mehl im Maul, sondern sagen frey vnd redlich herauss, was jhr Meynung sey'. Mathesius, *Historien*, 180.
48. 'Vnd wolt nicht gern, das E f g solten mit mir ynn den fedder kampff komen' (WB, 9, 3518, 24 July 1540, 200:28–29).
49. Philip's existing first wife was the daughter of Duke George of Saxony to whom he was therefore related by marriage; George died in 1539 and Philip immediately set about consulting leading theologians about bigamy.
50. WB, 9, 3458, 5 April 1540. Luther burnt the letter: see WB, 9 3464, 12 April 1540, and 3484, 24 May 1540; and WB, 9, 3491, 9 June 1540. See Roper, *Martin Luther*, 357–61.
51. 'Es ist aber mein meinung nit gewesen, mit euch Jnn federkampf zuschreiten noch ewer feder regig zumachen, Dan ich ewer geschicklicheit darin wol erkenne, bin auch gannz nit gemeinet, mit euch zuzanken' (WB, 9, 3520, 27 July 1540, 206:23–25).
52. WB, 9, 3502 (written in the landgrave's own hand) and 3503, 20 and 21 June 1540. See, on the affair, Rockwell, *Die Doppelehe des Landgrafen Philipp von Hessen*.
53. 'Jch wolte, das ich ein stunde bei euch were, wir wolten vns wol mit einander vertragen'. WB, 9, 3520, 27 July 1540, 208:91–92.
54. Interestingly, an anti-Lutheran Catholic polemic envisaged a drinking game in which Luther bests Agricola, a pointed slur since Agricola was reputed to be a drunkard: Flasch, *Zwey vnd zwaintzig Vrsachen*.
55. See the pioneering work of Puff, *Sodomy in Reformation Germany and Switzerland*, and Hendrix and Karant-Nunn, *Masculinity in the Reformation Era*.
56. On beards, see Hanß, 'Face-Work', esp. 7–9; Hanß, 'Hair, Emotions and Slavery'.
57. 'Wenn mir ein solcher Stoerenfried fur mein Hauss kem, wolt ich mit meinem Hausspiess zu ihm hinauss wischen, vnnd meinen Haussfried und Gemach (wie einem Haussvatter von recht zugelassen vnnd gebueret) vertheidigen. Stiess ich mien Spiess durch ein solchen Auffrhuerer, wolt ich still stehen vnd auffschreyen:

Hie Gottes vnd Keysers Recht, vor denen beiden ich solch mein Nothwehr vnnd Haussschutz, mit ehren vnnd gutem Gewissen Christlich vnnd rechtlich verantworten wolte' (Mathesius, *Historien*, 175 (1529)). The Luther household did in fact have a sword: *Luther und die Fürsten*, Catalogue volume, 292, Item 220; and Luther himself remarked in 1532, 'Wan ich plötzlich in meinen vier pfelen einen dieb antreffe, so muß ich mich weren, ne ipse me occideret' (WT 3, 2481 b, 20:23–24); and see also 2481 a.

58. 'Als wenn der Man feig wird, so zittern die Hende, die Beine beben, der Kopff hanget, das er weder Spies noch Schwert halten kan, viel weniger streiten oder sich weren, lesst in sich stechen und hawen, wie in einen klotz'. WS, 54, 410:19–21. Klotz can mean blockhead as well as block of wood.

59. See also, in particular, Karant-Nunn, 'The Masculinity of Martin Luther'.

60. See Thompson, *Studies in the Reformation: Luther to Hooker*.

61. Von Friedeburg, *Luther's Legacy*, 1:105–19, 382 ff.

62. Hall and Pick, 'Thinking about Denial', 1–23: I am using denial in the sense that explains why Luther has so much libidinal investment: he is denying something that another part of him knows to be true.

63. Although Chancellor Brück made a show of trying to keep Luther in line when he insulted George, he was not so concerned about his aggression towards Albrecht of Mainz, nor was he above advising Luther how to defend himself against George's complaints, WB, 7, 2161, 21 Dec. 1534, 137–39.

64. See, on this image, Christensen, *Princes and Propaganda*.

## CHAPTER 4. NAMES

1. Cochlaeus accused Luther of having changed his name because of this, picking up on an allegation originally made by Hieronymus Emser in 1521; see Wartenberg, 'Martin Luthers Kindheit'. Luther published the *Sieben Bußpsalmen* under the name 'Luder', apparently the last time he did so, VD 16, B 3483. See also Möller and Stackmann, 'Luder, Luther, Eleutherius'. Luther was christened 'Martin' because he was born on St Martin's eve and baptised the next day.

2. See Leppin, *Martin Luther*, 117–26; Roper, *Martin Luther*, 455, n. 64; Prinz, *Wie aus Martin Luther wurde*; Udolph, *Martinus Luder-Eleutherius-Martin Luther*; and Roper, 'The Seven-Headed Monster'.

3. Udolph, *Martinus Luder-Eleutherius-Martin Luther*, 33–49; the 'f' stands for 'frater', brother.

4. See Korsch, 'Luther's Seal'. Korsch speculates that it may have drawn on an old Luder family coat of arms which showed a crossbow on its side with two white roses. Interestingly, Luther's father Hans Luder had a seal or emblem showing two hammers, and Luther would certainly have known this. On the Luther rose, see Conermann, 'Die Lutherrose'.

5. Roper, *Martin Luther*, 143. On the rose, see Conermann, 'Die Lutherrose', 260–65. On the use of Luther's name on title pages, see Pettegree, *Brand Luther*, 157–63.

6. Letter to Lazarus Spengler 8 July 1530, WB 5, 1628, 444–5; this was probably so that it could be correctly made in Nuremberg. It was presented to him by the Electoral Prince Johann Friedrich in September at Coburg 1530. The ring is on display in the Grünes Gewölbe, Dresden, Inventar Nr. VIII 97; Luther may rarely have worn it because it was made to be worn over gloves, as aristocrats did, so when he put it on, it fell straight off his finger onto the floor. Luther joked that it showed he wasn't suited to gold and was, in the words of Psalm 22, a worm. See WB 5, 1719, 15 Sept. 1530, 623:33–38; 'Siegelring Martin Luthers' in Syndram, Wirth, and Wagner, eds., *Luther und die Fürsten*, Katalog, Kat. Nr. 155, p. 225. I have been unable to determine whether the dimensions of the ring were ever altered by Luther to fit his ungloved finger, or later by the Elector John George I, who owned it and wore it on his deathbed, to fit a gloved one: its dimensions remain large at a diameter of 27 mm. I am grateful to Ulrike Weinhold of the Grünes Gewölbe for the information, and to Julia Beusch, who showed me just how large it was, even with a glove. It could still of course have been used as a seal.

7. It is reminiscent of the language of the 95 Theses, where in Theses 93 and 94 Luther says: '7. Valeant itaque omnes illi prophete, qui dicunt populo Christi "Pax pax", et non est pax, 8. Bene agant omnes illi prophete, qui dicunt populo Christi "Crux crux", et non est crux', WS 1, 238:14–17; 'Away then with all those prophets who say to the people of Christ, "Peace, peace", and there is no peace! 93. Blessed be all those prophets who say to the people of Christ, "Cross, cross", and there is no cross!' LW 31, 33. The Weimar edition follows the numbering in batches of 25 of the Nuremberg edition, in which 93 and 94 are 7 and 8.

8. See, for example, Johannes Eck, *Inhalt bepstlicher Bull wider Martin Ludder auffs kürtzest geteuscht*; Eck, *Des heilgen Concilij tzu Costentz*. Johannes Nas provides a long passage on Luther's name, providing an acrostic which links each letter of the name with something negative (the 'u' or its 'v' equivalent, for example, stands for Vipera), and mocking the original name as proving he was a 'lotterbub': Johannes Nas, *Quinta Centuria*, ff. 40r–43(v).

9. See Udolph, *Martinus Luder*, 54, who points out that Lutherus is used in the Weimar edition of Luther's letters because it is taken over directly from Aurifaber's copies of the letters, who probably Latinised it; it is used in WB 5, 1584, 5 June 1530, 350–51, 350:29–33, when Luther is referring to himself as the last of the name. However, he kept 'Martinus' with its -*us* suffix and regularly used this in his signature.

10. It was also rather different from the common practice in some orders of changing one's baptismal name on entering religious life. So, for example, Luther's antagonist Thomas Cajetan was born Jacopo Vio but chose the name Thomas on becoming a Dominican out of admiration for Thomas Aquinas—which would not have recommended him to the reformer.

11. Trinkaus, *Erasmus. Controversies: Hyperaspistes 2*, 605–6.

12. See, on Spalatin, Kohnle, Meckelnbog, and Schirmer, eds, *Georg Spalatin*. English fifteenth-century new men also often made puns on their names as they devised their coats of arms: Gunn, *Henry VII's New Men*, 31.

13. On Jonas, see Kawerau, ed., *Der Briefwechsel des Justus Jonas*, vol. 2, Introduction, vii–lviii, and Mager, '"Das war viel ein andrer Mann".'

14. https://commons.wikimedia.org/wiki/File:Jonas-und-der-Wal.jpg.

15. Kramer and Eisenmenger, *Die Marktkirche*, 13, for an illustration of the whale.

16. See, for example, Martin Luther, *Von den Conciliis vnd Kirchen*, 1539, Hans Lufft, Wittenberg [VD 16 L 7158]; Philipp Melanchthon and Martin Luther, *Vnterricht der Visitatorn*, 1538, Hans Lufft, Wittenberg [VD 16 M 2603].

17. Interestingly, he had originally signed himself 'f.', as brother, in conventional Augustinian manner, with 'Augustinian' or 'August.' at the end of the name.

18. On Luther's background, see Fessner, 'Die Familie Luder und das Bergwerks', and Stahl, 'Baugeschichtliche Erkenntnisse zu Luthers Elternhaus'; Knape, *Martin Luther und Eisleben*; Treu, '. . . *von daher bin ich*'; Jankowski, *Zur Geschichte*; Kramm, *Oberschichten*, I, 109–33; Freydank, 'Vater Luther'; Freydank, *Martin Luther und der Bergbau*; Westermann, *Das Eislebener Garkupfer*; Mück, *Der Mansfelder Kupferschieferbergbau*; Möllenberg, *Urkundenbuch*; Fessner, 'Die Familie Luder in Möhra und Mansfeld'.

19. On the mining background and on Luther's brother, see Fessner, 'Die Familie Luder und das Bergwerks'; Stahl, 'Baugeschichtliche Erkenntnisse zu Luthers Elternhaus in Mansfeld'; and Fessner, 'Die Familie Luder in Möhra und Mansfeld'.

20. Siggins, *Luther and His Mother*; and see also Siggins, 'Luther's Mother Margarethe', 125–50.

21. The name may also have been in the Luder family since Luther's niece, daughter of the Kaufmanns, was also called Lene; Brecht, *Martin Luther*, vol. 3, 238.

22. WB 8, 3129 27, Jan. 1537, 18, to his son Johannes, *pater tuus carne et spiritu*, 18:20. There is some dispute over the date of the letter and it may be from 1543.

23. This must have been well known. Simon Lemnius, for one, rhymed pitilessly about his marriage to Katharina von Bora: 'Mit jr zeugt er der Kinder vil / Darunder keins gerahten wil'; Lemnius, Chronologia evangelica, fo. B ii (v).

24. Roper, *Martin Luther*, 413.

25. LW Letters 1, 329–36; WS 8, 654–69; Jonas soon produced a German translation, as did the Swiss reformer Leo Jud. In the German edition by Jud, Luther's father is referred to as 'Hans Luther' (*Ein gar schon nutzlich büchlin* . . . (Zurich, 1523), [VD 16 L 7328], fo. A ii (v)); and the Latin version gives his name as Johannes Luther (*De Votis Monasticis* (Wittenberg, 1522), [VD 16 L 7322], fo. Aaii (r)); but Jonas's translation carefully avoids giving Luther's father a surname. Interestingly, in Jonas's translation, Luther opens by explaining that he has not dedicated the book to his father: 'das ich deynen nahmen / hoch fur der welt berumbt macht. Vnnd alßo nach dem fleysch wider die lere des Apostel Pauli ehre suchet . . .', f. I v, *Uon den geystlichen vnd klostergelubden Martini Luthers vrteyll* (Wittenberg, 1522), [VD 16 7327], f. 1 v. Luther then opens the treatise itself by reflecting on names, explaining it is not written for those 'die auß allten gifftigen haß meins namens, vorlangst vmb meynnet willen verdampt haben, die offentlichen

warheyt', f. B r: they should not read the book because he does not wish to cast his pearls before swine; *De Votis*, fo. Bb (r).

26. 'Ego succedo nunc in haereditate nominis, ut senior sim fere Lutherus in mea familia. Mihi quoque nunc debetur non solum casus, sed ius sequendi eum per mortem in regnum Christi, quod nobis omnibus benigniter concedat ille, propter quem sumus miserabiliores cunctis hominibus, et totius mundi opprobrium'. LW Letters 2, WB 5, 1584, 5 June 1530, 350–51, 350:29–33; but the letter is not an autograph. In his last letter to his father, Luther—according to the Weimar edition—wrote to him as 'Luther' (WB 5, 1529, 15 Feb. 1530, 239:1); so also, his last letter to his mother in 1531. Both letters, however, are taken from the 1545 printed edition of letters of comfort compiled by Caspar Cruciger and not from original autographs. In WB 2125, 5 July 1534, Luther refers to his brother and father as Luder as he describes the will. He also uses the name Luder in writing to Kanzler Brück when referring to his paternal relatives, WB 10, 4058, 2nd half Dec. 1544; and he even signed himself, for example, as 'williges Landkind Martinus Luder D' when writing to Counts Philipp and Johann Georg of Mansfeld (7 Oct. 1545, WB 11, 4157). He also referred to his wife as 'Luderin' or 'Lüdherin'. Udolph, *Martin Luder*, 102–6.

27. WB 11, 4157, 7 Oct. 1545.

28. Mathesius, *Historien*, Vorrede, fo. B iii r–v.

29. Mathesius, *Historien*, 533: 'Heut an disem Schulfest dancken wir dem Herren Jesu, der die Christlich Schulz u Wittenberg durch theure Leut hat stifften vnd erhalten lassen, vnd der treffliche Wunderleut, dergleich in vil hundert Jaren auf Erden nicht gelebet, zu diser Kirch vnd Schul verordnet. . . .'

30. Georg Witzel, *Apologia: das ist: ein vertedigs rede Georgii Wicelii wider seie afterreder die Luteristen*, fos B ii (v), A i (v), [A iv (r)]; Nas used the term too, as did Petrus Sylvius.

31. 'Ein sect ist ein sect vnd bleibt ein sect, wie ein affe ein affe, man schmücke, preyse, Vnd verteydige sie so hoch man woell' (*Apologia*, f. B ii (v)). He also referred to it as the 'Luterischen Synagog' (fo. D (r)). He once mentions the 'Wittembergischen kirchen' (fo. F iii (r)).

32. Luther himself also occasionally used the term, referring ironically to the 'Lutherischen'—insisting for example that though they were called Lutheran by their opponents, they were 'Christlich'. See, for example, 'Beelzebub an die Heilige Bepstliche Kirche' (WS 50, 128–9), an imaginary letter of Beelzebub to the pope in which he complains about the disruption to his Reich caused by the 'Lutherischen ketzer'.

33. See Goertz, *Thomas Müntzer*. Müntzer used the conditional 'maneat' in place of 'manet'. It may well have been used by the Saxons before Speyer, in 1522–23.

34. See Beyer, 'A Public Mystery', 126.

35. WS 6, 135–36; *Doctor Martinus Luthers antword auff die zedel, szo unter des Officials zu Stolpen sigel ist aus gangen*, WS 6, 137–41.

36. See, for example, 'drecketal', WS 47, 568:21 (sermon 1539); 'drecketen und dreck-etaln', WS 50, 568:16 (1539 Preface to the collected edition of the German works); WS 54, 212:2; Die Luegend von St. Johanne Chrysostomo, 1537, in WS 50, 52–64.
37. WB 5, 1628, 8 July 1530, 445:22; 1649, 15 July 1530, 482:17; 1653, 20 July 1530, 487:30; Gruboco, 1644, 13 July 1530, 473:27; Gruboc, 1648, 15 July 1530, 480:49; Grubok, 1649, 15 July 1530, 482:2.
38. WB 5, 1554, 24 April 1530, 291:35–46.
39. WB 5, 1553, 24 April 1530, 286:27–28; see also 1558, 29 April 1530, 298:19–20; 1563, 8 May 1530, 309:27–28.
40. *Ein frage des gantzen heiligen Ordens der Kartenspiler vom Karnoeffel an das Concilium Mantua*, WS 50 (1537), 132–34.
41. See Buck, *The Roman Monster*, 8–48; 160–68.
42. 'Ey pfu Teufel, wie hat sich der Bapstesel beschiessen' (WS 54, 221:4–5).
43. 'da die foertze aus faren?' 'da scheis ein hund ein' (WS 54, 221:19).
44. He is a 'fart ass of Rome', 'fartz Esel zu Rom', farting out decrees (222:4; Eselfartz-Bapst, 266:19); the pope and his cardinals are 'coarse asses, unlearned in Holy Writ' ('grobe ungelerte Esel . . . in der Schrift', 227:7); and he addresses Paul III as the 'the bishop of Hermaphrodites and Pope of Buggers' ('Hermaphroditen Bischoff und Puseronen Bapst'; 227:8; 228:2).
45. WS 54, 212:2; and early on (205:12) he mocks the papal bull as 'eine Bulla (mit urlaub zu reden)', that is, 'a bulla (excuse me)', by which he probably intends a pun on 'bull', or vagina (Fischer, *Schwäbisches Wörterbuch*, 1, 1514).
46. 'Mügen in die bruch thun und an den hals hencken'; 'thesem apffel' or *Bisamapfel* (pomander); WS 54, 220:28–29. Interestingly, Luther had been given a pomander just two years earlier, in 1543, by Elector Johann Friedrich, which was inherited by his wife and children, so the idea of a pomander might have been on his mind; it is not an image he uses often. On the object, see Gutjahr, 'Pomander', 158.
47. 'Seiner klugheit sich beschmeißen' (WS 54, 272:35). Interestingly, the excremental images are often linked with discussions of learning.
48. 'Denn der Teufel mus es ja also machen, das er einen stanck hinder sich lasse, dadurch man wise, er sey da gewest' (WS 54, 279:1–2).
49. Two other pet phrases he repeats deserve note: he mentions the pope's 'masks', and he talks of how the pope 'laughs into his fist' ('in die Faust lachen'), meaning that the pope is a deceiver who is taking advantage of his flock. Both phrases can be found in Luther's early work too. On excremental and diabolic imagery, see Scribner, *For the Sake of Simple folk*, 129–33. On farting at the Devil to get rid of him, see WT 1, 122, p. 48.
50. He had first mooted this in a letter to Linck (WB 1, 121, 18 Dec. 1518), and then developed it in letters to Spalatin (WB 1, 161, 13 March 1519, 359:29–30). He became more convinced when he had received Lorenzo Valla's proof that the Donation of Constantine was a forgery (WB 2, 257, 24 Feb. 1520, 48:26–28),

promising to say more to Spalatin when they met. By August 1520, when Luther wrote to Johannes Lang (who had been shocked by the tone of *To the Christian Nobility of the German Nation*), he could state that 'we' were now certain that the papacy was the seat of the Antichrist and the pope was owed no obedience (WB 2, 327, 18 Aug. 1520, 167:13–14). By 11 October, when he knew the contents of the papal bull, he wrote to Spalatin that he was finally certain the pope was the Antichrist (WB 2, 341, 11 Oct. 1520), and by the end of October, he wrote *Wider die Bulle des Endchrists* (*Against the Bull of the Antichrist*), WS 6, 614:29. He also uses the word in *On the Babylonian Captivity*, LW 36, 12; WS 6, 498:9; Luther, *De captivitate babylonica ecclesiae praeludium*, fo. A ii (r). Luther explicitly uses the word Antichrist (as opposed to Nimrod), LW 36, 72; WS 6, 537:25. From then on it became inseparable from any of his attacks on the papacy.

51. 'Das Luther nicht ein schlechter ketzer sondern eygentlich der selbige langst vorhyn verkuendigter [illegible] . . . mischter Antichrist sey' (Petrus Sylvius, *Die letzen zwey geschlissliche vnd aller kreffigste buchleyn*).

52. See, for example, Johannes Nas, *Qvinta centvria*.

53. LW 31, 25; '[1] Dominus et magister noster Iesus Christus dicendo "Penitentiam agite & c." omnem vitam fidelium penitentiam esse voluit.
   '[2] Quod verbum de penitentia sacramentali (id est confessionis et satisfactionis, que sacerdotum ministerio celebratur) non potest intelligi'. WS 1, 233:10–13.

54. [92] 'Valeant itaque omnes illi prophete, qui dicunt populo Christi "Pax pax", et non est pax.
   '[93] Bene agant omnes illi prophete, qui dicunt populo Christi "Crux crux", et non est crux'. WS 1, 238:14–17; LW 31, 33.

55. 'szo ertichten sie, es muge niemant ein Concilium beruffen, den der Bapst'. LW 44, 126; WS 6, 406:28–29.

56. 'Alszo haben sie die drey rutten uns heymlich gestolen, das sie mugen ungestrafft sein, und sich in sicher befestung diszer dreyer maur gesetzt, alle buberey und boszheit zutreyben, die wir dan itzt sehen'. LW 44, 126; WS 6, 406:29–32.

57. 'propheten' (WS 15, 239:27); 'Wenn er dann saget, Got und sein geyst hab in gesand wie die Apostel, So last in dasselb beweysen mit zeychen und wunder, Oder weret im das predigen', 240:3–5, 'Dann ich mich nicht berhuemen kan, das mich Gott on mittel von hymel gesandt hat, wie sie thůn' (240:7–9).

58. 'moerdischen und blut gyrigen propheten' (*Eine schreckliche Geschichte und ein Gericht Gottes über Thomas Münzer*, 1525), WS 18, 367:5–6; 'so der teuffel durch seyne rottengeyster und moerdische propheten anrichtet' (Preface to the *Vertrag zwischen dem löblichen Bund zu Schwaben und den zwei Haufen der Bauern vom Bodensee . . .*, 1525), WS 18, 343:5–6; 'die blutduerstigen bawren und mord propheten', 'Drumb sol hie zuschmeyssen, wurgen und stechen heymlich odder offentlich, wer da kan' (*Wider die räuberischen und mörderischen Rotten der Bauern*, 1525), WS 18, 316:16; 358:14–16.

59. Roper, *Martin Luther*, 42–43.

60. These were produced in Joachimstal, a mining area. Wolf Milicz, Martin Luther, medal, gilt on silver, Dresden Kunstsammlungen, Münzkabinett, 1914/198b;
and there were also versions on lead, and on silver (Rijksmuseum Amsterdam,
NG-VG-1–213).

61. Vandiver, Keen, and Frazel, *Luther's Lives*, 38–39; Melanchthon, *Vita Lutheri*, fo.
24 (v).

62. Luther seems to have begun using it with frequency in his sermons of 1523;
certainly the council and community of Orlamünde were defending themselves
against this insult in 1524, WS 15, 343. Luther was soon writing provocatively
to the Strasbourgers, warning them against the 'schwermer geyst' (WS 15,
391–97).

63. Burnett, *Karlstadt and the Origins of the Eucharistic Controversy*, 71.

64. For example, WT 5, 6419, 653:24–28.

65. See Roper, *Martin Luther*.

66. LW 38, 81 ('Rhapsodies on the Marburg Colloquy'), WS 30, III, 157:22–28: 'verbum
dicit, Christum habere corpus, hoc credo, verbum dicit corpus Christi ascendisse
in coelum, sedere ad dexteram patris, hoc quoque credo, verbum dicit, hoc ipsum
corpus esse in coena, et hoc credo. Sed quod disputem, an sit extra locum vel
in loco, est mathematicae disputationis, supra quam est verbum dei, qui creavit
mathematicam et omnia, et hoc iubet vos de illo credere'.

67. WT 6, 6815, 208:32–34.

68. 'Lieber was ists doch vonnoeten, den Luther also loben, von seines Tauffs wegen?
Jst dann sunst niemannt getaufft worden, als er?', Nas, *Qvinta centvria*, 33 (r),
and 34 (r) for the apocryphal story about Luther's mother. Nas was using the
same rhetorical strategies as Luther—addressing the reader, inventing conversations, renaming Luther as 'Hutler', using humour, and moving rapidly to toilet
humour—but to less effect.

69. 'eym monchen vnd nonnen kinde' (WB 4, 1013, 26 May 1526, 80:5).

70. Rublack, 'Grapho-Relics', 144–66.

## CHAPTER 5. 'LIVING I WAS YOUR PLAGUE'

1. Neudecker, *Die handschriftliche Geschichte*, 138.

2. 'Das ist auff Deudsch / Bapst / Bapst / Da ich lebete / da war ich deine Pestilentz / wenn ich sterbe / so wil ich dir dein bitter tod sein'. In Jonas, Caelius,
Bugenhagen, Melanchthon, and Cruciger, *Vom Christlichen abschied*, fo. H 3 (r).

3. Neudecker, *Die handschriftliche Geschichte Ratzeberger's*; see Götze, *Lutheri*. Goetz
also wrote a history of the various relics of Luther and how they were used.

4. See Mathesius, *Historien*, 498–9, and WT 1, No. 844, 411. Linking Luther's death
with the prophecy was long-standing: see, for example, Luther's own *Wider den
Meuchler zu Dresden*, 1531, where he turns the table on the accusation that he
curses the papists by undertaking to do nothing but curse them, and immediately

links this to his own death (WS 30, III, 470:13–18): 'Nu aber, weil sie verstockt, schlecht kein gut, sondern eitel boeses zu thun beschlossen haben, das keine hoffnung da ist, wil jch auch hin furt mich mit den boesewichten zu fluchen und zu schelten bis jnn meine gruben, und sollen kein gut wort mehr von mir hören. Jch wil jn mit meinem donnern und blitzen also zum grabe leuten'. In 1537 when Luther recovered he (or his followers) extended the slogan into a longer Latin poem: WT 4, 6974, 301–2, text 302:5–8; WT 5, 5989 a, 417:21–24; and see Schmidt, *Luthers Bekanntschaft mit den alten Classikern*, 42–43. In the *Table Talk*, however, the verse is said to be Luther's own, and the reformer averred that he would die in the Pope's ban, but the Pope would die in God's ban; he entrusted himself entirely to God's grace, and would die in the hatred of the Pope, the scoundrel [Bösewicht] who exalted himself above Christ. The motto was apparently added by Luther or Rörer to the manuscript of the hymn 'Was furchtst du, Feind Herodes, sehr', perhaps in 1541, perhaps later; WS 35, 267–68. Versions of it can be found in WS 10, II, 107:14ff; WS 30, III, 280:8 ff; and it was included in Georg Walther's collection *Prophezeiungen D Martini Lutheri*, fo. F 7 (r). Similar maledictions updated to encompass Calvin as well as the pope include 'Gottes Wort vnd Lvtheri Schrift ist des Bapst vnd Calvini Gift', found on a sixteenth-century stone portal of a house in Wittenberg and renewed in gold in 1717; see Jöstel and Strehle, *Luthers Bild*, 25.

5. 'Mein epitaphium sol war bleyben: Pestis eram vivens, moriens ero mors tua, papa'; WT 3, No. 3543 A, 390:17–18. The verse was added to manuscript copies of the letter Luther wrote to Melanchthon describing what had happened: WB 8, 3139, 27 Feb. 1537, p. 50: footnote 10.

6. WT 3, 2922I and 2922b, p. 81:11–13; 90:2–4: 'der auch ein gutt starck buch wider den babst geschrieben hatt'. He was referring to Revelations. Luther was here coming to terms with not being a martyr, so the comparison with John, who had also not been martyred, was consoling; what linked their fates was that both wrote against the pope.

7. 'Betet fur vnsern Herrn Gott / vnd sein Euangelium / das jm wolgehe / Denn das Concilium zu Trent / vnd der leidige Bapst / zuernen hart mit jhm'; Jonas et al., *Vom Christlichen abschied* [VD 16 J 905], fo. B ii (v).

8. Bugenhagen, *Eine Christliche Predigt*, fo. D [i] (v).

9. Jonas et al., *Vom Christlichen abschied*, facing title page. An owner of the Munich copy has added comments to the title page, including 'Pestis eram viuus, moriens ero mors tua papa'.

10. Many of these have doubtless been lost. See, for example, the image of Luther in the Marienkirche, Göttingen, placed near the altar on the right wall of the choir, dating from the second half of the sixteenth century; Projekt Deutsche Inschriften Online, www.inschriften.net.

11. The text is included in the balcony of the Marktkirche Halle, DI 85, Nr. 152, adorning the image of Luther. This highly influential image was frequently copied, see DI 85, Nr. 265.

12. DI 58, Nr. 365; the Hildesheim image was part of a series of three, and the other two showed Duke Johann Friedrich of Saxony and the Emperor Charles V. The Hildesheim image was from 1550, that at Jena, 1549. See also Juncker, *Das Guldene*, 211–14: it was used on at least two commemorative medals.

13. See Bäck, *Martin Luther*, engraving by Johann Baptist Paravicini, 'Life of Martin Luther', c. 1674 (National Portrait Gallery, D33437); satirical print, 1730, Prey (grfl VI 1068 Lutherhaus, Wittenberg).

14. There is a sketch of Luther in the last year of his life by his student Johann Reiffenstein in the front of a Latin copy of the gospels which also has the inscription (Treu, *Martin Luther in Wittenberg*, 97). It was also pasted into the front of a Bible of 1545, under a pen drawing of a bust of Luther (now held in Berlin), WS 35, 598. See also WB 4, pp. 587–88: a similar sketch with the same motto is contained in a Latin New Testament given by Luther to Eberhard Brisger, WB 4, 588; and there is also a third in another collection, with the motto. It can be found written in Rörer's hand in a Bible of 1542, WS 48, 280; and a portrait of Luther as Junker Jörg dated 1537 (Cranach Digital Archive, US_MMA_39–5; now in the Muskegon Art Gallery) also includes the text, as the restoration discovered: http://www.baumanconservation.com/homefs.html. A closely-related image from the parish church of Penig also dated as 1537 bears the motto too; though it is possible that these texts were added later, after Luther's death.

15. Luther.—Martinus Lutherus, Islebiensis Theologus. Deutsche Handschrift auf Papier, zweite Hälfte des 16. Jhs. 2 S. Blattformat 34 : 20,5 cm. Mit mont. Holzschnitt-Porträt (10,2 : 8 cm), website of Ketterer Kunst Hamburg. https://www.the-saleroom.com/en-gb/auction-catalogues/ketterer/catalogue-id-ketter10006/lot-9b883762-7029-45d7-a1f0-a4230160aecc.

16. It is in the Leipzig Universitätsbibliothek: Inv Nr. 0633/090. See Stuhlfauth, *Die Bildnisse*, 31–32: it came from the Pauliner Library in Leipzig, and even though it had been painted over, the big black letters above the head and to both sides are still just visible, and are clearly so in the infrared photograph. See Cranach Digital Archive, DE_KSUL_0633–90.

17. See Mathesius, *Historien*, 498–99, and WT 1, No. 844, 411. Linking Luther's death with the prophecy was long-standing: see, for example, Luther's own *Wider den Meuchler zu Dresden*, 1531, where he turns the table on the accusation that he curses the papists by undertaking to do nothing but curse them, and immediately links this to his own death (WS 30, III, 470:13–18): see above, p. 231–32, n. 4.

18. LW 34, p. 49, 'Lebe ich, so bin ich ewr pestilentz, Sterbe ich, so bin ich ewer tod' (WS 30, II, 339 b:33–34).

19. See, for example, Wolf Milicz, Hans Reinhart, and Peter Flötner's anti-papal medals (Kluttig-Altmann, *Martin Luther. Treasures of the Reformation*, 314–5, nos. 325–27); anti-papal picture puzzle, 330, no. 343. See Andrew Morrall, 'Protestant Pots': many of these were produced in the wake of the Interim of 1548.

20. See, for example, Lake, 'Antipopery'; and Lake and Questier, *The Antichrist's Lewd Hat*.

21. Scribner, *For the Sake*, 59–147.
22. On Luther's antipapalism throughout his career, see Hendrix, *Luther and the Papacy*.
23. See, for example, the Muskegon portrait of Luther (Cranach Digital US_MMA_39–5).
24. For a fuller discussion of this image, see Roper and Spinks, '*Karlstadt's Wagen*'.
25. Karlstadt, *Auszlegung vnnd Lewterung*.
26. On the debate, see Hein and Kohnle, *Die Leipziger Disputation*, and Roper, *Martin Luther*, 125–44.
27. Roper and Spinks, '*Karlstadt's Wagen*'; WB vol. 1, No. 192, 18 Aug. 1519, Karlstadt and Luther to Frederick the Wise, 465–78, 466: 'Ich hab niemand genennt noch ausgemalt in den Bildern des Wagens, sondern die gemeine Jrrtumb der Theologen angezeigt' [466:48–49]; but this was in the context of excusing himself to his ruler. See also Hofmann, *Luther und die Folgen für die Kunst*, 192. Eck himself wrote 'dann ich mich ungern in sollich oder dergleichen Leichtfertigkeit merken wollt lassen, in den Druck ein Wagen zu geben, wie E. Ch. G Doctor Carlstat tan hat und mich ganz spöttlich mit ausgedruckten Namen darin verschmaecht. Ich Kuent auch wol ein Wagen machen, aber ich wollt ihn nit darinnen setzen; aber das ist sein Kunst' [461:76–81]; and he complained in his next letter, with heavy-handed irony, 'Jch hab nit geklagt über das Gemäl, dann ich acht, er sitz selb auf dem untern Wagen; aber daß er mich mit ausgedruckten Worten antast und schmächt: wann ich Esel in Wagen satzte, wollt er die Esel treiben; laß ich sein. Kann ers, so fiegt er wohl in das Welschland'; WB vol. 1, No. 192, 8 Nov. 1519, 480:39–43.
28. 'Vnßere augen bulen / vnd puben / vnd ist ye war / das sie allesampt huren vnd eheprecheryn sein / die bilder eheren / oder vmb hylff ansuchen. . . . mein hertz ist von Jugend auff yn eher erbiethung vnd wolachtung der bildnis ertzogen vnd auffgewachßen. vnd ist mir ein schedliche forcht eingetragen / der ich mich gern wolt endletigen / vnd kan nit. Alßo stehn ich in forcht / das ich keynen olgotzen dorfft verbrennen'. Furcha, *Carlstadt*, 115, 117; Karlstadt, *Von abtuhung der Bylder*, Wittenberg: Nickel Schirlentz 1522 [VD 16 B 6215] fos C iii (v); C iv (v).
29. On Karlstadt's theology, see Barge, *Andreas Bodenstein von Karlstadt*; Burnett, *Karlstadt*; and Bubenheimer, 'Andreas Rudolff Bodenstein von Karlstadt'. On Lutheran images, see Körner, *The Moment of Self-Portraiture*.
30. Stiftung Luthergedenkstätten in Sachsen-Anhalt, ed., *Passional Christi und Antichristi*; see Luther, *Passional Christi vnd Antichristi*, Wittenberg 1521 [VD 16 L5584, 5585, 5586, 5587]; it was copied with illustrations by a different artist in a Strasbourg edition (L 5583), and pirated in an Erfurt edition too (L 5581).
31. On the Passional, see Scribner, *For the Sake of Simple Folk*, 148–63.
32. See, for example, a copy held by the British Museum, 1895,0122.285.
33. On Law and Gospel, see the magnificent compilation and discussion in Reinitzer, *Gesetz und Evangelium*. See also Kluttig-Altmann, *Martin Luther*, 186–91: art historians distinguish two broad versions, the 'Gotha' and 'Prague' designs. The

Gotha type was most often used by the Cranach workshop, whilst the Prague variant was taken up by Erhard Altdorfer and Hans Holbein amongst others. See Messling, *Die Welt des Lucas Cranach*, 229–31. Often taken to be the only new iconography the Reformation introduced, it is to be found in a variety of sizes produced by the workshop, and inspired related iconographies from others. It was also used in oven tiles: see 191 for a fragment of one such tile, found in the Schlosshof, Wittenberg. The Hamburg artist Franz Timmermann, who studied with Cranach, also produced a version which uses largely half-length figures, but is evidently based closely on Cranach. See Wegmann, 'Franz Timmermann'.

34. 'Is tua dum uiuat, seu moriatur, habes. Mors tua tunc certe cum morietur, erit . . .', 'Eine waelsche Luegenschrift von Doctoris Martini Luthers Tod 1545', WS 54, 188–94: Luther printed the original Italian and a German translation, adding an 'Afterword' attesting he had read it, and that it hardly hurt him that the Devil and his associates, pope and papists, were so hostile. Writing to Philip of Hesse, who had sent him the pamphlet, Luther mused that it must have come from a 'barmhertziger schieispfaff', a 'pitiful shit cleric', who 'gerne wolte güt thun und hat doch nichts ym bauche' (188), that is, who would like to do [a] good [one] but has nothing in his stomach; the apparent excremental reference here is unlikely to be accidental. There were editions from Wittenberg, Nuremberg, Basel, and Frankfurt.

35. WS 54, 206–299; there were two editions from Wittenberg in 1545, an upper German one, and a fourth from Strasbourg; Justus Jonas translated the work into Latin, giving it an international audience, and it was published in Wittenberg and Strasbourg, 202–5.

36. 'Jungfraw Paula Tertius'; see, for example, WS 54, 214, 215 repeatedly; 218.

37. LW 41, 289, 'Denn mein kopff ist schwach, und füle mich also, das ichs villeicht nicht möchte hinaus fueren, und doch noch nicht bin komen dahin, das ich mir fuer genomen habe in diesem Büchlin zu schreiben, Welchs ich wil zuvor ausrichten, ehe mir die kreffte gar entgehen'. WS 54, 228:17–20.

38. LW 41, 334, 'Jst aber alles mit Teufels dreck versiegelt, und mit Bapstesels förtzen geschrieben'. WS 54, 265:16–17.

39. 'teufels synagoga' (WS 54, 245:25; LW 41, 311).

40. LW 41, 311. Much of the humour and insult is anal and sexual. He makes the old joke about decretals being 'drecketaln' (WS 54, 212:2); and mocks the papal Bull as 'eine Bulla (mit urlaub zu reden)', that is, 'bulla (excuse me)' (205:12), by which he probably intends a pun on 'bull', or vagina (Fischer, *Schwäbisches Wörterbuch*, vol. 1, 1514). For his use of the Papal Ass image, see Buck, *The Roman Monster*, 160–68.

41. Spending over 60 pages on the first point, he leaves himself a bit over 10 for the second, and barely 4 pages for the third. Even Luther admitted this: 'Es ist mir dis Büchlin zu gros unterhanden worden, und wie man sagt: Das alter ist vergessen und wesschicht' (283:26–27).

42. Everyone would say, Luther imagines, 'Ey pfu Teufel, wie hat sich der Bapstesel beschiessen' (221:4–5). Going a step further, Luther then asks which 'mouth' the

pope is speaking out of, 'da die förtze aus faren?', or the mouth into which the Corsican wine flows, adding the coarse imprecation, 'da scheis ein hund ein' (221:19).

43. 'Denn der Teufel mus es ja also machen, das er einen stanck hinder sich lasse, dadurch man wise, er sey da gewest' (279:1–2).

44. He repeats the metaphor he used in *Against Hanswurst*: if the papists are angry, then 'muegen in die bruch thun und an den hals hencken' and they should use this as a pomander (Bisamapfel) (220:289). He repeatedly calls the Pope a 'fartz Esel zu Rom', farting out decrees (222:4; Eselfartz-Bapst, 266:19), terms the Pope and his Cardinals 'grobe ungelerte Esel . . . in der Schrift' (227:7), and addresses the Pope as the 'Hermaphroditen Bischoff und Puseronen Bapst', 227:8, building up to his claim that they do not know 'ob sie Man oder Weib sind, oder bleiben wollen', 228:2. Two other rhetorical phrases are interesting: several times he talks of how the pope 'laughs into his fist', in die Faust lachen, meaning that the pope is a deceiver who is taking advantage of his flock, a saying Luther used quite frequently in many different contexts. There are also many animal images, not just of the ass, but of the sow. Repeatedly Luther talks of the pope's 'masks' ('Larven'), another favourite word which allows him to present himself as removing the mask to reveal reality. Interesting too is the fact that this is a remarkably pro-German tract, suggesting that much of it is about his own identity; it also allows Luther to position himself with the emperor and against the pope, defending him against the unedited crude first draft of the letter of Paul to Charles, a gift to the Lutherans, whose strategy consistently tried to drive a wedge between the emperor and the pope.

45. The original Papal Ass found in the Tiber in 1496 was interpreted by Melanchthon in 1523. See Scribner, *For the Sake of Simple folk*, 129–33.

46. So, for example, WS 54, 219: here he relates a story he claims he heard when he was in Rome back in 1510; 222–23, he cites the poet Mantuanus, whom we know was one of the favourites of his youth; he recalls the arguments at Augsburg in 1530 (288:5–11).

47. WS 54, 229:14–27.

48. WS 54, 244–55.

49. 'Sterbe ich in des, So gebe Gott, das ein ander tausent mal erger mache, Denn die teufelische Bepsterey ist das letzt unglueck auff Erden, und das neheste, so alle teufel thun koennen mit alle jrer macht' (WS 54, 299:5–8).

50. Grisar and Heege, *Luthers Kampfbilder*, vol. 4, 86. It is likely that Luther not only had a hand in commissioning the images, but that he even designed them. Certainly there is proof that he designed the image of the Papal Crossed Keys of 1538 as well as composing the verses and perhaps even the dramatic scene that accompany the image; see WS 54, 346–48. *Against the Roman Papacy* was published in late March; the pictures were circulating before then, WS 54, 352.

51. WS 54, 357.

52. WS 54, 356–57: some sets were pasted in by their owners or placed before the tract.
53. See Grisar and Heege, *Luthers Kampfbilder*, vol. 4, 17–34; all these images are clearly referenced in the text. So, for example, 'Lieber, male mir hie den Bapstesel mit einer sackpfeiffen' (270:23–25).
54. See Paas, *The German Political Broadsheet*, vol. 1, 222–38; 371–78; vol. 2, 94–103.
55. So, for example, in *Against the Roman Papacy*, Luther imagines 'Solch Decret, sihet jderman, das es mus von allen Teufeln, so allenthalben sind, mit einhelligem odem in den Bapst und Roemischen Stül geblasen sein' (225:12–4); and then says that they do not know 'ob sie Man oder Weib sind, oder bleiben wollen, sich nicht schemen dch fuer dem weiblichen Geschlecht, da jre Mutter, Schwester, Mumen. unter sind' (228:2–4). He asks 'Wo kompt das Bapstum her? . . . Es kompt vom Teufel' (237:37–238:1); and later declares that the pope and the papacy is 'dem Teufel aus dem hintern geborn' (260:16). 'Da ligt der Bapst in seinem eigen dreck, und wird eerfunden, das sein Regiment und stand sey nicht von Gott noch von Menschen, Sondern von allen Teufeln aus der Helle' (270:36–38); the Pope is 'von Teufel hinden aus geborn' (288:31).
56. 'Nepos tuus Georgius ostendit mihi picturam papę, Sed Meister Lucas ist ein grober maler . . . Poterat sexui feminino parcere propter Creaturam Dei & matres nostras'. He continued, 'Alias formas papa dignas pingere poterat, nempe magis Diabolicas. Sed tu Judicabis'. WB II, 4123, 3 June 1545, 115:17–21. On 15 June he wrote to Amsdorf again, 'Agam diligenter (si superstes fuero), vt Lucas pictor foedam hanc picturam mutet honestiore'. WB II, 4126, 15 June 1545, 120:11. See Grisar and Heege, *Luthers Kampfbilder*, vol. 4, 92–99; the editor of the Abbilding des Papstums in the Weimarer Ausgabe concurs with Grisar and Heege that these remarks refer to this double set of images now in the British Museum and not to the other set of eight or nine images, because that set was probably finished by early May; but he believes that they were commissioned by Amsdorf and not Luther. He agrees, however, that they came from the Cranach workshop, WS 357–8; and certainly they evidence the same close connection to Luther's text and were designed or printed very shortly after the other images.
57. Luther's contemporary Matthias Wanckel noted on the images themselves, after they had been bound together, in the copy held in the Lutherhalle, that Luther expressly said this shortly before he died in Eisleben. His words were: 'Ich hab den Bapst, mitt den bösen bildern sehr erzurnet, O wie wird die Saw den Burtzel regen, vnd wen sie gleich mich Tödten, so fressen sie den dreck, so der Bapst in der hand hatt', going on to explain that because his Lord was the God who would raise them all on the Last Day, he was unafraid, linking his thoughts about his imminent death and his faith directly to the images, WS 54, 346–73; 353.
58. This is the connection Justus Jonas made at the time, interpreting the pig as representing the Germans, WS 54, 352.
59. See, however, Grisar and Heege, *Luthers Kampfbilder*, vol. 4, 98, who state that the monogram, which might be that of the artist or cutter, is also to be found on the

left-hand post of the gallows on the other image. However, I cannot see such a monogram on the image. There is an unclear section of the image which appears to be a distortion of the join of the gallows; it is in the place where Grisar says there is a monogram. Moreover, the two letters do not look like a monogram, especially since the second 'b' is clearly smaller than the first.

60. 'Jch bin des bapsts laus, den tzwacke ich, der ernehret mich, vnd von seinem gutte nehre ich mich'. WT 5, 6374, 630:3–4.

## Chapter 6. Luther the Anti-Semite

1. The issue was first raised by Micha Brumlik in the summer of 2016: 'Was die AfD und Playmobil eint' (*Die Tageszeitung* (taz.de), 8 June 2016), and picked up by members of the Evangelical Church in Hesse and Nassau.

2. Oberman, *The Roots of Anti-Semitism*, 117: Oberman wants to contextualise Luther's anti-Semitism within his whole output and theology, relating it to his apocalypticism, rather than searching out anti-Semitic quotations; however, this also leads him to avoid repeating what Luther actually wrote about the Jews, and thus confront its nature. He does not, for example, quote from *Vom Schem Hamphoras*, or discuss it in his text. On the history of attitudes to Luther's anti-semitism, see Wiese, 'Überwinder des Mittelalters?'

3. Heinz Schilling, for example, writes of the 'historical distinction between the religiously determined anti-Jewishness of Old Europe and the racial anti-Semitism of the modern age' (Schilling, *Martin Luther*, 471); Oberman links it to Luther's concern with the Devil and with the Last Days (Oberman, *The Roots of Anti-Semitism*, 113–22).

4. Kaufmann, *Luther's Jews*. For an excellent discussion of the incidence of anti-Semitism amongst Catholic, Lutheran, and Reformed preaching, see Karant-Nunn, *The Reformation of Feeling*, 133–57. For a brief recent discussion of attitudes in the scholarship on Luther and the Jews see Osten-Sacken, 'Martin Luther's Position on Jews and Judaism'.

5. 'Der Teuffel hat in die N. geschmissen und den bauch abermal geleeret, Das ist ein recht Heiligthumb, das die Jueden, und was Juede sein wil, kuessen, fressen, sauffen und anbeten sollen' (WS 53, 587:2–4); Da schmeis und spruetzt er sie auch so vol, das es an allen oerten von jhnen ausschwadert und schwemmet eitel Teuffels dreck, ja, der schmeckt jhn jns hertz, da schmatzen sie wie die Sew. WS 53, 587:21–23; 'Jch verfluchter Goi kan nicht verstehen, woher sie solche hohe kunst haben, on das ich mus dencken, Da Judas Scharioth sich erhenckt hatte, das jhm die Darme zurissen und, wie den erhenckten geschicht, die Blase geborsten, Da haben die Jueden villeicht jre Diener mit guelden kannen und silbern schuesseln dabey gehabt, die Judas pisse (wie mans nennet sampt dem andern Heiligthumb auffgefangen, darnach unternander die merde gefressen und gesoffen, davon sie so scharffsichtige augen kriegt, das sie solche und dergleichen Glose jnn der Schrifft sehen, die weder Mattheus noch Jsaias selbs, noch alle Engel, schweige

wir verfluchten Goijm sehen koennen. Oder haben jrem Gott, dem Sched, jnn den hindern gekuckt und in demselben rauchloch solchs geschrieben funden'. WS 53, 636:33–637:5.

6. See, however, Katz, 'Shylock's Gender', 440–46, who argues that there was a widespread belief, dating from the thirteenth century, that male Jews menstruated.

7. Roper, *Witch Craze*.

8. Nirenberg, *Anti-Judaism*, 256, 260.

9. Kaufmann, *Luther's Jews*, 26–31: there was supposedly an encounter with some rabbis which happened at Worms during the Diet, for which Selnecker, writing over thirty years later, is the only source. Luther certainly does allude to disputing with Jews (see below). There was also a Jew named Bernhard who had converted to Christianity and formed part of the circle of Wittenberg acquaintances; see Kaufmann, *Luther's Jews*, 54; 56–58.

10. 'Und (wenn Jhr koenntet) all die Seine umb alles braechtet, was sie sind und was sie haben' (WB 8, 3157, 11 June 1537, 90:48–49). Luther had been asked by Wolfgang Capito in Strasbourg to intercede, and either to meet him in person or to intercede directly with the elector: WB 8, 3152, 26 April 1537. Josel had repeatedly written to Luther in the matter. According to the *Table Talk*, Luther's response was to exclaim, 'Was soll man den Buben vergunnen, die die Leute beschaedigen re et corporis et suis superstionibus multos Christianos avocant' (WT 3, 3597, 41:3–8); and he threatened to write to Josel 'ne redeat', that is, to write in such terms that he would not return with such an request.

11. Euling, *Chronik des Johan Oldecop*, 31.

12. I am grateful to David Katz for pointing this out.

13. 'Wenn ich jünger waere, so wollte ich diese Sprache lernen' (WT 1, 1040, 525:15–16). However, he also had great confidence in his knowledge of the language, and insisted that he was able to counter anyone in their interpretation of Greek or Hebrew. He translated freely, he argued, without following the letter of the rules, but 'ich las mich nirgenden binden, sondern ich gehe frei hindurch' (525: 21–22), a turn of phrase which on one level is just about translating the sense, not the letter of the words, but also echoes deep themes of his theology, as it can be understood in relation to his general hatred of laws and his emphasis on evangelical freedom. The rabbis stood for the old law, while he represented the freedom of the Christian. Indeed, Luther's translation of Hebrew was at times very non-literal, to the point that he even dispenses with the literal sense of the Hebrew.

14. 'Corrupte, vermischt und unrein, wie die Walen lateinisch reden' (WT 1, 1040, pp. 524:35–36). Luther claimed that Nicholas of Lyra was the best Hebraist. Lyra had been rumoured to be of Jewish parentage; however, he was a Franciscan and therefore a Christian Hebraist in Luther's eyes.

15. The chair in Hebrew at Wittenberg was a new creation; Luther at first secured Johann Böschenstein for the position, but he left after three months in early 1519, apparently because Luther and Melanchthon saw Hebrew as the servant of theology and not important in its own right. Böschenstein was rumoured to

be of Jewish parentage, which he denied. His successor was Mathias Adrianus, a converted Spanish Jew, who secured the post in April 1520 but stayed less than a year: he was immediately given permission to leave when he requested it, and Luther commented that they were 'freed of this man' (WB 2, 377, 17 Feb. 1521 'liberati sumus ab homine isto', 266:17). He was replaced by the Czech scholar Matthaeus Aurogallus in 1521, who also saw the point of Hebrew study was to contribute to Christian theology and biblical interpretation; see also Brecht, *Martin Luther*, vol. 1, 282.

16. 'Viel weniger gehe ich damit umb, das ich die Jueden bekeren wolle, Denn das ist ummueglich' (WS 53, 417:22–4; LW 47, 137).

17. 'Welchs eben so mueglich ist, als den Teuffel zu bekeren. . . . Denn ein Juede odder Juedisch hertz ist so stock, stein, eisen, Teuffel hart, das mit keiner weise zu bewegen ist' (WS 53, 579:15–6; 21–2); 'nicht mehr zu tun haben', 'Welche sich bekeren wollen, Da gebe Gott seine gnade zu, das sie (doch etliche) mit uns erkennen und loben Gott den Vater, unsern Schepffer, sampt unserm Herrn Jhesu Christo und dem heiligen Geist, jnn ewigkeit, Amen'. WS 53, 648:11;12–15; 'So schendlich haben sie jn besueddelt mit jhrer Judas pisse'. WS 53, 647:11–12.

18. 'Wenn ich aber einen frommen Juden mehr uberkomme zu täufen, so will ich ihn balde auf die Elbbrücke führen und ein Stein an Hals hängen und in die Elbe werfen' (WT 1, 299, 124:22–24). Luther was reacting to a request for advice from Justus Menius on how to baptise Jews; he feared that Menius would be taken in by the 'flattery' ('Schmeichelworte') of the Jews and so provides the banter after having given a serious reply. See also WT 2, 1795: the Jew to be drowned should be baptised in the name of Abraham, since the Jews do not keep the faith (WT 2, 2634 a and b for another version). Luther also alleged that Jews would get themselves baptised for money: WT 6, p. 171, 6762.

19. WB 7, 24 Aug, 6 Sept. 1535; 7 1937, 2227, 2228, 2235.

20. For example, WT 3, 2912 b, pp. 76, 77; WT 3, pp. 599, 600, 601; 3768; the arrogance of the Jews comes from their pride in circumcision, which is exclusive to them and which Luther believes has been replaced by baptism. On 'verstockt', see, for example, WB 8, 90:35; 91:13, where he condemns the rabbis for failing to be moved by Christ's suffering—'even if I were horns and stones it would have moved me'; and imagines that if he were to show mercy and intercede, it would be used to 'euer Verstockung'. See also Rublack, 'Fluxes', 1–16.

21. WB 3, 656, 2 Sept. 1523, 147, n. 4: this concerns rumours of an attempt by a nun in Rome who was a former mistress of the elector and had then been unhappily married off. Hearing of Luther, she was attempting to use her contacts with the elector to get an introduction to him.

22. Juncker, *Das guldene und Silberne Ehren-Gedächtniß*, 90–93. Luther refers to the incident in two letters at the time, saying the man had been promised two thousand gold coins: WB 3, 821, 23 Jan. 1525, 428; WB 3, 829, 11 Feb. 1525, 439. Luther did not want the men to be tortured but was convinced they were the ones about whom he had been warned. See also WT 2, 2501 a and b, 493, 494.

23. Mathesius, *Historien*, ch. 14. See also on this story WT 5, p. 83, 5354, where Luther supposedly said that only when cats and mice agree—that is, never—will the Jew become truly Christian.

24. Jonas and Celius, *Vom Christlichen abschied*, in Freybe, *Drei zeitgenössische Texte*, fo. B i (v)–B ii (r).

25. WT 3, p. 76, 2912 a; 2192 b; in these comments from 1533 he also mentions the Jewish statue on the outside of the Wittenberg church. Luther is surprised by how so many Jews could fit into the tiny space of Judea, WT 5, p. 126, 5396: Luther may be referring to another Ambrosius here, but he does mention Reutter's house in other contexts, which seems to have been a landmark for him.

26. There is a version from around 1470 of a Judensau similar to that on the Wittenberg church which shows the Jew poking out his tongue in the direction of the pig's anus, whilst there is a heap of excrement beneath his foot, alluding to the idea that Jews ate excrement. The Wittenberg Judensau also featured in a single sheet broadside of 1596, published in Wittenberg; this image adds a young Jewish boy who looks in the anus of a piglet. See also Shachar, *The Judensau*.

27. 'Ein gelerter ehrlicher Man . . . der den unfletigen luegen der Jueden feind gewest ist' (WS 53, 601:1–3).

28. WS 54, 21: 4–6: 'niemand je wuester, groeber und unziemlicher wider christliche Zucht und Bescheidenheit . . . geschrieben habe, denn Luther'. They name two other writings against Jews, including the 'schweinisches, kotiges Schemhamphorasch' (21:8).

29. In *That Jesus Christ Was Born a Jew*, Luther does interpret Daniel to mean that Gabriel is speaking about Christ, and that when he talks about those who 'cut off' the Messiah he means that 'die yhn creutzigen und auß dißer wellt treyben, werden nicht mehr yhn angehoren und seyn volck seyn, sondern wirt eyn ander volck annemen' (WS 11, 335:8–10); 'those who crucify him and drive him from this world will no more belong to him and be his people, but he will take unto himself another people' (LW 45, 227).

30. 'davon er in einer stund, in einem Monat, in einem Jar, ja in zehen oder zwentzig jaren sterben mus' (WS 51, 195: 35–36). Luther promises that Jews who convert and 'give up their usury' will be treated as brothers, but that those who tolerate Jews are guilty of their sins. On the myth of ritual murder, see Rubin, *Gentile Tales*, and Hsia, *The Myth of Ritual Murder*.

31. WS 53, 523–26: On the Jews and their Lies: here Luther sets out his seven-point programme of measures to be taken against the Jews; and he repeats it with variations, 536–40.

32. 'als weren es hunde und nicht menschen' (WS 11, 315:3–4); 'das man sie gleich fur hunde hellt, Was sollten wyr guttis an yhn schaffen? Item das man yhn verbeutt, untter uns tzu erbeytten, hantieren und andere menschliche gemeynschafft tzu haben, da mit man sie tzu wuchern treybt, wie sollt sie das bessern?' (WS 11, 336:26–29; LW 45, 229).

33. 'Denn unsere narren die Bepste, Bischoff, Sophisten und Munche, die groben esels kopffe, haben bis her also mit den Juden gefaren, das, wer eyn gutter Christ were geweßen, hette wol mocht eyn Jude werden. Und wenn ich eyn Jude gewesen were, und hette solche tolpell und knebel gesehen den Christen glauben regirn und leren, so were ich ehe eyn saw worden denn eyn Christen'. WS 11, 314:28–315:2; LW 45, 200.

34. 'es sollten yhr viel rechte Christen werden und widder tzu yhrer vetter, der Propheten unnd Patriarchen glauben tretten, davon sie nur weytter geschreckt werden, wenn man yhr ding furwirfft und ßo gar nichts will seyn lassen und handelt nur mit hohmut und verachtung gegen sie'. WS 11, 315:15–19; LW 45, 200.

35. 'Eyn newe lugen ist aber uber mich aus gangen' (WS 11, 314:3); sind auch rechte Christen geweßen wie wyr (WS 11, 317:26; LW 45, 199; 203).

36. Rubin, *Mother of God*, 228–29; 301–2.

37. Rubin, *Gentile Tales*, 138–39; and Rubin, *Mother of God*, 301.

38. See Creasman, 'The Virgin Mary against the Jews'; the woodcut is by Michael Ostendorfer.

39. LW 45, 197 (Introduction).

40. 'die verkereten preyßer der mutter gottis . . . Denn die unverstendigen gotzen diener thuns nicht weytter denn nur der mutter gottis tzu ehren, das sie die selben hoch heben umb der jungfrawschafft willen und gleich eyn abgott draus machen'. WS 11, 319:3–7; LW 45, 205.

41. 'laß sie tzuvor milch saugen und auffs erst dißen menschen Jhesum fur den rechten Messiah erkennen. Darnach sollen sie weyn trincken und auch lernen, wie er warhafftiger Gott sey'. WS 11, 336:16–19; LW 45, 229.

42. Israel, *European Jewry in the Age of Mercantilism*, 15–17; Edwards, *The Jews in Christian Europe*, 105–6.

43. 'Wie jnn den Lendern hin und widder die Jueden mit jrem geschmeisʒund lere ein reissen, auch etliche Christen schon verfueret haben, das sie sich beschnitten lassen'(WS 50, 312:8–10); LW 47, 65. See also WT 3, p. 441, 3597 (from 1537), where his immediate association with Jewish wickedness is that they have circumcised many Christians in Moravia.

44. 'Nostris temporibus in Moravis natum est stolidum hominum genus, Sabbatharii, qui Iudaeorum exemplo Sabbathum servandum contendunt, et forte circumcisionem quoque pari ratione urgebunt'(WS 42, 520:22–24); he mentioned them again, 603:20; LW 47, 60; LW 2, 361, Lectures on Genesis, ch. 13.

45. 'So bitte ich gar freundlich, jr wollet mir die selbige eilend zu schreiben, So will ich alter narr vnd barmhertziger Christ, flugs lassen ein steinern messer machen, vnd ein Jude werden, vnd solt ich nicht allein das glied, sondern auch nasen vnd ohren beschneitten lassen . . .'(fo. B (r)). He made a similar comment at table in 1538, again discussing the circumcision of Moravian Christians, and imagining that he and others might be forced to undergo circumcision (WT 3, 3768, 600); and in 1537 he had talked about Christians in Moravia undergoing circumcision and calling themselves by a new name, 'Sabbatarians' (WT 3, 3597, 441): in this

earlier remark the agency is less clear. Luther hoped he himself would not be so crazy as to get circumcised; 'you'd have to cut off my Katy's and all women's left breast first' ('Jch hoff nicht, das ich so thorecht werdt werden, ut circumcisionem susciperem. Ehr must ir mein Keth vnd alle weiber die linck brust lassen abschneiden', 600:4–5). Again, the comparison Luther makes is very sexual and is connected to gender identity itself; losing the foreskin is as bad as losing the left breast. Luther may also be thinking of the one-breasted Amazons here, though they supposedly cut off their right breasts. At any rate, he clearly sees circumcision as a diminution of sexual identity.

46. 'ist mir vnter der hand gewachssen . . . weil die fedder so lauffen must'; WS 50, 337:3–5; LW 47, 97, translates this as 'I was quite unaware of it, so quickly did my pen skim over the paper', omitting the possible phallic reference. In his anti-Semitic outpourings, Luther often says that his works simply grew or poured out of his pen. See also the close of *On the Jews and Their Lies*: 'So viel schreibens . . . habt jr mir ausgezwungen' (WS 53, 552:29–30), 'So long an essay, dear sir and good friend, you have elicited from me . . .' (LW 47, 305).

47. 'Teufelischem zusatz' (WS 53, 430:17); 'Welche uber das, das sie dem Kneblin die Vorhaut abschneiten, Weiter das heutlin an seinem schwentzlin zurueck auffreissen mit scharffen Finger negelin, Wie man lieset in jren Buechern Und thun dem Kindlin damit uber die massen wehe, on und uber Gottes befehl, also, das dem Vater, so sich der Beschneittung frewen solt, da stehet und hoeret das Kindlin schreien, die augen ubergehen und durchs hertz gehet' (WS 53:439:8–14; LW 47, 152–53). Anton Margaritha's text also has extensive sections on the legacies of circumcision, in which he imagines a circumcised Jew being unable to urinate in a straight line, or father children and so forth: *Der gantz Jüdisch glaub mit sampt ainer gründtlichen und warhafften anzaygunge* (fo. B ii (r)). It is also illustrated and attacks many 'superstitions' which Margaritha argues are associated with particular festivals. On the relationship of Luther's text to Margaritha's, see Peter von der Osten-Sacken, *Martin Luther und die Juden*.

48. WS 26, 634 ff., 638:14–15: 'Es ist freylich solch rottwelsche sprache von den Juden komen, den viel Ebreischer wort drynnen sind' (preface to his edition of the classic *Von der falschen Betler buberey*). The remark follows straight after he warns the reader to beware of the Devil.

49. 'Und diese betruebte neige, garstrige hefen, verdorreter schaum, schimlichte grund suppe und moesichtiger pful vom Juedenthum solten mit jrer busse und gerechtigkeit der gantzen Welt reich, das ist Messiam und der Prophetien erfuellung, verdienen, da sich doch oberzeleter stueck keins haben, nichts denn eine faule, stinckende, verworffen neige sind, vom Veterlichen gebluet'. WS 53, 510:22–26; LW 41, 241. There is a good deal about smell in the tract as well: the Jews 'stink' and Luther ironically imagines them finding that the gentiles 'stink' because they are not circumcised. See also WS 51, 195: in his *Admonition Against the Jews*, the conclusion to his final four sermons, he terms their blood 'wesserig', watery, and 'wild': 195:14.

50. 'quin cogantur fateri se non esse amplius populum Dei, quia, si essent populus Dei, haberent terram illam' (WS 42, 520:19–20; LW 2, 361).

51. WS 50, 322; LW 47, 78.

52. 'faule, unnuetze luegen und falsch geschwetze'; 'das sie mit teidingen und luegen umb gehen' (WS 50, 323:3; and 6–7; LW 47, 78).

53. LW 47, 268–70; 285–87; WS 53, 523–26; 536–37.

54. Kaufmann, *Luther's Jews*, 48–50.

55. 'Ja wol, sie halten uns Christen in unserm eigen Lande gefangen, Sie lassen uns erbeiten im nasen schweis, gelt und gut gewinnen, Sitzen sie die weil hinter dem Ofen, faulentzen, pompen und braten birn, fressen, sauffen, leben sanfft und wol von unserm ererbeitem gut, Haben uns und unser gueter gefangen durch jren verfluchten Wucher, spotten dazu und speien uns an'. WS 53, 521: 9–14; LW 47, 266. Luther also accuses them of being the most avaricious of peoples, guilty of accursed usury: 'Denn kein Volck unter der Sonnen geitziger, denn sie sind, gewest ist, noch sind und jmer fort bleiben, wie man sihet an jrem verfluchten Wucher'. WS 53:477:21–23.

56. 'Glaub keinem wolffe auff wielder heyden, / Auch keinem Juden auff seinen eydt, / Gleub bapst auff seine gewissen, / Du wirst sonst von allen dreyen beschissen'. WT 5, 6172, 522:33–6. He recited a similar rhyme equating the Jews' constant petitioning, lawyers' books, and 'that which is under the maid's apron' as the three things that drive the world mad: 'Der juristen buch, Der Juden gesuch / Vnd das vnter der magd schurztuch / Seindt drey geschirr, / Machen die gantze welt irr' (WT 5, 5655, 292:8–12); and see for a slightly different version WT 5, 5609, 276:19–22.

57. 'Wenn ich wäre an der Herren zu N. N. Statt, so wollte ich alle Jüden zusammenfordern, und sie fragen: Warum sie Christum ein Hurenkind heißen, seine Mutter eine Hure, und Hariam, ein Scheißhaus? Könnten sie es probiren und beweisen, so wollte ich ihnen tausend Gülden schenken; könnten sie es aber nicht probiren, so wollte ich ihnen die Zunge zum Nacken heraus reißen lassen. WT 5, p. 248:10–4, 5567. In this passage Luther also seems to deny that the Jews will be converted before the Last Judgement. Here Luther's attack on the Jews mentions Mary, and to this extent it shares medieval currents; but it is their denial of Mary's virginity and their insult to Christ that is key, not reverence for Mary. As an Oedipal theme, it raises issues of both parental figures.

58. See, however, Katz, 'Shylock's Gender', which argues that the widespread belief that male Jews menstruated was linked to beliefs about circumcision, and that this was thought to be the reason why Jews stole Christian children for their blood. Luther, however, does not seem to have believed in the Jewish blood libel.

59. So also in 1542 Luther had said: 'The Jews think that we have to learn to study the Bible from them. What? Should we learn the Bible from them, who are its greatest enemies?' (Die Juden meinen, wir mussen von inen die bibliam studirn. Ja wol! Solten wir bibliam lernen ab eis, qui sunt summi hostes bibliae?); WT 5, pp. 220:25–26, 5535. Luther was responding to the translation of the Bible into Latin by Sebastian Muenster, which he held to be too keen to follow rabbinical

interpretation. See also WS 53, 647. WS 48, 702: here Luther wrote that just as flies dirty a room, leaving it covered in excrement so that it becomes black with fly dung and must be washed, so also the Jews dirty Scripture.

60. WS 43, 575:8–11; he refers to Jacob's Ladder as Christ, WT 2, 2631 a, 1532, p. 561:27; WT 6, 6558, pp. 38:21–22, and see Steinmetz, 'Luther and the Ascent of Jacob's Ladder'.

61. In *On the Jews and Their Lies*, he asserts 'Viel weniger gehe ich damit umb, das ich die Jueden bekeren wolle, Denn das ist unmueglich'; WS 53, 417:23–6 ('Much less do I propose to convert the Jews, for that is impossible', LW 47, 137).

62. LW 47, 192 (lies); WT 5026: here Luther starts by saying that the Jews insult Mary as a whore and latrinam, and call Christ Thola, that is, a hanged highwayman. The issue over which he says they insisted on the authority of their rabbis was the status of the meaning of virgin.

63. WS 53, 634–42.

64. Nikolaus Selnecker, *Historica oratio vom Leben . . . d. Mart. Lutheri*, fo. 34 (r)–35 (v); having given Luther some sweet wine, they debate the meaning of 'virgin'. The account of the meeting with Cochlaeus follows straight on; Selnecker claims to have heard both stories from Caspar Sturm, the imperial herald.

65. 'Propheta Germaniae' is written around the circle of Wolf Milicz of St Joachimstal's medals of Luther from 1537, based on the Brosamer version of Cranach's original, Dresden Kunstsammlungen, Münzkabinett, 1914/198b, silver gilded, and B1D2545 for the same design in lead. The designation of Luther as a prophet became particularly important after his death, but Luther himself was interested in it, and it circulated during his lifetime.

66. Melanchthon in Vandiver, Keen, and Frazel, *Luther's Lives*, 38–39; Melanchthon, *Vita Lutheri*, fo. 24 (v). See also Petersen, 'The Apocalyptic Luther', 83–84.

67. WS 51, 148–96; 195–96.

68. 'Villeicht euch nicht mehr predigen moecht'(WS 51, 195:3); 'Darumb solt jr Herren sie nicht leiden, sondern sie weg treiben' (195:25); 'das er ein verboester Juede ist, der nicht ablassen wird Christum zu lestern, dich aus zu saugen und (wo er kan) zu toedten' (196:1–3).

69. Luther/Walther, *Prophezeiungen D. Martini Lutheri, Zur erinnerung und anreitzung zur Christlichen Busse ordentlich und mit vleiß zusamen getragen*, Wittenberg, 1559 [VD 16 L 3491], fo. A I r ff. Walther uses the same digestive imagery that we will see later: believers ought to hunger for the Word, but 'Die Jueden aber sinds so sat / voll vnd truncken / das sie goecken vnd vbergehen', fo. A i (v). The *Table Talk* also included a section on the Jews, providing a handy compilation of Luther's anti-Semitism; this was particularly important because the work's sub-headings by topic made it easy to locate the anti-Semitic comments; and the widespread diffusion within Lutheranism of the *Table Talk* meant that it was particularly influential.

70. Johannes Aurifaber, ed., Martin Luther, *Tischreden*, Eisleben 1566, fo. 588 (r)–595 (v), [VD 16 L 6748].

71. See Nikolaus Selnecker, a strong proponent of Luther's commemoration, *Von den Jueden . . .* , Leipzig 1577 [VD 16 L 7155], Preface, fo. ii (r)–xv (r).

72. One of the allegations made against Johannes Agricola, Luther's former close associate, was that he publicly defended Jews: WB 10, 3909 [c. 1 Sept. 1543], p. 388, n. 12.

73. Interestingly, *On the Jews and Their Lies* was translated into Latin by Justus Jonas, appearing in 1544 in Frankfurt and dedicated to Duke Moritz of Saxony; *Vom Schem Hamphoras* was not. See WS 53, 415.

74. 'Hie dreck, nicht der auff der Gassen ligt, Sondern aus dem bauch kompt, "Scham" heisst: hie oder da, "Peres", das der Saw und allen Thieren jnn den Dermen ist'. WS 53, 601:12–15.

75. LW 45, 200.

76. Hans-Jürgen Döhle, 'Schwein, Geflügel und Fisch'.

77. 'Als ein wilde schwartze Sau' (Mathesius, *Historien*, 481).

78. 'Fallen . . . wie die unfletigen Sew in den trog lestern und schenden, das sie nicht wissen noch verstehen wollen' (WS 53, 541:2–3); 'oder mit Sew dreck auff jn werffe' (WS 53, 537:15); 'Jr soltet allein die Biblia lesen, die der Saw unter dem Schwantz stehet, und die buchstaben, so da selbs heraus fallen, fressen und sauffen' (WS 53, 478:30–33; LW 47 291; 286; 212); he also insists that the Jews must be 'driven out like mad dogs', 'so muessen wir sie, wie die tollen hunde aus jagen' (WS 53, 541:36–542:1), the simile he had also used in relation to the peasants in his infamous tract *Against the Murdering Thieving Hordes of Peasants* of 1525 (LW 47, 292).

79. 'Wenn mir Gott keinen andern Messia geben wolt, denn wie die Jueden begeren und hoffen, So wolt ich viel, viel lieber eine Saw, denn ein Mensch sein' (WS 53, 542:5–7); 'Denn eine Saw ligt in jrem pflaum feddern bette, auff der gassen oder misten, ruget sicher, schnarcket sanfft, schlefft suesse, fuercht keinen Koenig noch Herrn, keinen tod noch Helle, keinen Teufel noch Gottes zorn. Lebet so gar on sorge, das sie auch nicht dencket, wo Kleien sind' (WS 53: 542:35–543:2; WS 53 543:10–13; LW 47, 292–4).

80. We know from archaeology on the house that the Luther household in Wittenberg kept pigs close to the house, Mirko Gutjahr, 'The first protestant parsonage? Luther's House and Household according to Archaeological Evidence', in Harald Meller, Colin Bailey, Martin Eberle, and Stefan Rein, eds., *Martin Luther and the Reformation* (Exhibition Accompanying Volume), Dresden 2016, p. 169; they had their own swineherd. Domestic pigs in this period looked rather like wild pigs: they had long legs and long snouts: Antje Heling, *Zu Haus bei Martin Luther*, 27–28. Money could also be saved in 'piggy boxes', ceramic containers in the shape of pigs: see, for an example of a green-glazed pig found in Dresden, Gutjahr et al, eds., *Luther!*, 131.

81. Luther could also use the pig to represent Germans: see WS 54, 354: in his 'Images of the Papacy' which he designed to accompany his 1545 work, *Against the Roman Papacy*, the rhyme makes it clear that the sow on which the pope rides

represents the Germans, exploited by the papacy. The idea is that to ride a sow you should put excrement in your mouth/hand, so that the sow smells it and tries to eat it and will not bite the rider: there is a pamphlet which explains this: *New Raeterschbuechlin Kurtzweilig zügerichtet Mit scharpffsinnigen verborgenen Fragen vnd Antworten*, produced in Frankfurt in 1541 [VD 16 ZV 26661].

82. 'Der Teuffel hat in die N. geschmissen und den bauch abermal geleeret, Das ist ein recht Heiligthumb, das die Jueden, und was Juede sein wil, kuessen, fressen, sauffen und anbeten sollen. Und widderumb der Teuffel auch fressen und sauffen, was solche seine Juenger speien, oben und unten auswerffen koennen'; WS 53, 587:2–6.

83. WT 3, pp. 355, 3491. Bugenhagen was the parish priest of Wittenberg and Luther's confessor.

84. 'Woher sie solche hohe kunst haben, on das ich mus dencken, Da Judas Scharioth sich erhenckt hatte, das jhm die Darme zurissen und, wie den erhenckten geschicht, die Blase borsten, Da haben die Jueden villeicht jre Diener [Bl. O 1] mit guelden kannen und silbern schuesseln dabey gehabt, die Judas pisse (wie mans nennet sampt dem andern auffgefangen, darnach unternander die merde gefressen und gesoffen, davon sie so scharffsichtige augen kriegt, das sie solche und dergleichen Glose jnn der Schrifft sehen, die weder Mattheus noch Jsaias selbs, noch alle Engel, schweige wir verfluchten Goijm sehen koennen. Oder haben jrem Gott, dem Sched, jnn den hindern gekuckt und in demselben rauchloch solchs geschrieben funden'. WS 53, 636:32–637:5.

85. Aber wenn du werest da gewest, so hettestu gesagt, Es were der Juden oder ires Gottes schuld gewest. Denn wir musten durch ein Dorff hart vor Eisleben, da viel Juden innen wonen, vielleicht haben sie mich so hart angeblasen. LW Letters III, 290–91; WB 11, 1 Feb. 1546, 4195, 275; the American translation does not quite capture the sense. In this letter Luther also writes that the 'beautiful women', that is, the prostitutes, can no longer tempt him; and in the following letter to his wife, he mentions his impotence and apologizes for it, after having reverted to discussing his illness and the village through which they went: now he says that 400 Jews are rumoured to go in and out there, and accuses the Countess of Mansfeld of being their protector. WB 11, 4201, 7 Feb. 1546, 286–87.

86. This was his criticism of Münster's bible: it gave too much respect to rabbinical interpretation. Instead the Old Testament had to be understood as being about Christ.

87. *Biblia, Die Luther-Bibel von 1534. Vollständiger Nachdruck*, vol. 2, fo. CVI (r–v); A I (r).

## Chapter 7. Luther Kitsch

1. Buc, *The Dangers of Ritual*. Buc's book offered a persuasive attack on the anthropological idea that rituals work automatically in creating unity; they are, he claims, contested discourses.

2. There were even printed Luther tour guides, which offered illustrated itineraries through the places with connections to Luther and his Reformation, and dedicated Luther tours by bicycle or bus. The ultimate development of this came with Steiger, *Gedächtnisorte der Reformation*, two gigantic tomes published by Schnell und Steiner, the firm responsible for the art-historical church guide booklets found in every German church. This massive work of scholarship, covering over 280 places, is richly illustrated and finally provides a definitive, encyclopaedic survey of Lutheran art and the Lutheran aesthetic; it was published in 2016 in time for the celebrations. Its importance is impossible to overstate, because the ecclesiastical art it documents was not systematically captured when Germany was split between East and West (indeed it spread beyond the boundaries of Germany), and after the War, the richness of German Lutheran art was simply forgotten. See also, for its first major scholarly analysis, Heal, *A Magnificent Faith*.

3. The Wittenberg statue is by Johann Gottfried Schadow, and it was given an iron baldachin by Johann Friedrich Schinkel. The monument's foundation was laid to mark the anniversary of 1817, and it was finished in 1821; its installation coincided with the King's assumption of overall Church authority in a united Lutheran Church in Prussia, in a Wittenberg which had only become part of Prussia in 1814. On monuments to Luther, see Lehmann, *Luthergedächtnis 1817 bis 2017*, and Rößler, 'Martin Luther'; and Buss, 'Die Deutschen und Martin Luther'.

4. Mai, 'Von Luther zu Hitler?', 64, 133; Laube, 'Homely Audacity': both Luther and Bismarck carry swords and Luther carries the banderole 'Ein feste Burg' while the other banderole states, 'Wir Deutsche fürchten Gott sonst nichts auf dieser Welt'; Bering, *Luther im Fronteinsatz*. Images from the celebrations of 1917 and from Lovis Corinth's cycle were displayed in the exhibition *Martin Luther: Sein Leben in Bildern*, held at the Augusteum Wittenberg in 2016–17, and curated by Jutta Strehle. In the USA and in Australia, by contrast, the First World War and anti-German feeling led to a distancing from Luther (Lehmann, *Luthergedächtnis*, 110–25).

5. I am grateful to Diarmaid Macculloch for bringing the existence of this church to my attention. See also Großmann, 'Lutherkirchen', 374–76.

6. For a reflection on the Lutherans in Britain and over the world, see Long, *Martin Luther and His Legacy*.

7. On Lutheran culture and what it might encompass, see Hill, 'Introduction: Making Lutherans'; and see her 'Fun and Loathing in Later Lutheran Culture', ibid.

8. Rabus, *Historien*. The fourth volume (1556) contains a biography of Luther.

9. The format continued into the nineteenth century, and there were printed and coloured versions from 1817 produced in Nuremberg that show many of the same scenes: see Wartburg-Stiftung, *Luther und die Deutschen*, 128–29, for illustrations. There were medieval small round boxes for holding the host. I am grateful to Ryan Asquez for this information.

10. WB 4, 1164, 1 Nov. 1527, 274:26–27.

11. WS 54, 179–87.
12. For a diagram illustrating how representations of the 'posting' changed between 1617 and 2014, see Wendebourg, 'Reformation Anniversaries', 439. On the posting of the 95 Theses, see Volz, *Martin Luthers Thesenanschlag*, Iserloh, *Luther zwischen Reform und Reformation*; Iserloh, *Luthers Thesenanschlag*; Ott and Treu, *Luthers Thesenanschlag*; Marshall, *Nailing the Myth*; and Pettegree, *Brand Luther*, 70–73, for a pithy summary. The exhibition 'Martin Luther: Sein Leben in Bildern' held in the Augusteum Wittenberg in 2016–17 and curated by Jutta Strehle vividly demonstrated the absence of such images. For a brilliant discussion of the episode, which puts it in its wider cultural context, see Jütte, *The Strait Gate*, 175–208. From the copies which have survived: in the Leipzig one, the printer has made mistakes in numbering, ending up with an apparent 87; in another from Nuremberg the Theses are numbered in batches of 20; and in the Basel printing, the numerals are Roman and the format is that of a small pamphlet, which could not have been displayed or posted. It is likely that other printings of the Theses have been lost. For photographs of the known copies, see Kluttig-Altmann, *Martin Luther*, 154–56.
13. Rabus, *Historien*; Spalatin, *Annales Reformationis*; Seidel, *Historia und Geschicht* [VD 16 S 5354], 59–60, moves seamlessly from the Peasants' War of 1525 to the Confession of Augsburg without mentioning it; Mathesius, *Historien*, 118, 119; so also does Selnecker, *Historica oratio* [VD 16 S 5557], fo. 44 (r).
14. Vandiver, Keen, and Frazel, *Luther's Lives*, 130.
15. Cochlaeus (Vogelsang), 'Ein Heimlich Gespräch'. See also the manuscript image by Kilian Leib of Luther's Bath and Mirror, University Library Graz, Cod. 1227; Cgm 6551 [http://daten.digitale-sammlungen.de/bsb00105115/image_6.], which shows a balding, bearded Luther holding the hand of 'Ket von bora', both in habits, clearly indicating that both are breaking vows of chastity.
16. Hasenberg, *Ludus ludentem luderum ludens* [VD 16 H 715]; and Hasenberg, *Czwen sendbrieffe* [VD 16 H 713].
17. See Seidel and Spehr, *Das evangelische Pfarrhaus*; and on the first generation of pastors' wives, Plummer, *From Priest's Whore to Pastor's Wife*.
18. Preface to the Complete Edition of Luther's Latin Writings, 1545. LW 34, 337; WS 54, 176–87, 185:18; 186:8–9.
19. Melanchthon, *Vita Lutheri*, Frankfurt am Main 1555 [VD 16 M 3428].
20. On Bugenhagen, see Schmid, 'Luther im Norden'; on the incident, Roper, *Martin Luther*, ch. 17, n. 22.
21. See, for example, Fitschen, 'Vorbild oder Abbildder Gesellschaft?'. Gustav König's saccharine mid-century etching shows him at Christmas.
22. Though some depictions managed to incorporate a market-day crowd in Renaissance dress! On WWI, see Bering, *Luther im Fronteinsatz*: as Bering shows, Luther and the hammer became incorporated into WWI propaganda, the hammer taking on a life of its own. Luther was used to justify the war, his masculinity was underlined, and the 1917 anniversary of the posting was celebrated in

militaristic fashion. By contrast, the lithograph series of Luther's life by the artist Lovis Corinth in the wake of the German defeat depicts a more ambiguous, less triumphalist vision of the reformer with the hammer.

23. *Die Bibel nach Martin Luthers Übersetzung*: the material is on special high-quality paper that enables coloured photograph material.

24. See Kasten, '"Was ist Luther?".'

25. Melanchthon in Vandiver, Keen, and Frazel, *Luther's Lives*, 16; 21; 38–9; Philipp Melanchthon, *Vita Lutheri*, fo. 24 (v). For an example of how early biographers of Luther repeated the idea that his attack on the Church had been foretold by Hilten and others, see Seidel, *Historia und Geschicht* [VD 16 S 5354], 11–13; Mathesius, *Historien*, 8–9; for Luther's interest in the prophecies, WT 3, 3795; WB 5, 1480, 17 Oct. 1529; and 1491, 7 Nov. 1529; Myconius's full reply, 1501, 2 Dec. 1529.

Dingel, *Die Bekenntnisschriften*, 378. Hilten predicted that the assault on the papacy would last thirty years—and so Lutheran hagiographers could link it precisely with Luther's death in 1546. Hilten thus took his place as an important forerunner of Luther, a St John the Baptist figure predicting the coming of the new prophet. Nikolaus Rebhan, the seventeenth-century Lutheran theologian and Superintendent of Eisenach's account, even had Hilten perish in his cell refusing to receive the sacrament in one kind only, as if he were an adherent of Hus, WB 5, 1501, *Beilage* II, 195.

26. There were three such major collaborations: one at the Minneapolis Institute of Art, 'Martin Luther: Art and Reformation'; one at the Morgan Library and Museum New York, 'Word and Image: Martin Luther's Reformation'; and one at the Pitts Theology Library, Emory University, Atlanta, 'Law and Grace: Martin Luther, Lucas Cranach and the Promise of Salvation'. The combined catalogue is Kluttig-Altmann, *Martin Luther: Treasures of the Reformation*. The exhibition was also made available online through Google, and was financially supported by the German Federal Foreign Office.

27. It was named *Der Luther Effekt*. Instead of providing descriptions of each of the exhibits, the visitor was given a small printed brochure with which to walk around the exhibition, matching object with number—it was as if the visitor had to encounter the objects through printed research. In many respects it was a highly original exhibition, which deliberately refused to provide a conventional Luther blockbuster with Berlin as the centre. Breaking with the nineteenth-century tradition of celebrating Luther as Prussian/German, it attempted to present Lutheranism as an international phenomenon, not primarily a German one, and to showcase Berlin as an international city, rather than as the capital of Germany.

28. Rößler, *Luthermania*.

29. On some routes into town you also passed the 'Luther oak' on the site where Luther burnt the bull of excommunication and the books of Canon Law. Luther oaks, planted in 1893 and again in 1917, are an interesting commemorative form. The original marks a significant historic site, but there are Luther oaks all over

Germany. Like relics they have multiplied so that everyone can have their own, and you don't have to be in Wittenberg to plant one. Natural objects to which commemorative significance was attached, Luther oaks planted Luther in the landscape, not unlike the way-crosses and shrines that dot Catholic landscapes. The deliberate choice of non-man-made objects linked Luther yet more closely to German terrain—and it was a German oak which was used in the World War I postcard (Mai, 'Von Luther zu Hitler?', 64).

30. The Luther socks are a long-standing souvenir, available in both English and German. It was rumoured that there was a variant of these, a condom inscribed 'Here I stand . . .', which was discontinued; I like to think Luther would have been amused.

31. I am indebted to Hole Rößler of the Herzog August Bibliothek Wolfenbüttel, who gave me his own duck.

32. I am grateful to Johannes Paulmann for supplying me with a packet.

33. Courtesy of Philip Booth.

34. Grebe and Thiele, *LUTHER*. Asisi explains in an interview that he oriented himself on the colours Cranach used, but that the image is intended to be hyper-realist. A couple of evenings spent in Wittenberg enabled him to absorb the 'genius loci', 15; on his view of the Panorama as not showing 'einen bestimmten Zeitpunt' but an epoch, 17; and on his technique of conducting photoshoots with real performers in costume, 33.

35. Grebe and Thiele, *LUTHER*, 67; 85 for photographs of these scenes; Asisi explains the fires are also meant to represent witch hunting, and he refers to the Cranach woodcut of the three condemned witches. Asisi's team worked with the archive, and much of the Panorama has historically correct references.

36. On the sources for Tübke's artwork see Ulrike Eydinger, 'Motive historischer Flugblätter und Druckgraphiken im Bauernkriegspanorama von Werner Tübke': chief amongst them was the richly illustrated commemorative volume of 1974, Laube, Steinmetz, and Vogler, eds., *Illustrierte Geschichte der deutschen frühbürgerlichen Revolution*.

37. Kober, *Werner Tübke: Monumentalbild Frankenhausen*; Lindner, *Vision und Wirklichkeit*; on Tübke, see Tübke-Schellenberger, *Werner Tübke. Das malerische Werk*, esp. 122–32; there are also paintings which are designs for the Frankenhausen monument, Neue National Galerie Berlin. A major exhibition of his work was held in 2017 at the Museum de Fundatie, Zwolle: 'Werner Tübke. Zeichnungen und Aquarelle'.

38. Kluttig-Altmann, *Martin Luther*, 376, for a pottery swan probably sold at Eisleben; on Luther and swan imagery, see Strehle, *Luther mit dem Schwan*. Another very popular format was the Luther medal, closely related to the Cranach portraits and often in the three-quarter-face format he favored. These were produced during Luther's lifetime as well, and could be worn on the hat.

39. See Laube, 'Süchtig nach Splittern und Scherben'. On the Lutheran cult of memory, see Boettcher, 'Late Sixteenth-Century Lutherans', 121–41. One interesting

object type is the Luther competitive drinking glass, which also developed a print version: the glass (and the Luther household owned at least one) had ridges at intervals and the object of the game was to drink to exactly the next ridge. The print version produced for 1618 celebrations divided the sections of the print glass into 'Our Father', 'Catechism', and so on (Laube, 'Süchtig nach Splittern und Scherben', 85). For Luther stove tiles, see, for example, Kluttig-Altmann, *Martin Luther*, 379: they are often in medal form, green in colour, and based on the Cranach portrait. Recent investigations suggest that they were produced in bulk shortly after Luther's death in 1546. The fact that they were used on stoves is particularly interesting, because German tiled stoves were a widely used and highly effective form of heating. They formed the convivial centre of the house, and so the placement of tiles there meant they were literally at its heart. On Luther beer mugs see Kluttig-Altmann, *Martin Luther*, 375, 383; and there is one from c. 1620 in the Berlin Kunstgewerbe Museum, Ident. Nr. K 1459, probably from Creußen, Franconia.

40. See Wartburg-Stiftung, *Luther und die Deutschen*, 317, for a photograph of a nineteenth-century framed print of the house in Eisleben where Luther was born, which includes three mementos or relics: a piece of tablecloth from Eisleben, part of a pen, and a fragment of the table on which Luther translated the New Testament. For Luther postcards, and their use on the front in World War I, see Laube, 'Homely Audacity'. Luther porcelain was produced for the celebrations in 1817 and later, Bauer, 'Das Luther-Jahrhundert'; and see p. 130 for further examples.

41. See Götze, *De Reliquiis Lutheri*. On the relationship between relics, magic, and religion in Protestantism, see Scribner, *Religion and Culture*, 275–365, and his classic essay, 'Incombustible Luther'. See also Roper, 'Luther Relics', and Rublack, 'Grapho-Relics'.

42. The 'cult' truly took off after mid-century, and 100,000 people supposedly celebrated the unveiling of the massive Luther statue in Worms in 1868 (Buss, 'Die Deutschen'). The largest Reformation monument in the world, it contains twelve massive statues. From the last quarter of the nineteenth century on, many 'Martin Luther' churches were built; for a complete list covering the twentieth century too, see Großmann, 'Lutherkirchen', esp. 377–83. The Wartburg became a monument in the nineteenth century, thoroughly Gothicised in nineteenth-century taste; Jacobs, 'Ein nationales Monument'. Luther's ring is still on display in the Dresden Green Vault entrance hall (Inv. Nr. VIII 97) having been acquired in 1650 by the Elector John George I, who wore it on his finger on his deathbed.

43. See Kornmeier, 'Luther in Effigie'. That Halle became a Luther pilgrimage/tourist site is thanks to Justus Jonas's prompt decision to commission the plaster casts as the funeral procession made its way to Wittenberg from Eisleben.

44. One instance of how this might take popular form is a tapestry by Anna Bump on show in the Berlin Museum of European Cultures. This extraordinary work comes from the region of Dithmarschen and commemorated the 150th anni-

versary of the Reformation in 1667; Anna Bump illustrated key biblical scenes and complex theological concepts in her tapestry in simple folk style, adding her own initials in the work as its creator at several points. See Neuland-Kitzerow, Binroth, and Joram, *Anna webt Reformation*.

45. Heal, *A Magnificent Faith*; Spicer, 'Martin Luther'; on the material culture of Lutheranism in Eastern Europe, see Bahlcke, Störtkuhl, and Weber, *The Luther Effect*, which also includes photographs of remarkable former Prussian and Silesian churches; on the material culture of Prussia and Brandenburg, see Slenczka, *Reformation und Freiheit*; and see Steiger, *Gedächtnisorte der Reformation*, which finally makes plain the extent of the sacral Lutheran cultural heritage.

One of the most remarkable artistic creations to which Lutheranism gave rise is the Silver Library of Duke Albrecht of Prussia: twenty Lutheran devotional printed books were bound in costly silver and gold bindings, with superb engravings and reliefs: Slenczka, *Die Silberbibliothek aus Königsberg*. Church plate, fonts, and altars were also made in Lutheran style resulting in superb works of art. The new theological and liturgical emphases required new forms: pre-Reformation chalices, for example, no longer sufficed once the congregation received communion in both kinds, and a larger jug was needed to hold the wine; better pulpits were needed, and they needed to be positioned where people could hear. For a thirteenth-century chalice extended in 1590 so that it could contain enough, see Syndram, Wirth, and Wagner, *Luther und die Fürsten*, vol. 1, 160–61.

46. See Roper, *Martin Luther*; Roper 'The Stout Doctor'; and Karant-Nunn, 'The Mitigated Fall of Humankind'.

47. 'Hie radt ich: wenn du weyßlich geloben wilt, ßo gelobe, die naßen dyr selb nicht ab beyssen, das kanstu halten' (WS 10, II, 284:21–22).

48. See Roper, 'Luther Relics'. Although they share some similar features, the Luther kitsch objects are not relics. First, they are funny. Second, they do not have any healing functions and are not devotional objects (some of the early Luther relics, however, were put to use in healing, much to the alarm of Lutheran pastors, who considered such usages superstitious). Third, their focus on eating, pleasure, and play differentiates them from relics and they include such objects as beer bottle openers.

49. Karl Friedrich Schinkel had made a visit to Wittenberg back in 1815, in order to check the state of the Castle Church for the Prussian government; and he also used the occasion to visit another 'Heiligtum', namely, the Lutherstube. Neser, *Luthers Wohnhaus*, 80–81. He chose the site of the monument; originally a much larger hall was planned for it. The bronze statue was poured in a Berlin cannon works. Originally it was surrounded by a protective railing, removed in 1928; and the baldachin was apparently replaced in 1967 (Bellmann, Harksen, and Werner, *Die Denkmale der Lutherstadt*, 47).

# BIBLIOGRAPHY

## Primary Works

Arnoldi, Franciscus. *Auff das Schmaebuchlein, welches Martin Luther widder den Meuchler zu Dreßden . . . hat lassen außgehen.* Dresden, 1531.

Bugenhagen, Johannes. *Eine Christliche Predigt vber der Leich vnd begrebnis des Ehrwirdigen D. Martini Luthers.* Wittenberg, 1546.

Cochlaeus, Johannes. *Hertzog Georgens zu Sachssen Ehrlich vnd grundtliche entschuldigung, wider Martin Luthers Auffruerisch vn[d] verlogenne brieff vnd Verantwortung.* Dresden, 1533. VD 16 C 4324.

Cochlaeus, Johann (Vogelsang). 'Ein Heimlich Gespräch von der Tragedia Johannis Hussen, 1538'. In *Flugschriften aus der Reformationszeit* 17, edited by Hugo Holstein. Halle, 1900.

Confessio Augustana. In *Die Bekenntnisschriften der evangelisch-lutherischen Kirche.* 7th ed. Göttingen: Vandenhoeck & Ruprecht, 1976.

Eck, Johannes. *Des heilgen Concilij tzu Costentz, der heylgen Christenheit, vnd hochlöblichen keyßers Sigmunds, vn[d] auch des Teutzschen Adels entschüldigung, das in bruder Martin Luder, mit vnwarheit, auffgelegt, Sie haben Johannem Huß, vnd Hieronymu[m] von Prag wider Babstlich Christlich, Keyserlich geleidt vnd eydt vorbrandt.* Leipzig, 1520.

Eck, Johannes. *Inhalt bepstlicher Bull wider Martin Ludder auffs kürtzest geteuscht.* Ingolstadt, 1520. VD 16 K 284.

Euling, Karl, ed. *Chronik des Johan Oldecop.* Tübingen: Literarischer Verein in Stuttgart, 1891.

Fischer, Hermann, ed. *Schwäbisches Wörterbuch,* 7 vols. Tübingen: 1901–36.

Flasch, Sebastian. *Zwey vnd zwaintzig Vrsachen, warumb er die Lutherisch Ketzerey . . . verlassen hab (etc.) Mit sampt angehencktem kurtzweiligen Lesen, von ermeldten Luthers guten muth, starcken trincken vnd zuesauffen.* Munich 1584. VD 16 L 3562.

Freybe, Peter, ed. *Drei zeitgenössische Texte zum Tode D. Martin Luthers.* Stuttgart: Joachim W. Siener, 1996.

Götze, Georg Henrich. *De Reliquiis Lutheri, Diversis in locis asservatis, singularia.* Leipzig, 1703.

Götze, Georg Heinrich. *Lutheri: Pestis eram vivus, moriens ero mors tua, Papa!* Lübeck, 1712.

Hasenberg, Johann. *Czwen sendbrieffe, Latein vn[d] deutzsch dem Lutther vnd seynem vormeynthem ehelichem Weybe Kethen von Bhore sampt einem geschenck, freundtlicher meynung tzuuuorfertiget: Anno 1.5.28.* Leipzig, 1528. VD 16 H 713.

Hasenberg, Johann. *Ludus ludentem luderum ludens....* Landshut, 1531. VD 16 H 715.

Jonas, Justus, Michael Celius, Johannes Bugenhagen, Philipp Melanchthon, and Caspar Cruciger. *Vom Christlichen abschied auß diesem tödlichen leben....* Nuremberg, 1546. VD 16 J 904.

Juncker, Christian. *Das Guldene und Silberne Ehren-Gedächtniß des Theuren Gottes-Lehrers D. Martini Lvtheri.* Frankfurt and Leipzig, 1706.

Karlstadt, Andreas. *Auszlegung vnnd Lewterung etzlicher heyligenn geschrifften ... in den figurn vnd schrifften der wagen....* Leipzig, 1519. VD 16 B 6113.

Karlstadt, Andreas. *Von abtahung der Bylder....* Wittenberg, 1522. VD 16 B 6215.

Lehmann, Christian. *Historischer Schauplatz derer natürlichen Merckwürdigkeiten in dem Meißnischen Ober-Ertzgebirge.* Leipzig, 1699. VD 17 3:302104H.

Lemnius, Simon. *Chronologia evangelica. Das ist ein Summarischer Auszug der Neweuangelischen Chronicken, ... des newen Christenthumbs, wie es Martin Luther selbst gepflanzt hat.* Weissenhorn, 1570. VD 16 V 2119.

Margaritha, Anton. *Der gantz jüdisch Glaub: mit sampt einer gründlichen vnd warhafftigen anzaygunge, aller Satzungen, Ceremonien, Gebetten, Haymliche vnd offentliche Gebreüch (etc.).* Augsburg, 1530. VD 16 M 972.

Mathesius, Johannes. *Historien von dem Leben und den Schicksalen des grossen Reformators Doctor Martin Luther Im Jahr 1565 in 17 Predigten beschrieben.* 1566. Repr. Leipzig: Salomo Lincke, 1806.

Matheson, Peter, ed. *The Collected Works of Thomas Münzter.* Edinburgh: T. & T. Clark, 1988.

Mayer, Johannes Friedrich. *De Catharina Lutheri coniuge dissertatio.* Hamburg, 1698.

Melanchthon, Philipp. *Vita Lutheri.* Frankfurt am Main, 1555. VD 16 M 3428.

Müntzer, Thomas. *Auszlegung des andern vnter||schyds Danielis,* Allstedt, 1524. VD 16 M 6746.

Müntzer, Thomas, *Thomas-Müntzer-Ausgabe. Kritische Gesamtausgabe,* 3 vols. Edited by Armin Kohnle et al., Evangelische Verlagsanstalt: Leipzig, 2004–2017.

Nas, Johannes, *Qvinta Centvria....* Alexander II and Samuel Weissenhorn: Ingolstadt, 1570. VD 16 N 105.

*New Räterschbüchlin Kurtzweilig zügerichtet Mit scharpffsinnigen verborgenen Fragen vnd Antworten.* Frankfurt, 1541. VD 16 ZV 26661.

Rabus, Ludwig. *Historien: Der Heyligen Außerwölten Gottes Zeügen/ Bekennern vnd Martyrern,* 8 vols. Strasbourg, 1552–58.

Seidel, Paul. *Historia und Geschicht ... Doctoris Martini Lvtheri.* Wittenberg: Simon Gronenberg, 1581. VD 16 S 5354.

Selnecker, Nikolaus. *Historica oratio vom Leben ... d. Mart. Lutheri.* Leipzig, 1576. VD 16 S 5557.

Spalatin, Georg. *Annales Reformationis Oder Jahr-Bücher von der Reformation Lvtheri,* edited by Ernst Salomon Cyprian. Leipzig, 1718.

Stiftung Luthergedenkstätten in Sachsen-Anhalt, ed. *Passional Christi und Anti-christi*. Wittenberg, 1998.

Sylvius, Petrus. *Die letzen zwey geschlissliche vnd aller kreffigste buchleyn*. Leipzig, 1534. VD 16 P 1296.

Walther, Georg. *Prophezeiungen D. Martini Lutheri. Zur erinnerung und anreitzung zur Christlichen Busse ordentlich und mit vleiß zusamen getragen*. Wittenberg, 1559. VD 16 L 3491.

Witzel, Georg. *Apologia: das ist: ein vertedigs rede Georgii Wicelii wider seine afterreder die Luteristen*. Leipzig, 1533.

Zwingli, Huldrych. *Huldrici Zuinglii Opera*, 8 vols. Edited by Melchior Schuler and Johannes Schulthess, Zürich: Schulthess und Höhr, 1829–42.


## SECONDARY WORKS

Amelang, James. 'Sleeping with the Enemy: The Devil in Dreams in Early Modern Spain'. *American Imago* 69, no. 3 (Fall 2012): 319–52.

Bahlcke, Joachim, Beate Stoertkuhl, and Matthias Weber, eds. *The Luther Effect in Eastern Europe: History, Culture, Memory*. Translated by Sarah Patey. Oldenbourg: De Gruyter, 2017.

Barge, Hermann. *Andreas Bodenstein von Karlstadt*, 2 vols. Leipzig: Friedrich Brandstetter, 1905 (repr. Leipzig, 2007).

Barrett, Lois. *Wreath of Glory: Ursula's Prophetic Visions in the Context of Reformation and Revolt in Southwestern Germany, 1524–30*. PhD diss., Union Institute, Cincinnati, OH, 1992.

Bauer, Joachim. 'Das Luther-Jahrhundert. Luther als deutscher Nationalheld im 19. Jahrhundert'. In *Luther und die Deutschen. Begleitband zur Nationalen Sonderausstellung auf der Wartburg 4. Mai—5. November 2017*. Petersberg: Michael Imhof Verlag, 2017.

Baumann, Kirsten, Joachim Krüger, and Uta Kuhl, eds. *Luthers Norden*. Petersberg: Michael Imhof Verlag, 2017.

Bellmann, Fritz, Marie-Luise Harksen, and Roland Werner, eds. *Die Denkmale der Lutherstadt Wittenberg*. Weimar: Herrmann Böhlaus Nachfolger, 1979.

Bering, Dietz. *Luther im Fronteinsatz: Propagandastrategien im Ersten Weltkrieg*. Göttingen: Wallstein, 2018.

Beyer, Oswald. 'A Public Mystery'. *Lutheran Quarterly* 26 (2012): 125–41.

Boettcher, Susan. 'Late Sixteenth-Century Lutherans: A Community of Memory'. In *Defining Community in Early Modern Europe*, edited by Karen Spierling and Michael Halvorsen. Farnham: Ashgate, 2008.

Braunfels, Veronika. *Mit Luther durch die Kunstsammlungen: Ein Führer zu den Luther-Zeugnissen in den Kunstsammlungen der Veste Coburg*. Coburg: Kunstsammlungen d. Veste Coburg, 1996.

Brecht, Martin. *Martin Luther*, 3 vols. Translated by James L. Schaaf. Minneapolis: Fortress Press, 1985–93.

Brinkmann, Bodo. *Cranach*. London: Royal Academy of Arts, 2008.

Brumlik, Micha. 'Was die AfD und Playmobil eint', *Die Tageszeitung (taz.de)*, June 8, 2016.

Bubenheimer, Ulrich. 'Andreas Rudolff Bodenstein von Karlstadt'. In *Theologische Realenzyklopädie*, edited by Gerhard Müller, vol. 17, 649–57. Berlin and New York: Walter de Gruyter, 1988.

Buc, Philippe. *The Dangers of Ritual: Between Early Medieval Texts and Social Scientific Theory*. Princeton: Princeton University Press, 2001.

Buck, Lawrence P. *The Roman Monster: An Icon of the Papal Antichrist in Reformation Polemics*. Kirksville, MO: Truman State University Press, 2014.

Burke, Peter. 'L'histoire sociale des rêves', *Annales* 28, no. 2 (March 1973): 329–42.

Burnett, Amy Nelson. *Karlstadt and the Origins of the Eucharistic Controversy: A Study in the Circulation of Ideas*. Oxford and New York: Oxford University Press, 2011.

Buss, Hansjörg. 'Die Deutschen und Martin Luther. Reformationsjubiläen im 19. und 20. Jahrhundert'. In *Luthermania. Ansichten einer Kultfigur*, edited by Hole Rößler. Wolfenbüttel: Herzog-August-Bibliothek: 2017.

Christensen, Carl. *Princes and Propaganda: Electoral Saxon Art of the Reformation*. Kirksville, MO: Sixteenth Century Journal Publishers, 1992.

Conermann, Klaus. 'Die Lutherrose. Luthers Markzeichen im Kontext der Reformationskunst und—theologie. Zur Entstehung des Lutherkults'. In *Luthermania: Ansichten einer Kultfigur*. Virtuelle Ausstellung der Herzog August Bibliothek im Rahmen des Forschungsverbundes Marbach Weimar Wolfenbüttel 2017. Online: http://www.luthermania.de/exhibits/show/klaus-conermann-die-lutherrose [Accessed 4 January 2019].

Cranach-Stiftung, ed. *Lucas Cranach d. Ä und die Cranachhöfe in Wittenberg*. Halle: Mitteldeutscher Verlag, 1998.

Creasman, Allyson F. 'The Virgin Mary against the Jews: Anti-Jewish Polemic in the Pilgrimage to the Schöne Maria of Regensburg, 1519–25'. *The Sixteenth Century Journal* 33, no. 4 (Winter 2002): 963–80.

De Luca, Francesca. 'I volti della Riforma nelle collezioni granducali'. In *I volti della Riforma. Lutero e Cranach nelle collezioni medicee*, edited by Francesca de Luca and Giovanni Maria Fara. Florence: Giunti, 2017.

De Luca, Francesca, and Giovanni Maria Fara, eds. *I volti della Riforma: Lutero e Cranach nelle collezioni medicee*. Florence: Giunti, 2017.

Dettmann, Ingrid. 'Martin Luther as a Saint? The Portrait of the Reformer between Holy Icon and Denominational Identity in the Sixteenth Century'. In *Martin Luther and the Reformation*, edited by Anne-Marie Rous. Dresden: Sandstein, 2016.

*Die Bibel nach Martin Luthers Übersetzung—Lutherbibel revidiert 2017. Jubiläumsausgabe 500 Jahre Reformation, Mit Sonderseiten zu Martin Luthers Wirken als Reformator und Bibelübersetzer*. Stuttgart: Deutsche Bibelgesellschaft, 2017.

Döhle, Hans-Jürgen. 'Schwein, Geflügel und Fisch—bei Luthers zu Tisch'. In *Luther in Mansfeld, Forschungen am Elternhaus des Reformators*, edited by Harald

Meller. Halle an der Saale: Landesamt für Denkmalpflege und Archäologie Sachsen-Anhalt, 2007.

Edwards, John. *The Jews in Christian Europe*. London: Routledge, 1988.

Enke, Roland, Katja Schneider, and Jutta Strehle, eds. *Lucas Cranach der Jüngere: Entdeckung eines Meisters*. Munich: Hirmer, 2015.

Ermischer, Gerhard, and Andreas Tacke, eds. *Cranach im Exil: Aschaffenburg um 1540. Zuflucht, Schatzkammer, Residenz*. Regensburg: Schnell und Steiner, 2007.

Eser, Thomas, and Stephanie Armer, eds. *Luther, Kolumbus und die Folgen: Welt im Wandel, 1500–1600*. Nuremberg: Germanisches Nationalmuseum, 2017.

Eydinger, Ulrike. 'Motive historischer Flugblätter und Druckgraphiken im Bauern-kriegspanorama von Werner Tübke. Zur Genese des Kunstwerkes'. In *Reformation und Bauernkrieg*, edited by Werner Greiling, Thomas T. Müller, and Uwe Schirmer. Cologne: Böhlau, 2019.

Fauth, Dieter, 'Träume bei religiösen Dissidenten in der frühen Reformation'. In *Religiöse Devianz in christlich geprägten Gesellschaften*, edited by Diether Fauth and Daniela Müller. Würzburg: Religion und Kultur Verlag, 1999.

Fessner, Michael. 'Die Familie Luder und das Bergwerks–und Hüttenwesen in der Grafschaft Mansfeld und im Herzogtum Braunschweig-Wölfenbüttel'. In *Martin Luther und Eisleben*, edited by Rosemarie Knape, 11–31. Leipzig: Evangelische Verlangsanstalt, 2007.

Fessner, Michael. 'Die Familie Luder in Möhra und Mansfeld. Archivalische Überlieferungen zum Elternhaus von Martin Luther'. In *Fundsache Luther: Archäologen auf den Spuren des Reformators*, edited by Harald Meller, 79–85. Halle Saale, 2008.

Fischer, Hermann. *Schwäbisches Wörterbuch*, 6 vols. Tübingen: Laupp, 1901–36.

Fitschen, Klaus. 'Vorbild oder Abbild der Gesellschaft? Einblicke in die Geschichte des evangelischen Pfarrhauses in Deutschland'. In *Luther und die Deutschen: Begleitband zur Nationalen Sonderausstellung auf der Wartburg 4. Mai–5. November 2017*, edited by Wartburg-Stiftung, 202–7. Petersberg: Michael Imhof Verlag, 2017.

Freud, Sigmund. *Die Traumdeutung*. Leipzig and Vienna: Franz Deuticke, 1899.

Freydank, Hanns. 'Vater Luther der Hüttenmeister'. In *Das Eisleber Lutherbuch 1933*, edited by Hermann Etzrodt and Kurt Kronenberg. Eisleben: Ernst Schneider, 1933.

Freydank, Hanns. *Martin Luther und der Bergbau*. Eisleben: Ernst Schneider, 1939.

Friedeburg, Robert von. *Luther's Legacy: The Thirty Years War and the Modern Notion of 'State' in the Empire, 1530s to 1790s*. Cambridge: Cambridge University Press, 2016.

Furcha, Edward J., ed. and tr. *The Essential Carlstadt*. Waterloo, Ontario: Herald Press, 1995.

Gantet, Claire. 'Dreams, Standards of Knowledge and "Orthodoxy" in Germany in the Sixteenth Century'. In *Orthodoxies and Heterodoxies in Early Modern German Culture: Order and Creativity, 1550–1750*, edited by Randolph C. Head and Daniel Christensen, 69–88. Leiden: Brill, 2007.

Gantet, Claire. *Der Traum in der frühen Neuzeit. Ansätze zu einer kulturellen Wissenschaftsgeschichte*. Berlin and New York: De Gruyter, 2010.

Geisberg, Max, and Walter L. Strauss. *The German Single-Leaf Woodcut, 1500–1550*, 4 vols. New York: Hacker Art Books, 1974.

Goertz, Hans-Jürgen. 'Träume, Offenbarungen und Visionen in der Reformation'. In *Reformation und Revolution: Beiträge zum politischen Wandel und den sozialen Kräften am Beginn der Neuzeit*, edited by Rainer Postel, 171–92. Stuttgart: Steiner, 1989.

Goertz, Hans-Jürgen. *Thomas Müntzer: Revolutionär am Ende der Zeiten*. C. H. Bleck, 2015.

Gordon, Bruce. 'Huldrych Zwingli's Dream of the Last Supper'. In *Crossing Traditions: Essays on the Reformation and Intellectual History*, edited by Maria-Cristina Pitassi and Daniela Solfaroli Camilocci, 296–310. Leiden: Brill, 2017.

Grebe, Karsten, and Mathias Thiele, eds. *LUTHER. Yadegar Asisi 360° Panorama*. Berlin: Asisi, 2016.

Grimm, Claus. 'Die Anteile von Meister und Werkstatt. Zum Fall Lucas Cranach d. Ä'. In *Unsichtbare Meisterzeichnungen auf dem Malgrund. Cranach und seine Zeitgenossen*, edited by Ingo Sandner, 67–82. Regensburg: Schnell und Steiner, 1998.

Grisar, Hartmann, and Franz Heege. *Luthers Kampfbilder*, 4 vols. Freiburg im Breisgau: Herder & Co., 1923.

Großmann, G. Ulrich. 'Lutherkirchen und andere Beispiele öffentlichen Luthergedenkens in Deutschland'. In *Luther und die Deutschen: Begleitband zur Nationalen Sonderausstellung auf der Wartburg 4. Mai–5. November 2017*, edited by Wartburg-Stiftung, 371–85. Petersberg: Michael Imhof Verlag, 2017.

Gruau, Élise, ed. *Palazzo Farnese (English Edition)*. Milan: 5 Continents Editions, 2007.

Gunn, Steven. *Henry VII's New Men and the Making of Tudor England*. Oxford: Oxford University Press, 2016.

Gutjahr, Mirko. 'Pomander'. In *Luther! 95 Treasures—95 People*, edited by Mirko Gutjahr, Benjamin Hasselhorn, Catherine Nichols, and Katha Schneider. Munich: Hirmer, 2017.

Gutjahr, Mirko, Benjamin Hasselhorn, Catherine Nichols, and Katha Schneider, eds. *Luther! 95 Treasures—95 People*. Munich: Hirmer, 2017.

Hall, Catherine, and Daniel Pick. 'Thinking About Denial'. *History Workshop Journal* 84, no. 1 (October 2017): 1–23.

Hanß, Stefan. 'Face-Work: Making Hair Matter in Sixteenth-Century Central Europe'. In *Das Haar als Argument: Zur Wissensgeschichte von Bärten, Frisuren und Perücken*, edited by Martin Mulsow. Gotha: in press.

Hanß, Stefan. 'Hair, Emotions and Slavery in the Early Modern Habsburg Mediterranean'. *History Workshop Journal* 87 (2019): 160–87.

Heal, Bridget. *A Magnificent Faith: Art and Identity in Lutheran Germany*. Oxford: Oxford University Press, 2017.

Hecht, Christian. 'Luther bekommt Hörner'. In *Luthermania. Ansichten einer Kultfigur*, edited by Hole Rößler, 223–37. Wolfenbüttel: Herzog-August-Bibliothek: 2017.

Hein, Markus, and Armin Kohnle, eds. *Die Leipziger Disputation 1519.* Leipzig, 2011.

Heling, Antje. *Zu Haus bei Martin Luther. Ein alltagsgeschichtlicher Rundgang.* Wittenberg: Stiftung Luthergedenkstätten in Sachsen-Anhalt, 2003.

Hendrix, Scott H. *Luther and the Papacy: Stages in a Reformation Conflict.* Philadelphia: Fortress Press, 1981.

Hendrix, Scott H., and Susan Karant-Nunn, eds. *Masculinity in the Reformation Era.* Kirksville, MO: Truman State University Press, 2008.

Hennen, Insa Christiane. '"Cranach 3D": Häuser der Familie Cranach in Wittenberg und das Bild der Stadt'. In *Das ernestinische Wittenberg: Spuren Cranachs in Schloss und Stadt,* edited by Heiner Lück, Enno Bünz, Leonhard Helten, Armin Kohnle, Dorothée Sack, and Hans-Georg Stephan, 313–62. Petersberg: Michael Imhof Verlag, 2015.

Heydenreich, Gunnar. '". . . That You Paint with Wonderful Speed": Virtuosity and Efficiency in the Artistic Practice of Lucas Cranach the Elder'. In *Cranach,* edited by Bodo Brinkman, 29–47. London: Royal Academy of Arts, 2008.

Heydenreich, Gunnar. *Lucas Cranach the Elder: Painting Materials, Techniques and Workshop Practice.* Amsterdam: Amsterdam University Press, 2007.

Hill, Kat. *Baptism, Brotherhood, and Belief in Reformation Germany: Anabaptism and Lutheranism, 1525–1585.* Oxford: Oxford University Press, 2015.

Hill, Kat. 'Introduction: Making Lutherans'. In *Cultures of Lutheranism: Reformation Repertoires in Early Modern Germany* (Past and Present Supplement 12), edited by Kat Hill, 9–32. Oxford: Oxford University Press, 2017.

Hill, Kat. 'Fun and Loathing in Later Lutheran Culture'. In *Cultures of Lutheranism: Reformation Repertoires in Early Modern Germany* (Past and Present Supplement 12), edited by Kat Hill, 67–89. Oxford: Oxford University Press, 2017.

Hofmann, Werner, ed. *Luther und die Folgen für die Kunst.* Munich: Prestel-Verlag, 1983.

Hsia, Ronnie Po-Chia. *The Myth of Ritual Murder. Jews and Magic in Reformation Germany.* New Haven and London: Yale University Press, 1988.

Hsia, Ronnie Po-Chia. 'Dreams and Conversions: A Comparative Analysis of Catholic and Buddhist Dreams in Mind and Qing China: Part I', *The Journal of Religious History* 29, no. 3 (October 2005): 223–40.

Hsia, Ronnie Po-Chia. *A Jesuit in the Forbidden City: Matteo Ricci 1552–1610.* Oxford: Oxford University Press, 2010.

Iserloh, Erwin. *Luthers Thesenanschlag, Tatsache oder Legende?* Wiesbaden: Steiner, 1962.

Iserloh, Edwin. *Luther zwischen Reform und Reformation. Der Thesenanschlag fand nicht statt.* Münster: Aschendorff, 1966.

Israel, Jonathan. *European Jewry in the Age of Mercantilism.* Oxford: Oxford University Press, 1985.

Jacobs, Grit. 'Ein nationales Monument. Die Neugestaltung der Wartburg im 19. Jahrhundert'. In *Luther und die Deutschen: Begleitband zur Nationalen Sonderausstellung auf der Wartburg 4. Mai–5. November 2017,* edited by Wartburg-Stiftung, 297–303. Petersberg: Michael Imhof Verlag, 2017.

Jankowski, Günter, ed. *Zur Geschichte des Mansfelder Kupferschieferberghaus*. Clausthal-Zellerfeld: Gesellschaft Deutscher Metallhütten- und Bergleute, 1995.

Jöstel, Volkmar, and Jutta Strehle. *Luthers Bild und Lutherbilder: Ein Rundgang durch die Wirkungsgeschichte*. Wittenberg: Stiftung Luthergedenkstätten, 2003.

Junghans, Helmut. 'Die Tischreden Martin Luthers'. In *D. Martin Luthers Werke: Sonderedition der kritischen Weimarer Ausgabe. Begleitheft zu den Tischreden*. Weimar: H. Böhlaus Nachfolger, 2000.

Jütte, Daniel. *The Strait Gate. Thresholds and Power in Western History*. London and New Haven: Yale University Press, 2015.

Kagan, Richard L. *Lucrecia's Dreams. Politics and Prophecy in Sixteenth-Century Spain*. Berkeley and Los Angeles: University of California Press, 1990.

Kalkoff, Paul. *Die Depeschen des Nuntius Aleander vom Wormser Reichstage 1521*. Halle: Verein, 1886.

Karant-Nunn, Susan. 'The Masculinity of Martin Luther: Theory, Practicality, and Humor'. In *Masculinity in the Reformation Era*, edited by Scott Hendrix and Susan Karant-Nunn, 167–89. Kirksville, MO: Truman State University Press, 2008.

Karant-Nunn, Susan. *The Reformation of Feeling. Shaping the Religious Emotions in Early Modern Germany*. Oxford: Oxford University Press, 2010.

Karant-Nunn, Susan. 'The Mitigated Fall of Humankind: Martin Luther's Reconciliation with the Body'. In *Cultures of Lutheranism: Reformation Repertoires in Early Modern Germany* (Past and Present Supplement 12), edited by Kat Hill, 51–66. Oxford: Oxford University Press, 2017.

Karant-Nunn, Susan. 'The Tenderness of Daughters, the Waywardness of Sons: Martin Luther as a Father'. In *The Personal Luther: Essays on the Reformer from a Cultural Historical Perspective*, edited by Susan Karant-Nunn, 141–54. Leiden: Brill, 2017.

Kasten, Ingrid. '"Was ist Luther? Ist doch die lere nitt meyn": Die Anfänge des Luther-Mythos im 16. Jahrhundert'. In *Magister et amicus: Festschrift für Kurt Gärtner zum 65. Geburtstag*, edited by Vaclav Bok and Frank Shaw, 899–931. Vienna: Edition Praesens, 2003.

Katz, David. 'Shylock's Gender: Jewish Male Menstruation in Early Modern England'. *The Review of English Studies* 50, no. 200 (November 1999): 440–62.

Kaufmann, Thomas. *Luther's Jews: A Journey into Anti-Semitism*. Translation by Lesley Sharpe and Jeremy Noakes of his 2014 book *Luthers Juden*. Oxford: Oxford University Press, 2017.

Kaufmann, Thomas, *Neues von 'Junker Jörg'. Lukas Cranachs frühreformatorische Druckgraphik. Beobachtungen, Anfragen, Thesen und Korrekturen'. In *Konstellationen*, edited by Reinhard Laube, vol. 2. Weimar: Herzogin Anna Amalia Bibliothek, 2020.

Kawerau, Gustav, ed. *Der Briefwechsel des Justus Jonas*, 2 vols. Halle: O. Hendel, 1884–85.

Kluttig-Altmann, Ralf. 'Archäologische Funde von Grundstücken der Familie Cranach in Wittenberg'. In *Das ernestinische Wittenberg: Spuren Cranchs in Schloss und*

*Stadt,* edited by Heiner Lück, Enno Bünz, Leonhard Helten, Armin Kohnle, Dorothée Sack, and Hans-Georg Stephan, 363–400. Petersberg: Michael Imhof Verlag, 2015.

Kluttig-Altmann, Ralf, ed. *Martin Luther: Treasures of the Reformation. Catalogue.* Dresden: Sandstein, 2016.

Knape, Rosemarie, ed. *Martin Luther und Eisleben.* Leipzig: Evangelische Verlagsanstalt, 2007.

Kober, Karl-Max. *Werner Tübke: Monumentalbild Frankenhausen.* Dresden: Verlag der Kunst, 1989.

Kohnle, Armin, Christina Meckelnborg, and Uwe Schirmer, eds. *Georg Spalatin: Steuermann der Reformation.* Halle: Stadt Altenburg, 2014.

Körner, Joseph Leo. *The Moment of Self-Portraiture in German Renaissance Art.* Chicago: University of Chicago Press, 1993.

Körner, Joseph. *The Reformation of the Image.* London: Reaktion, 2004.

Kornmeier, Uta. 'Luther in Effigie, oder: Das "Schreckgespenst von Halle".' In *Lutherinszenierung und Reformationserinnerung,* edited by Stefan Laube and Karl-Heinz Fix, 343–70. Leipzig: Evangelische Verlagsanstalt, 2002.

Korsch, Dietrich. 'Luther's Seal as an Elementary Interpretation of His Theology'. In *Harvesting Martin Luther's Reflections on Theology, Ethics and the Church,* edited by Timothy J. Wengert, 56–77. Minneapolis, MN: Fortress Press, 2017.

Kramer, Sabine, and Karsten Eisenmenger, eds. *Die Marktkirche unser Lieben Frauen zu Halle.* Halle: Janos Stekovics, 2004.

Kramm, Heinrich. *Studien über die Oberschichten der mitteldeutschen Städte im 16. Jahrhundert: Sachsen, Thüringen, Anhalt,* 2 vols. Cologne: Böhlau, 1981.

Lake, Peter. 'Antipopery: the Structure of a Prejudice'. In *Conflict in Early Stuart England: Studies in Religion and Politics, 1603–1642,* edited by Richard Cust and Ann Hughes, 72–106. London: Longman, 1989.

Lake, Peter, and Michael Questier. *The Antichrist's Lewd Hat: Protestants, Papists and Players in Post-Reformation England.* New Haven and London: Yale University Press, 2002.

Lang, Thomas, 'Simprecht Reinhart: Formscheider, Maler, Drucker, Bettmeister—Spuren eines Leben sim Schatten von Lucas Cranach d. Ä'. In *Das ernestinische Wittenberg: Spuren Cranachs in Schloss und Stadt,* edited by Heiner Lück, Enno Bünz, Leonhard Helten, Armin Kohnle, Dorothée Sack, and Hans-Georg Stephan. Petersberg: Michael Imhof Verlag, 2015.

Laube, Adolf, Max Steinmetz, and Günter Vogler, eds. *Illustrierte Geschichte der deutschen frühbürgerlichen Revolution.* Berlin: Dietz, 1974.

Laube, Stefan, ed. *Von der Reliquie zum Ding. Heiliger Ort—Wunderkammer—Museum.* Berlin: De Gruyter, 2011.

Laube, Stefan. 'Homely Audacity: Memories of Luther between Hero Worship and Enchanted Idyll'. In *Martin Luther and the Reformation,* edited by Anne-Marie Rous, 440–50. Dresden: Sandstein, 2016.

Laube, Stefan. 'Süchtig nach Splittern und Scherben. Energetische Bruchstücke bei Martin Luther'. In *Luthermania. Ansichten einer Kultfigur*, edited by Hole Rößler. Wolfenbüttel: Herzog-August-Bibliothek: 2017.

Laven, Mary. *Mission to China: Matteo Ricci and the Jesuit Encounter with the East*. London: Faber & Faber, 2011.

Lehmann, Hartmut, *Luthergedächtnis 1817 bis 2017*, Göttingen: Vandenhoeck & Ruprecht, 2012.

Leppin, Volker. *Martin Luther: Gestalten des Mittelalters und der Renaissance*. Darmstadt: Wissenschaftliche Buchgesellschaft 2006.

Lindner, Gerd. *Vision und Wirklichkeit: Das Frankenhausener Geschichtspanorama von Werner Tübke*, Frankenhausen: Panorama Museum, 2006.

Long, Roy. *Martin Luther and His Legacy: A Perspective on 500 Years of Reformation*. London: Council of Lutheran Churches, 2017.

Mager, Inge. '"Das war viel ein andrer Mann". Justas Jonas—Ein Leben mit und für Luther'. In *Luther und seine Freunde*, edited by Peter Freybe. Wittenberg: Drei Kastanien Verlag, 1998.

Mai, Gunther. 'Von Luther zu Hitler? Luther-Rezeptionen 1883–1945'. In *Luther und die Deutschen: Begleitband zur Nationalen Sonderausstellung auf der Wartburg 4. Mai—5. November 2017*, edited by Wartburg-Stiftung. Petersberg: Michael Imhof Verlag, 2017.

Marshall, Peter. *Nailing the Myth. 1517: Martin Luther and the Invention of the Reformation*. Oxford: Oxford University Press, 2017.

Marx, Harald, and Ingrid Mössinger. *Cranach: Gemaelde aus Dresden*. Cologne: Wienand, 2005.

Mayer, Alicia. '"The Heresiarch That Burns in Hell": The Image of Martin Luther in New Spain'. In *Luther zwischen den Kulturen. Zeitgenossenschaft—Weltwirkung*, edited by Hans Medick and Peer Schmidt, 119–40. Göttingen: Vandenhoeck & Ruprecht, 2004.

McLellan, Josie. 'Visual Dangers and Delights: Nude Photography in East Germany'. *Past and Present* 205 , no. 1 (November 2009): 143–74.

Meller, Harald, ed. *Fundsache Luther: Archäologen auf den Spuren des Reformators*. Halle, Saale: Konrad Theiss, 2008.

Meller, Harald, Colin Bailey, Martin Eberle, and Stefan Rein, eds. *Martin Luther and the Reformation* (Volume Accompanying Exhibition). Dresden, 2016.

Messling, Guido. *Die Welt des Lucas Cranach. Ein Künstler im Zeitalter von Dürer, Tizian und Metsys*. Brussels: Palais des Beaux-Arts, 2010.

Morrall, Andrew, 'Protestant Pots: Morality and Social Ritual in the Early Modern Home'. *Journal of Design History* 15, no. 4 (2002): 263–73.

Möllenberg, Walter. *Urkundenbuch zur Geschichte des Mansfeldischen Saigerhandels im 16. Jahrhundert*. Halle an der Saale: Otto Hendel, 1915.

Möller, Bernd, and Karl Stackmann, 'Luder, Luther, Eleutherius. Erwägungen zu Luthers Namen'. In *Nachrichten der Akademie der Wissenschaften in Göttingen, Philologisch–Historische Klasse* 7 (1981): 167–203.

Mück, Walter. *Der Mansfelder Kupferschieferbergbau in seiner rechtsgeschichtlichen Entwicklung*, 2 vols. Eisleben: Selbstverlag des Verfassers, 1910.

Mundt, Lothar. *Lemnius und Luther. Studien und Texte zur Geschichte und Nachwirkung ihres Konflikts (1539–9)*, 2 vols. Bern, Frankfurt am Main, and New York: Peter Lang, 1983.

Neser, Anne-Marie. *Luthers Wohnhaus in Wittenberg. Denkmalpolitik im Spiegel der Quellen*. Leipzig: Evangelische Verlaganstalt, 2005.

Neudecker, Christian Gotthold, ed. *Die handschriftliche Geschichte Ratzeberger's über Luther und seine Zeit*. Jena: Friedrich Mauke, 1850.

Neugebauer, Anke, and Thomas Lang, 'Cranach im Schloss. Das Wirken und die Werke Lucas Cranachs d. Ä. und seiner Werkstatt in Schloss und Schlosskirche Wittenberg'. In *Das ernestinische Wittenberg: Spuren Cranachs in Schloss und Stadt*, edited by Heiner Lück, Enno Bünz, Leonhard Helten, Armin Kohnle, Dorothée Sack, and Hans-Georg Stephan. Petersberg: Michael Imhof Verlag, 2015.

Neuland-Kitzerow, Dagmar, Christine Binroth, and Salwa Joram ed. *Anna webt Reformation. Ein Bildteppich und seine Geschichten*. Dresden: Verlag der Kunst, 2017.

Nickel, Heinrich, ed. *Das Hallesche Heiltumbuch von 1520. Nachdruck zum 450. Gründungsjubiläum der Marienbibliothek zu Halle*. Halle: Stekovics, 2001.

Nirenberg, David. *Anti-Judaism: The Western Tradition*. New York: W. W. Norton, 2013.

Oberman, Heiko. *The Roots of Anti-Semitism in the Age of Renaissance and Reformation*. Translated by James I. Porter. Philadelphia: Fortress Press, 1984 (German, 1981).

Osten-Sacken, Peter von der. *Martin Luther und die Juden. Neu untersucht anhand von Anton Margarithas 'der gantz Jüdisch glaub' (1530/31)*. Stuttgart: Kohlhammer, 2002.

Osten-Sacken, Peter von der. 'Martin Luther's Position on Jews and Judaism'. In *Martin Luther and the Reformation*, edited by Anne-Simone Rous, 323–30. Dresden: Sandstein, 2016.

Ott, Joachim, and Martin Treu, ed. *Luthers Thesenanschlag—Faktum oder Fiktion*. Leipzig: Evangelische Verlagsanstalt, 2008.

Ottomeyer, Hans, Jutta Goetzmann, and Ansgar Reiß, eds. *Heiliges Römisches Reich Deutscher Nation 962 bis 1806*. Dresden: Sandstein, 2006.

Ozment, Steven. *The Serpent and the Lamb. Cranach, Luther, and the Making of the Reformation*. New Haven and London: Yale University Press, 2011.

Paas, John Roger. *The German Political Broadsheet 1600–1700*, 12 vols. Wiesbaden: Harrassowitz Verlag, 1985–2014.

Petersen, Rodney L. 'The Apocalyptic Luther: Exegesis and Self-Identification'. In *The Myth of the Reformation*, edited by Peter Opitz, 71–91. Göttingen and Bristol: Vandenhoeck & Ruprecht, 2013.

Pettegree, Andrew. *Brand Luther: 1517, Printing, and the Making of the Reformation*. New York: Penguin, 2015.

Pick, Daniel, and Lyndal Roper, eds. *Dreams and History: The Interpretation of Dreams from Ancient Greece to Modern Psychoanalysis*. London: Routledge, 2003.

Plane, Ann Marie, and Leslie Tuttle, eds. *Dreams, Dreamers and Visions: The Early Modern Atlantic World*. Philadelphia: University of Pennsylvania Press, 2013.

Plummer, Marjorie E. *From Priest's Whore to Pastor's Wife. Clerical Marriage and the Process of Reform in the Early German Reformation*. Farnham: Ashgate, 2012.

Posset, Franz. *The Front-Runner of the Catholic Reformation. The Life and Works of Johann von Staupitz*. Aldershot: Ashgate, 2003.

Price, Simon. 'The Future of Dreams: From Freud to Artemidorus', *Past and Present* 113 (November 1986): 3–37.

Prinz, Alois. *Wie aus Martin Luther wurde*. Berlin: Insel, 2016.

Projekt Deutsche Inschriften Online, www.inschriften.net, Niedersachsen/ Goettingen.

Puff, Helmut. *Sodomy in Reformation Germany and Switzerland, 1400–1600*. Chicago: University of Chicago Press, 2003.

Purvis, Zachary. 'Martin Luther in German Historiography'. In *Oxford Research Encyclopaedia of Religion*. Online publication, November 2016. DOI: 10.1093 /acrefore/9780199340378.013.379.

Rankin, Alisha. *Panaceia's Daughters: Noblewomen as Healers in Early Modern Germany*. Chicago and London: University of Chicago Press, 2013.

Ratzeberger, Matthäus. *Luther und seine Zeit*. Jena: F. Mauke, 1850.

Reinitzer, Heimo. *Gesetz und Evangelium: über ein reformatorisches Bildthema, seine Tradition, Funktion und Wirkungsgeschichte*, 2 vols. Hamburg: Christians Verlag, 2006.

Rockwell, William Walker. *Die Doppelehe des Landgrafen Philipp von Hessen*. Marburg: N. G. Elwert, 1904.

Roper, Lyndal. *Oedipus and the Devil. Witchcraft, Sexuality, and Religion in Early Modern Europe*. London: Routledge, 1994.

Roper, Lyndal. *Witch Craze: Terror and Fantasy in Baroque Germany*. New Haven: Yale University Press, 2004.

Roper, Lyndal. 'Venus in Wittenberg: Cranach, Luther, and Sensuality'. In *Ideas and Cultural Margins in Early Modern Germany*, edited by Marjorie E. Plummer and Robin Barnes. Farnham: Ashgate, 2009, 81–98.

Roper, Lyndal. 'Martin Luther's Body: The Stout Doctor and His Biographers'. *American Historical Review* 115, no. 2 (April 2010): 351–84.

Roper, Lyndal. 'The Seven-Headed Monster: Luther and Psychology'. In *History and Psyche: Culture, Psychoanalysis and the Past*, edited by Sally Alexander and Barbara Taylor, 219–40. Basingstoke: Palgrave Macmillan, 2012.

Roper, Lyndal. 'Luther Relics'. In *Religion, the Supernatural and Visual Culture in Early Modern Europe*, edited by Dagmar Eichberger and Jenny Spinks, 330–53. Leiden: Brill, 2015.

Roper, Lyndal. *Martin Luther: Renegade and Prophet*. London: The Bodley Head, 2016.

Roper, Lyndal, and Jenny Spinks. '*Karlstadt's Wagen*: The First Visual Propaganda for the Reformation'. *Art History* 40, no. 2 (April 2017): 256–85.

Rößler, Hole. 'Martin Luther—eine Kultfigur und ihr Sockel'. In *Luthermania. Ansichten einer Kultfigur*, edited by Hole Rößler. Wolfenbüttel: Herzog-August-Bibliothek: 2017.

Rößler, Hole, ed. *Luthermania. Ansichten einer Kultfigur*. Wolfenbüttel: Herzog-August-Bibliothek: 2017.

Rubin, Miri. *Gentile Tales. The Narrative Assault on Late Medieval Jews*, New Haven and London: Yale University Press, 1999.

Rubin, Miri. *Mother of God: A History of the Virgin Mary*. London: Penguin, 2009.

Rublack, Ulinka. 'Fluxes: the Early Modern Body and the Emotions'. *History Workshop Journal* 53 (Spring 2002): 1–16.

Rublack, Ulinka. 'Grapho-Relics: Lutheranism and the Materialization of the Word'. *Past and Present* 206, Supplement 5 (January 2010): 144–66.

Rublack, Ulinka. *Dressing Up: Cultural Identity in Renaissance Europe*. Oxford: Oxford University Press, 2011.

Rublack, Ulinka. *The Astronomer and the Witch. Johannes Kepler's Fight for his Mother*. Oxford: Oxford University Press, 2015.

Sandner, Ingo, ed. *Unsichtbare Meisterzeichnungen auf dem Malgrund. Cranach und seine Zeitgenossen*. Regensburg: Schnell und Steiner, 1998.

Schilling, Heinz. *Martin Luther: Rebel in an Age of Upheaval*. Translated by Rona Johnston. Oxford: Oxford Unviersity Press, 2017.

Schilling, Johannes. 'Bibliographie der Tischredenausgaben'. In WA 59, 747–760.

Schmid, Hans Ulrich. 'Luther im Norden', *Jahrbuch für Germanistische Sprachgeschichte* 9, no. 1 (2018): 172–89.

Schmidt, Oswald Gottlob. *Luthers Bekanntschaft mit den alten Classikern: Ein Beitrag zur Lutherforschung*. Leipzig: Veit & Comp., 1883.

Scribner, Robert W. *For the Sake of Simple Folk. Popular Propaganda for the German Reformation*. Cambridge: Cambridge University Press, 1981.

Scribner, Robert W. 'Incombustible Luther: The Image of the Reformer in Early Modern Germany'. In *Popular Culture and Popular Movements in Reformation Germany*, edited by Robert W. Scribner, 323–53. London: The Hambledon Press, 1987.

Scribner, Robert W. *Religion and Culture in Germany (1400–1800)*. Leiden: Brill, 2001.

Seidel, Thomas A., and Christopher Spehr, eds. *Das evangelische Pfarrhaus: Mythos und Wirklichkeit*. Leipzig: Evangelische Verlagsanstalt, 2013.

Shachar, Isaiah. *The Judensau: A Medieval Anti-Jewish Motif and its History*. London: Warburg Institute, 1974.

Siggins, Ian. 'Luther's Mother Margarethe'. *Harvard Theological Review* 71, no. 1 (January 1978): 125–50.

Siggins, Ian. *Luther and his Mother*. Philadelphia: Fortress Press, 1981.

Slenczka, Ruth. 'Die Reformation als Gegenstand der Herrschaftsrepresentation. Luther und die Fürsten in der Bildausstattung von Schloss Hartenfels'. In *Luther und die Fürsten*, edited by Dirk Syndram, Yvonne Wirth, and Iris Yvonne Wagner. Dresden: Sandstein, 2015.

Slenczka, Ruth, ed. *Reformation und Freiheit. Luther und die Folgen für Preußen und Brandenburg*. Petersberg: Michael Imhof Verlag, 2017.

Slenczka, Ruth, ed. *Die Silberbibliothek aus Königsberg* (1545–1562). Petersberg: Michael Imhof Verlag, 2017.

Smerling, Walter, ed. *Luther und die Avantgarde: Zeitgenössische Kunst im alten Gefängnis in Wittenberg mit Sonderpräsentationen in Berlin und Kassel. Katalog zur Ausstellung*. Cologne: Weinand, 2017.

Smith, Jeffrey Chipps. 'Dürer's Losses and the Dilemmas of Being'. In *Enduring Loss in Early Modern Germany: Cross Disciplinary Perspectives*, edited by Lynne Tatlock, 71–101. Leiden: Brill, 2010.

Spicer, Andrew. 'Martin Luther and the Material Culture of Worship'. In *Martin Luther and the Reformation*, edited by Anne-Marie Rous, 250–60. Dresden: Sandstein, 2016.

Spinks, Jennifer. 'Monstrous Births and Counter-Reformation Visual Polemics: Johann Nas and the 1569 *Ecclesia Militans*'. *The Sixteenth Century Journal* 40, no. 2 (July 2009): 335–63.

Stahl, Andreas. 'Baugeschichtliche Erkenntnisse zu Luthers Elternhaus in Mansfeld'. In *Martin Luther und Eisleben*, edited by Rosemarie Knape, 353–90. Leipzig: Evangelische Verlangsanstalt, 2007.

Steiger, Johann Anselm. *Gedächtnisorte der Reformation. Sakrale Kunst im Norden (16.-18. Jahrhundert)*, 2 vols. Regensburg: Schnell und Steiner, 2016.

Steinmetz, David. 'Luther and the Ascent of Jacob's Ladder'. *Church History* 55, no. 2 (June 1986): 179–92.

Strehle, Jutta. *Luther mit dem Schwan: Tod und Verklärung eines grossen Mannes : Katalog zur Ausstellung in der Lutherhalle Wittenberg anlässlich des 450. Todestages von Martin Luther vom 21. Februar bis 10. November 1996*. Wittenberg: Schlezky & Jeep, 1996.

Stuhlfauth, Georg. *Die Bildnisse D. Martin Luthers im Tode*. Weimar: Böhlau, 1927.

Syndram, Dirk, Yvonne Wirth, and Iris Yvonne Wagner, eds. *Luther und die Fürsten*, 2 vols. Dresden: Sandstein, 2015.

Tacke, Andreas. 'Agnes Pless und Kardinal Albrecht von Brandenburg'. *Archiv für Kulturgeschichte* 72, no. 2 (December 1990): 347–65.

Tacke, Andreas. 'Luther und der 'Scheissbischof' Albrecht von Brandenburg'. In *Luther und die Fürsten: Selbstdarstellung und Selbstverständnis des Herrschers im Zeitalter der Reformation Aufsatzband*, edited by Dirk Syndram, 114–25. Dresden: Sandstein, 2015.

Thompson, W. D. J. Cargill. *Studies in the Reformation: Luther to Hooker*. Edited by C. W. Dugmore. London: Athione Press, 1980.

Toussaint, Gia. 'Luther und der Teufel'. In *Luthermania. Ansichten einer Kultfigur*, edited by Hole Rößler, 213–5. Wolfenbüttel: Herzog-August-Bibliothek: 2017.

Toussaint, Gia. 'Luther wird heilig'. In *Luthermania. Ansichten einer Kultfigur*, edited by Hole Rößler, 150–3. Wolfenbüttel: Herzog-August-Bibliothek: 2017.

Treu, Martin. '. . . *von daher bin ich*'. *Martin Luther und der Bergbau im Mansfelder Land, Rundgang durch die Ausstellung*. Eisleben: Stiftung Luthergedenkstätte, 2000.

Treu, Martin. *Martin Luther in Wittenberg: Ein biographischer Rundgang*. Wittenberg: Stiftung Luthergedenkstätte, 2006.

Trinkaus, Charles, ed. *Collected Works of Erasmus. Controversies: Hyperaspistes Book 2*. Translated by Clarence H. Miller. Toronto: University of Toronto Press, 2000.

Tübke-Schellenberger, Brigitte. *Werner Tübke. Das malerische Werk: Verzeichnis der Gemälde 1976 bis 1999*. Amsterdam and Dresden: Verlag der Kunst, 1999.

Tudor-Craig, Pamela. 'Group Portraits of the Protestant Reformers'. In *Art Re-Formed: Re-assessing the Impact of the Reformation on the Visual Arts*, edited by Tara Hamling and Richard Williams, 87–102. Newcastle: Cambridge Scholars Publishing, 2007.

Udolph, Jürgen. *Martinus Luder-Eleutherius-Martin Luther: Warum änderte Martin Luther seinen Namen?* Heidelberg: Universitätsverlag Winter, 2016.

Vandiver, Elizabeth, Ralph Keen, and Thomas D. Frazel, eds. and trans. *Luther's Lives: Two Contemporary Accounts of Martin Luther*. Manchester and New York: Manchester University Press, 2002.

Volz, Hans. *Martin Luthers Thesenanschlag und dessen Vorgeschichte*. Weimar: Böhlau, 1959.

Volz, Hans. 'Der Traum Kurfürst Friedrichs des Weisen vom 30./31. Oktober 1517. Eine bibliographisch-ikonographische Untersuchung'. *Gutenberg Jahrbuch* 45 (1970): 174–211.

Walsham, Alexandra. 'Domesticating the Reformation: Material Culture, Memory and Confessional Identity in Early Modern England'. *Renaissance Quarterly* 69, no. 2 (June 2016): 566–616.

Warnke, Martin. *Cranachs Luther: Entwürfe fuer ein Image*. Frankfurt: Broshiert, 1984.

Wartburg-Stiftung, ed. *Luther und die Deutschen: Begleitband zur Nationalen Sonderausstellung auf der Wartburg 4. Mai–5. November 2017*. Petersberg: Michael Imhof Verlag, 2017.

Wartenberg, Günther. 'Martin Luthers Kindheit, Jugend und erste Schulzeit in frühen biografischen Darstellungen des Reformators'. In *Martin Luther und Eisleben*, edited by Rosemarie Knape, 143–62. Leipzig: Evangelische Verlangsanstalt, 2007.

Wegmann, Susanne. 'Franz Timmermann, Fall and Redemption'. In *Luther! 95 Treasures—95 People*, edited by Mirko Gutjahr, Benjamin Hasselhorn, Catherine Nichols, and Katha Schneider, 102–3. Munich: Hirmer, 2017.

Wendebourg, Dorothea. 'Reformation Anniversaries and Images of Luther'. In *Martin Luther and the Reformation*, edited by Anne-Marie Rous, 432–39. Dresden: Sandstein, 2016.

Westermann, Ekkehard. *Das Eislebener Garkupfer und seine Bedeutung für den europäischen Kupfermarkt 1460–1560*. Cologne and Vienna: Böhlau, 1971.

Wiese, Christian. 'Überwinder des Mittelalters? Ahnherr des Nationalsozialismus? Zur Vielstimmigkeit und Tragik der jüdischen Lutherrezeption im wilhelminischen Deutschland und in der Weimarer Republik'. In *Lutherinszenierung und Reformationserinnerung*, edited by Stefan Laube and Karl-Heinz Fix, 165–97. Leipzig: Evangelische Verlagsanstalt, 2002.
Wolter, Gundula. *Die Verpackung des männlichen Geschlechts: Eine illustrierte Kulturgeschichte der Hose*. Marburg: Jonas, 1988.

# INDEX

Note: Page numbers in italic type indicate illustrations.